HISTORY OF
CHRISTIAN EDUCATION

HISTORY OF
CHRISTIAN EDUCATION

BY

PIERRE J. MARIQUE, PD.D., PH.D.

*Professor of the History and Philosophy
of Education in Fordham University*

VOLUME III

FORDHAM UNIVERSITY PRESS
NEW YORK
1932

PREFACE

This volume, the third one of the series on the History of Christian Education, covers a period of approximately two hundred years, from the middle of the eighteenth century to the present time, and thus, for the time being at least, brings to a close this survey of western education during the Christian era.

It had been the fond hope of the author that the volume would appear two or three years ago, but many urgent, exacting duties have compelled him to delay the preparation from year to year. He, none the less, still entertains the hope that he has not exhausted the patience of the many friends who for several years have awaited the appearance of Volume III, and that they will welcome "Education in Modern Times" as favorably as they did its two companion volumes.

The plan and method of treatment are essentially the same as before. It is the same endeavor to present the trends and facts of education in their relation to the general trend of western thought and the facts of western history, more particularly their relation to the three great revolutions that have made the eighteenth century even more important in western history than the fifteenth or the sixteenth. It may not be amiss to remark again that the volume "can be used as a reference work, or as a text book with classes that make a more comprehensive study of the history of education. . . . But whatever the particular purpose for which the book might be used it is the earnest hope of its author that it be an incentive to much collateral reading, especially of sources, the surest way if not the only one, of reaching an adequate conception of our indebtedness to the past."

The author gratefully acknowledges his general indebtedness to the many historical writers whose works have in any way contributed in the preparation of this survey of Christian education. He is particularly and deeply grateful to the Reverend Aloysius J. Hogan, S.J., President of Fordham University, for his hearty encouragement and the interest which time and again he evinced in the progress and successful completion of the present volume. He also gratefully confesses his debt to Dr. William P. Finley, of the Fordham University staff, for painstaking assistance in the dreary task of proof reading.

PIERRE J. MARIQUE.

New York, September 8, 1931.

TABLE OF CONTENTS

TABLE OF CONTENTS

LIST OF ILLUSTRATIONS

x   LIST OF ILLUSTRATIONS

To My Very Dear Friend

REVEREND EDWARD P. TIVNAN, S.J.

GENERAL BIBLIOGRAPHY

General Histories of Education.

1. CUBBERLY, E. P., *The History of Education, Readings in History of Education*, 2 Vols. New York, 1920.
2. DAVIDSON, THOMAS, *History of Education*. New York, 1900.
3. GRAVES, F. P., *A History of Education*, 3 Vols. New York, 1913.
4. McCORMICK, P., *History of Education*. Washington, 1915.
5. MONROE, PAUL, *Text Book in the History of Education*. New York, 1909.
6. SCHMID, K. A., *Geschichte der Erziehung vom Anfang an bis auf unsere Zeit*. 5 Vols. Stuttgart, 1884-1902.

Bibliographies, Cyclopedias, Magazines.

1. *American Journal of Education*. (Henry Barnard, Ed.) 31 Vols. Syracuse, 1902.
2. *Bibliothek der katholischen Pädagogik*. (F. X. Kuntz, Ed.) 14 Vols. Freiburg, 1888-1902.
3. *Catholic Encyclopedia*. 16 Vols. New York, 1907-1914.
4. *Cyclopedia of Education*. (Paul Monroe, Ed.) 5 Vols. New York, 1911-1913.
5. *Dictionnaire de Pédagogie et d'Instruction primaire*. (F. Buisson, Ed.) 2 Vols. Paris, 1886-1887.
6. *Encyklopädisches Handbuch der Pädagogik*. (G. W. Rein, Ed.) 7 Vols. Langensalza, 1895-1899.
7. *Lexikon der Pädagogik*. (E. M. Roloff, Ed.) 5 Vols. Freiburg, 1913.
8. *Sammlung der bedeutendsten pädagogischen Schriften aus alter und neuer Zeit*. (Schulz, Gansen and Keller, Eds.) 28 Vols. Paderborn, 1888-1902.
9. *Syllabus of Lectures on the History of Education*, by E. P. Cubberly. New York, 1904.

CHAPTER I

THE BEGINNINGS OF THE MODERN ERA

FIFTY YEARS AGO IT STILL WAS THE FASHION, as it had been for generations before, to trace to the fifteenth century the beginnings of what goes by the name of "modern times." The taking of Constantinople by the Turks in 1453 or, better still, the discovery of America in 1492, were suggested as convenient and fairly accurate landmarks to start from in the teaching of modern history. By that time, it was argued, the triumph of the Renaissance had been assured by the printing press, the death knoll of the Middle Ages had been sounded and a new era in Western culture ushered in. It was pointed out further, that in the wake of the Renaissance there had come great geographical and astronomical discoveries which had changed man's conception of his own habitat and of the whole universe, and there had also come a great revolution which had broken up the religious unity of the West. To-day, however, with the better perspective and more dispassionate attitude towards historical events which come to us with the lapse of time, there is a clearer and more accurate view of the immediate influence of these events and a realization, that in spite of geographical discoveries, of the Renaissance and Reformation, the life of the average person at the beginning of the eighteenth century did not essentially differ from what it had been three centuries before.

The whole economic and social fabric of eighteenth cen-

The former conception of the modern era was inaccurate.

tury Europe was still much the same as in feudal times.
Towns had multiplied and there were a few cities counting
their inhabitants by the hundred thousands, but the great
majority of the population still lived in the country, deriving
their sustenance from the land, the greater part of which
was possessed by the aristocracy. The estates of the nobility
were parceled out into small farms which were worked by
tenant-farmers. Most of them, in some countries, were still
serfs bound to the farm, and like the land itself, a part of
the lord's property. The methods of cultivation were still
the same as centuries before, and so was, in the greater part
of Europe, the economic relation of lord to tenant. Part of

SEDAN CHAIRS

the produce of the farm
went to the lord's table, or
to his barnyard and
stables; the tenant owed
his lord several days of
free service every year
and, in many places, he
was still obliged to grind
his wheat at the lord's
mill, to bake his bread at
the lord's oven, to press his grapes at the lord's wine-
presses, and in each case he had to pay a special tax determined by the lord; he also had to pay toll for driving on
the highway, passing a bridge, or crossing a stream. The
means of communication and transportation, the methods
of metal melting, metal working, garment making were
still on the whole those used in the fifteenth century and before. Commerce and industry still retained their medieval
organization. Each trade was organized into a guild which
regulated the professional training of its members, the
quality and quantity of articles to be produced, and the
conditions of labor. For generations, in the medieval stage
of their evolution, the craft guilds had remained true to the

purpose of their foundation; they had been a powerful agency for the support and defense of the laboring class in towns and cities. By the beginning of the eighteenth century however, the guilds had long since lost their earlier character; they were then trade monopolies in the hands of a few families and they were used by the government to regulate industry to the best of its fiscal interests.[1]

The great geographical discoveries of the fifteenth and sixteenth centuries had opened new trade routes and given a new impetus to commerce. Italy had lost her commercial supremacy to Holland and England. Sea trade, which formerly had been only coastwise, had now ventured on the high seas. The docks of London, Rotterdam, Antwerp, Lisbon were crowded with the shipping from European countries as well as America, Asia and Africa. Like the craftsmen, the merchants were still organized into guilds, but those associations of merchants had preserved a greater degree of elasticity and individual initiative than the crafts' guilds; it was due partly to that fact that merchants' guilds were more prosperous and had greater economic and social influence. The volume of trade was now several times what it had been at the close of the Middle Ages but only a fraction as yet of what it is today, and the art of shipping was still, in all essentials, the same as in the days of Columbus.[2]

In one respect, religion, eighteenth century Europe decidedly differed from the medieval society. "One world, one faith, one Church" had been the religious status of the West for more than a thousand years. For this religious unity the Protestant Revolution had substituted the principle of national religious independence:[3] "One nation, one faith." In practice, however, this came to mean that the religion of the

---

[1] See Cambridge Modern History, Vol. VI or Lavisse and Rambaud, Histoire Générale, Vol. VII.
[2] See Day, Clive, History of Commerce.
[3] Cf. Vol. II, chs. IV and V.

king or princeling became by law the religion of their subjects, and official churches were established to preach it. The
North and East of Germany, together with some districts
of the South and the Rhineland, Scandinavia, Holland, England, Scotland, and parts of France, Poland, Bohemia, Switzerland and Hungary had followed the standard of revolt;
Russia, just emerging from a state of semi-barbarism, was of
the Greek Schismatic Rite; the Balkans were under Turkish
rule and many of its inhabitants had turned Mohammedan;
the rest of Europe had, on the whole, remained faithful to
the See of Peter. Religious toleration, such as we understand
it today, was then as yet a thing of the distant future, but
there was still everywhere much religious fervor and a deep
sense of the importance of religion in education.

The strong democratic tendencies of the twelfth and thirteenth centuries were obliterated in the course of the next
two hundred years and they were not to be revived before
the closing years of the eighteenth century. Nearly everywhere around 1750, as around 1500, the government was
monarchical and, with the exception of England, the mon-
arch was an autocrat who legally could do no wrong because
he reigned by "divine right."[1] If he happened to be of a
benevolent disposition the lot of his subjects might at least
be bearable. Some of those despots,[2] though unwilling to
share their power with representatives of the nation, realized
that good government, by advancing the welfare of the
country, would give greater stability to the throne, and they
did what they could to mitigate abuses, reform laws, abolish
privileges, develop the natural resources of the nation, and

[1] One of the stanchest defenders of this "divine right of kings" idea was James I
of England. "As it is atheism to dispute what God can do," he declared in
1604, "so it is presumption and a high contempt in a subject to dispute
what a king can do." Suarez' "De Defensione Fidei," in which the doctrine
is admirably refuted, had the distinction of being burned at London by
royal command and of being prohibited by the Parliament of Paris.

[2] *E.g.*, Frederick II of Prussia and the czar Peter the Great.

improve the condition of the masses,[1] which at times was a hard one, as, for that matter, it sometimes is today. France was probably the most striking illustration of this autocratic form of government. Louis XIV may not have uttered the famous "I am the State" but so he was in fact, and so were his successors, Louis XV and Louis XVI.[2] Aside from the Netherlands, Switzerland and a few Italian States, the only country where the democratic promises of the Middle Ages had to some extent come true was England. The Magna Charta, extorted from King John by the English barons and clergy in 1215, had been the corner stone of English constitutional liberty. Slowly but steadily there had developed from its provisions a type of government which in the eighteenth century was the nearest approach to the present day form of government for the people and by the people. Alongside this movement towards political liberty there had developed in England a spirit of tolerance that was still foreign to most eighteenth century states, and it was to lead before long to the removal of the civic and political disabilities under which had long remained all those dissenting from the State Church. Another sign of the rise of liberalism in England was the growth and gradual emancipation of the forces which for good or evil were to wield such a

[1] Much of what has been said and written in the last one hundred and fifty years on the condition of the masses in the eighteenth century, particularly in France, leaves the impression of a wretched condition in the populous sections of the large cities and even the countryside. La Bruyère's famous passage (Les Caractères, Vol. XI, page 128), Rousseau's sentimental vaporings, and the humanitarian declamations of politicians during the French Revolution and after, have been used time and again to draw a dramatic picture of high lights on the side of the upper classes and low darks on that of the common folks. The truth of the matter is that while there was great political and social inequality and a heavy burden of taxation unevenly divided, the masses, especially the peasants, managed to live on the average in no particular discomfort.

[2] See Sorel, Albert, L'Europe et la Révolution française, Vol. I; de Tocqueville, Alexis, The State of Society in France before the Revolution of 1789; Taine, H. A., The Ancient Régime.

tremendous educative influence on the following generations.[1] Newspapers of various descriptions had been published in England and elsewhere long before the eighteenth
century. Their appearance was sporadic, they were small
in size and dealt with local gossip. The newspaper, as we
know it today, is an English product of the middle of the
eighteenth century. By that time the freedom of the press
had been completed in
England and the news-
paper had become the ex-
ponent of public opinion.
Because it treated subjects
of interest to the whole
community the newspa-
per developed an interest
in reading among the
masses, and it gradually
helped to extend the
range of public opinion
from the educated classes
to the whole nation. The
art of printing which had
been confined almost en-
tirely to London began
to be practiced in country

FONTENELLE

towns; local newspapers were founded, at first appearing
on Sunday, because that was the only day on which they
could be read by the industrial class; societies for the pur-
chasing of books, circulating libraries, reading clubs, debating societies were organized, and in 1769 there was held
the first public meeting in which an attempt was made
to "enlighten Englishmen respecting their political rights."
Literature also underwent a remarkable change in those
years. Hitherto writers of plays, essays, poems, scholarly

[1] See Lecky, W. E. H., A History of England in the Eighteenth Century, 7 vols.

works, had suited their subject and style to the life, taste, interest, passions, whims and prejudices of the restricted public centering around the court where they hoped their productions would find patrons. Now efforts are made to popularize literature and the sciences. Literary periodical reviews begin to appear, which in selection of subject and style of treatment try to appeal to the general public. Treatises are written on the sciences, philosophy, theology in an easy non-technical style, that will place within the reach of the average person some acquaintance with subjects which previously had been restricted to the initiated.[1] Likewise novels begin to appear that make a strong appeal to the masses. Bunyan's Pilgrim had been published in the latter part of the seventeenth century; Defoe's Robinson Crusoe and Swift's Gulliver's Travels appeared in the early part of the eighteenth. Newspapers, books, essays, plays, debates, while contributing their share to the education of the nation, awakened a desire for more schools and learning.

The modern era was really ushered in by three great revolutions which exerted a deep and far-reaching influence upon the material, institutional and spiritual life of the Western nations: an intellectual revolution which was decidedly anti-Christian and is sometimes referred to as the Enlightenment; a political revolution which, in theory at least, substituted the government of the many for that of the few; the industrial revolution which was to replace hand work by machine work. With the exception of the advent of Christianity no event in the history of the Western World has more deeply affected the life and the trend of

The three modern Revolutions.

---

[1] The tendency to popularize science was not, of course, confined to England. One of the earliest and best known of those "popularizers" was Bernard Le Bovier, sieur de Fontenelle (1657-1757), a member of the French Academy, of the Academy of Inscriptions and Belles Lettres, of the Royal Society of London, of the Academy of Berlin.

educational theory and practice than this three-fold revolution of the eighteenth century. The following chapters will be devoted to a brief consideration of each, and its consequences for education in general and particularly for the school.

REFERENCES

The following list of references in general history is not, of course, and it could not be intended to be an adequate bibliography on the subject. The chief purpose of its being appended to the introduction is to remind the reader, from the very start, of the necessity of having a broad and solid background in general history for a fruitful study of the history of education.

Cambridge Modern History, 12 vols.
Catholic Encyclopedia, 15 vols.
Encyclopedia Britannica, 29 vols.
Hayes, Carlton I. H., A Political and Social History of Modern Europe, 2 vols.
Helmolt, H. F. (editor), Weltgeschichte, 8 vols.
Langlois, C. V., Manuel de bibliographie historique, 2 vols.
Lavisse, Ernest, et Rambaud, Alfred, Histoire générale du IVᵉ siècle à nos jours, 12 vols.
Oncken, Wilhelm (editor), Allgemeine Geschichte in Einzeldarstellungen, 50 vols.

CHARIOT WITH RUNNING FOOTMEN

CHAPTER II

WESTERN EDUCATION AROUND 1750

OUR SURVEY OF THE HISTORY OF EDUCA-tion in the fifteenth, sixteenth and seventeenth cen-turies[1] has shown us that the Renaissance, the Protestant Revolution and early scientific movement had brought some changes in educational aims and ideals, in curriculum and methods of teaching, in the organization and control of the schools. The ancient striving after fame, the desire to be praised, the tendency to limit one's world view to the things of this life, had, to some extent, supplanted the sterner but higher medieval ideals, and in the ranks and files of the upper classes there were now many who were openly skep-tics, or even downright materialists. The vernacular ele-mentary school had in many places taken the place of the former Latin school. The elegant expression of thought was now the chief purpose of the secondary school, instead of a formal preparation for the subtleties of dialectic which had been its main concern in medieval times. More attention was now given to the study of the mother tongue; there was a tendency to treat history and geography as separate sub-jects, and to introduce the new sciences into the curriculum. Hebrew, classical philology and literature were taught in the Faculty of Arts, and in some universities the traditional scholastic philosophy had been replaced by some system of natural philosophy together with lectures on the new mathe-matics and physics. In Protestant lands support and control of the schools had passed, nominally at least, from Church

[1] See Vol. II.

9

to State. On the whole however, at the beginning of the eighteenth century, the school system of the West, like its
Elementary political and economic systems, was still in
education: many ways medieval. No change worth
purpose, mentioning had taken place in elementary
education as a whole during the two hundred years following the sixteenth century revolution. Everywhere its purpose was still essentially religious, as we can gather from school regulations still in full force around 1750, or from text books that have come down

FATHER OF FAMILY READING THE BIBLE

to us. Thus the Connecticut law of 1650, which remained in force until 1792, provided that "All masters of families do, once a week, at least, catechise their children and servants, in the grounds and principles of religion, and if any be unable to do so much, that then, at the least, they procure such children or apprentices to learn some short orthodox catechism, without book, that they may be able to answer to the questions that shall be propounded to them out of such catechism by their parents or masters. . . ."[1] A circular of the Consistory of Gotha, dated September 11, 1741, complains that many teachers ". . . are unable to awaken in the children's heads a true understanding of the catechism, unable to jot down the sermon. . . ."[2] Noah Webster replying to a request sent by Barnard states that in his childhood or around 1760 the books used in the American Colonies were Dilworth's Spell-

[1] Barnard's American Journal of Education, Vol. IV, p. 660.
[2] Ibid., Vol. XX, p. 584.

ing Books, the Psalter, Testament and Bible.[1] We read in
the regulations of Charity Schools, which became quite
common in England and the American Colonies in the
eighteenth century, that the school master "shall be a
member of the Church of England, of a sober life and
conversation, not under the age of 25 years, one that fre-
quents the Holy Communion . . . one who understands
well the Ground and Principles of the Christian Religion,
and is able to give a good account thereof to the Minister
of the Parish or Ordinary on Examination."[2] Some of the
books used in those Charity Schools were the Bible, Testament and Common Prayer Book, the Church Catechism,
the Church Catechism broken into short questions, Lewis'
Exposition of the Church Catechism, Worthington's Scrip-
ture-Catechism, the First Principles of practical Christianity,
Dr. Woodward's Short Catechism with an Explanation of
divers hard Words . . . ;[3] the list is a rather long one. A
still better illustration of the religious purpose of elementary school education in the eighteenth century is the reading matter of its primers and spellers. The New England
Primer, for instance, was intensely religious throughout
and it has been computed that more than 3,000,000 copies
of the book were sold in America alone in 150 years. In
Catholic elementary schools, of course, religion was then
as it is today the center around which were grouped the
other subjects. But as the century is drawing to its end
signs begin to appear of a weakening of the hold of the
old religious traditions on the elementary schools, particularly in Germany and English speaking countries. Greater
tolerance is shown in licensing teachers, dissenting sects
are allowed to have their own schools, new text books are
published and used, in which the former religious mate-

---

[1] *Ibid.*, Vol. XXVI, pp. 195-196.
[2] An Account of Charity Schools, etc., p. 4, London, 1709.
[3] Allen, W. O. B., and McClure, E., History of the S. P. C. K. (Society for the
    Promotion of Christian Knowledge), p. 187, London, 1898.

rial has been curtailed and receded into the background. Some of the causes of this change were local; in the American Colonies, for instance, the decline of the once paramount religious motive in education could be partially ascribed to the rude frontier life of the pioneers; but the main cause of the decline there as everywhere else was the slow but steady progress of the philosophy of the age.[1]

The content of elementary school education was still substantially what it had been for centuries before, including everywhere at its best the elements of religion, reading, arithmetic, writing and music. That, however, should not convey the impression that there was a uniform elementary course of study. In fact, there was great diversity, even in the same country, as to what was actually taught in elementary schools. All of them provided some instruction in the elements of religion and reading, the free subjects—free in the sense that usually no fee was charged for those studies; arithmetic and writing, on the other hand, were in many places considered extra subjects, taught by specialists, who would go from one school to another according to the demand, and charge a special fee; music, and not very much music at that, was hardly taught outside of Teutonic countries. The "Conduct of the Schools"[2] could be taken as a fair description of elementary school work at its best in Latin countries, the school regulations of Frederick II and Maria Theresa[3] would answer the same purpose for Teutonic countries, and those of the English Charity Schools,[4] for England and the American Colonies; but it must be borne in mind that those regulations merely expressed a desideratum and do not describe actual conditions, which in many cases fell far short of the mark.

content,

[1] See ch. III.
[2] See Vol. II, p. 241.
[3] See Barnard's American Journal, Vol. XXII, pp. 861-868 and 879-884.
[4] See Allen and McClure, *op. cit.*

The elementary school was known under various names: parish school, little school, town or village school, trivial school seem to have been the more common names on the Continent; parish school, Charity school, Dame school, in England and the American Colonies. The last two deserve a few words of explanation. The Dame school[1] had its origin in post-Reformation days. As its name would suggest it was conducted by a woman, often a widow, who managed to eke out a small additional income by looking after the children of the neighborhood for a few hours every week-day, and imparting to them the rudiments of reading, sometimes writing and arithmetic. The Dame school has a special significance for the United States in this that it was in many localities the forerunner of the nineteenth century elementary school. The Charity schools owed their origin to two Societies founded in England around 1700: the Society for the Promotion of Christian Knowledge (S.P.C.K.) and the Society for the Propagation of the Gospel in Foreign Parts (S.P.G.). The Charity school[2] was a parish school expressly maintained for the benefit of poor children, to teach them reading, writing and the Catechism of the Anglican Church, in the words of the second Society, "to make them loyal church members and to fit them for work in that station of life in which it had pleased their Heavenly Father to place them." In some schools arithmetic was also taught and there was given some manual training either at the schools or at some nearby "school of industry" (work house).[3] Boys and girls were provided with books and clothing and wore a regular uniform. Charity schools rapidly multiplied in England and her American Colonies. By the middle of the eighteenth century there were approximately 2,000 caring

[1] Bartley, Geo., The Schools for the People; Sydney, Wm., England and the English in the Eighteenth Century.
[2] See Allen and McClure, *op. cit.*
[3] Fox, Bourne, H. R., Life of John Locke, Vol. II, p. 383.

for some 50,000 children. Another type of elementary school which was quite common in the eighteenth century was the private adventure, sometimes called the "hedge school." It was very similar to the Dame school but was taught by an itinerant schoolmaster, now in one place, now in another. The name "hedge school" seems to have originated in Ireland when the English repressive laws compelled Catholics to receive their instruction in hiding, "on the highways and on the hillsides, in ditches and behind hedges, in the precarious shelter of the ruined walls of some ancient abbey, under the roof of a peasant's cabin."[1]

The quality of the elementary school teaching body was, on the whole, of the poorest. Outside the Catholic teaching congregations very few teachers had received teachers, any professional training worth mentioning, and fewer still looked to teaching as their only, or at least their chief occupation. In the common run of things the elementary school teacher was the church sexton, or bell ringer, or beadle, or gravedigger, or some shoemaker, tailor, barber, crippled soldier, old dame, who considered teaching as a useful adjunct to their main employment, a means of making both ends meet. Nor was this attitude towards the profession confined to the ranks of teachers; we find it in higher official circles. Schoolmasters in Prussia had to be selected from tailors, carpenters, wheelwrights, weavers, blacksmiths. Later on Frederick the Great ordered that his crippled and superannuated soldiers should enjoy the same privilege. Hermann Krüsi, who was for sixteen years Pestalozzi's main helper, has left us an interesting account of the way he became a schoolmaster in 1793 at the age of eighteen. The following passage deserves quotation here because of the first hand information it supplies concerning the preparation of elementary school teach-

[1] McCarthy, Justin H., Ireland since the Union, p. 13.

ers in central Europe, and other lands as well, at the close of the eighteenth century. ". . . Since my leaving the day school, where I had learned and practiced only reading, learning by rote, and mechanical copying, and while I was growing up to adult age, I had so far forgotten to write that I no longer knew how to make all the capital letters; my friend, Sonderegger, therefore procured me a copy from a teacher in Altstättin well known as a writing master. This single copy I wrote over as often as a hundred times, for the sake of improving my handwriting. I had no other special

A SCHOOLMASTER

preparation for the profession; but, notwithstanding, I ventured, when the notice was given from the pulpit, to offer myself as a candidate for the position, with but small hope of obtaining it, but consoling myself with the thought that at least I should come off without shame."[1] In the American Colonies teachers were advertised for let like servants, and were rated as such. Little wonder that under such conditions elementary school instruction was of the most rudimentary character, the method crude, and the discipline harsh.

School books were few, costly and none too attractive.

[1] Barnard's American Journal, Vol. V., pp. 162-163.

The young scholar would master his letters and begin to
read from some (alphabet) A B C book. A
school books,   very simple contrivance for that purpose was
known in English speaking countries as the
"Horn book."[1] It consisted of a thin board of oak, sometimes with, sometimes without a handle, upon which was
pasted a printed slip bear-
ing the alphabet and the
Lord's Prayer, the whole
covered with a sheet of
translucid horn. From
this most elementary of
readers the child would
pass on to the reading of
extracts from the Bible,
more commonly though
to the Catechism, which
of course varied from
country to country or
rather from one Church
to another, and was the
very core around which
centered the whole of
elementary education.

Children were drilled
upon its contents, had to memorize its questions and answers, and were constantly reminded of the doctrines therein
expounded by teachers and preachers. The following extract from the Conduct of Schools fairly well expresses the
common practice in Catholic lands for religious instruction,
"They (the Brothers) shall teach them (the pupils) also
orthography, and arithmetic, the matins and vespers, the
Lord's Prayer and Hail Mary, the Apostle's Creed and Con-
fiteor and the French translations of these prayers, the Com-

[1] See Tuer, A. W., History of the Horn Book, 2 Vols.

mandments of God and of the Church, the responses at the Holy Mass, the Catechism, the duties of a Christian, and the maxims and precepts that Our Lord has left us in the Holy Testament. They shall teach the Catechism half an hour daily."[1]

In England and her colonies, towards the end of the seventeenth century, the Catechism as a book for beginners was gradually replaced by the illustrated primer. Originally a book of devotion for the use of adults, this new reader was adapted to school use by the insertion of the alphabet, some syllables and words, the figures, list of the books of the Bible and poems. The first English primer, the Protestant Tutor, appeared in London in 1685; an abridged edition of it was published in Boston around 1690 under the name of The New England Primer and it became at once very popular. For the next hundred years it was the most widely used school book in the American Colonies. The Boston Dame schools still used it as late as 1806.

Other primers followed it, such as The History of Genesis, a collection of short stories   method, based on the first book of the Bible, The Child's Weeks Work, a little compendium of fables, proverbs, maxims, extracts from the Catechism, but none of those subsequent primers attained the popularity of the first one. The next type of reader was the so-called speller. Dilworth's *A New Guide to the English Tongue* superseded by Noah Webster's *American Spelling Book* (1783) were very popular forms of this reading text book in the eighteenth and nineteenth centuries. Text books in arithmetic were few and seldom used by pupils; each one made up his own notebook under the dictation of the teacher, or copied from the blackboard. The work was too often of a most mechanical character, a matter of words and rules to be committed to memory, though we find here and there attempts at a more

[1] See Vol. II, p. 241.

rational teaching of the subject; thus Christian Trapp, a co-worker of Basedow at the Dessau Philanthropinum, advocated the teaching of the fundamental operations with nuts and other objects before figures were learned.[1] Writing, like arithmetic, was an educational luxury to be procured by going after school hours to the school of an arithmetic teacher or of a scrivener, sometimes from an itinerant teacher.

In spite of the fact that nearly three quarters of a century had elapsed since St. Jean Baptiste de La Salle had introduced the simultaneous or grading method of teaching in the schools of the Brothers of the Christian Schools, elementary instruction in the second half of the eighteenth century was still chiefly individualistic. The schoolmaster was occupied not so much in actual teaching as in dictating words, sentences, rules, sums, assigning tasks, cutting quills, examining the work of some pupil, or listening to his recitation. The pupils came individually to the teacher, to submit their written work to his perusal, or to read, or to recite something they had committed to memory. Appeal to the interest of the child, his imagination, reasoning powers, in other words, a real technique of instruction was something unknown. If we add to this the fact that school buildings were rather the exception, that school sessions had to be held in the kitchen or living room of the teacher, we can form some idea of the kind of discipline which perforce must prevail in eighteenth century schools. Speaking of the schools which he had actually known, Diesterweg says, "Stern severity and cruel punishments were the order of the day, and by them the children were kept in order. Parents governed children, too young to attend, by threats of the schoolmaster and the school, and when they went it was with fear and trembling. The rod, the cane, the rawhide were necessary apparatus in each school. The punishments

[1] Trapp, E. C., Versuch einer Pädagogik.

of the teacher exceeded those of a prison. Kneeling on peas, sitting on the shame bench, standing in the pillory, wearing an ass-cap, standing before the school door in the open street with a label on the back or breast, and other similar devices were the remedies which the rude men of the age devised . . . the learning and training correspond; the one was strictly a mechanical process, the other only bodily punishment."[1]

It must be borne in mind, however, that the school provided but a part, and a small one at that, of the education which the children of the masses received.

Country life was in itself an excellent   other
schooling for the sons and daughters of the   agencies,
peasant class. They had then, as they have
today, the benefits of an open air life, of a constant, first

FENCING SCHOOL

hand contact with nature, and they received a training which partly at least is denied country boys and girls of our own time, as a consequence of the introduction of machinery in farming and the invasion of the home by manufactured goods. Boys and girls had all their little share in the work on the farm and in the home, which was still then to a large extent a self producing and self supporting com-

[1] See Barnard's American Journal, Vol. IV, pp. 343-345.

munity, mending and repairing its own clothing, footwear, tools and implements, even manufacturing much of it. This life on the farm not only afforded for the younger generation the best kind of manual training, with all its physical and intellectual benefits, but it developed self-reliance, the sense of duty and responsibility to the community. In towns and cities the apprenticeship system still provided a remarkable training for boys intending to enter the trades.[1] Eighteenth century records show that the apprenticing of boys had

JOHN LYONS' SCHOOL

then everywhere become a well-organized institution. By the indenture of apprenticeship[2] the master was bound not only to train the boy for his trade but to act in all things in loco parentis, feed and clothe him, look after his morals and start him in life at the end of the period of apprenticeship, which varied according to trade and country from three to seven years. In England and the American Colonies apprenticing was compulsory for the children of the poor.[3] The origin of the institution went back to the reign of Elizabeth. It will be remembered that, as a consequence of the whole-

[1] See Vol. I, pp. 155 ff.
[2] See Dunlop and Denman, English Apprenticeship and Child Labor, p. 352.
[3] See Dunlop and Denman, op. cit.

sale robbery of Church property by the sixteenth century reformers thousands of people, who had depended upon that property for work or relief were deprived of all means of sustenance. The blow had come as a climax to a long crisis in English economic life, which began in the four-teenth century and was brought about mainly by the change of England from a farming to a sheep raising country, and by the growth of trade and manufacture. Thousands of peasants flocked to towns and cities in search of work, but the growth of manufacture was not rapid enough to give employment to all newcomers and there was an alarming increase in the number of people who were in need of poor-relief. The result of it all, insofar as education is concerned, was that there were at the close of the sixteenth century a large number of children who were not properly cared for, and a series of laws was enacted to remedy this situation: laws restricting begging, ordering church collections for the relief of the poor, the establishment of workhouses, the so-called schools of industry, for the poor and their children, and the taxation of the owners of property for poor-relief. In the eighteenth century the practice of conducting "schools of industry," supported by the parish "rates," had become quite common in England and the American Colo-nies. For many years to come the State will go no further in England in its support of elementary schools. Education will continue to be re-   school sup-garded as a concern of the Church, or some-   port. thing which belongs to the province of private initiative, and thus we find in eighteenth and nine-teenth century England endowed schools founded to take, so far as possible, the place of those which the Reformation had closed, schools for the poor supported from the parish rates, subscriptions, church tithes, charity schools and pri-vate adventure schools of various types deriving their support from fees. The same condition existed in the American Colonies, though there, as we have seen,[1] there was in the north a marked tendency towards state support and state control of elementary education. In Continental Europe the clearest evidence of such a tendency is found in the Dutch Provinces and some German States like Prussia. Even there, however, as everywhere else, church funds, lotteries, subscription lists, supplied most of the means of support.

There is no gainsaying that in some respects the child is today better taken care of, better educated than one hundred

OLD KINGS SCHOOL FROM THE MINT YARD

and fifty years ago. His physical welfare, his regular attendance at school, are looked after by an army of physicians, trained nurses, truant officers, and his labor is regulated by laws. As a consequence, child mortality has been greatly reduced. Boys and girls who do not know the rudiments of reading, writing and arithmetic are today the exception, whereas they seem to have been the majority one hundred and fifty years ago; nay, the stock of book knowledge of the ordinary child today is amazingly large, even when compared with that of many eighteenth century elementary school teachers; corporal punishment is unknown, at least forbidden, in the classroom today; the playground is a fea-

[1] See Vol. II, pp. 176 ff.

ture of the school plan, and our school buildings would be mistaken for palaces by eighteenth century folks. Every true friend of the child and the race will rejoice at this bettering of the conditions surrounding child life. And yet one may be pardoned for wondering if the child is better prepared to face the hardships of life today than he was one hundred and fifty years ago.

Secondary schools were still overwhelmingly of the humanistic, classical or "grammar school" type, though here and there could be found, in the name or curriculum of an institution, a reminder of the influence of realism. In England the greater number of secondary schools were known as grammar schools, the others being academies. At the beginning of the century the grammar schools were still in a fairly good condition of efficiency, but by 1750 they had fallen into a state of decay which became more and more pronounced as years went by. The only exceptions in this general condition of decline were the larger grammar schools like Winchester and Eton to which flocked the sons of the aristocracy and became known as Public Schools.[1]

Secondary education: in England,

Academies of the French and German type never flourished in England or her Colonies, but many "Dissenters'" academies were founded in the seventeenth and eighteenth centuries; their student body, drawn at first from the wealthy or well-to-do, came later from a poorer class, and funds for their support had to be provided. The subjects taught in those "Dissenters'" academies were, in addition to the classics and Hebrew, theology, logic, ethics, natural philosophy, somatology, pneumatology and chronology. The students were not only prepared for the ministry, but for medicine and public life. For over a hundred years those

the American colonies,

[1] See Vol. II, p. 72.

non-conformist academies did a good service to English
education in offering facilities for secondary and even higher
education to a large section of the population to whom the
Act of Uniformity (1662) had closed the doors of secondary
schools and universities. The example of their progressive,
liberal course of studies also contributed to the introduction
into the curriculum of secondary schools and universities,
of subjects to which the narrow humanism of the seventeenth century had paid scant attention.

  With the close of the eighteenth century the activity of
the academy in England came to an end. At that time it

was becoming more and
more the typical secondary
school in the young American Republic. During the
Colonial period the Latin
grammar school, a direct
importation f r o m t h e
homeland, had been in all
Colonies the typical secondary institution. It was

SALEM SCHOOL HOUSE WITH
THE WHIPPING POST IN NEAR STREET

under the direct control of
the local Church, and its
function was to prepare for the college and to perpetuate
the religious denomination which controlled and supported it. Latin, Greek and religion were for a time the
only subjects taught, but the exigencies of practical life
compelled the grammar school to introduce instruction in
English, reading, writing and arithmetic. The purpose of
the school, however, was still the same as before. It prepared for the college, and therefore ministered only to the
needs of a minority. The need of a type of school that
would provide some preparation for life for those who did
not intend to enter the professions, and which would receive
non-conformists was responsible for the rise of the academy.

The first one was Franklin's Philadelphia Academy founded in 1751 and the progenitor of the University of Pennsylvania.[1] By the close of the eighteenth century this new type of school was definitely established in all the States. Like the English institution of the same name, the American academy had a much more flexible course of study than the old Latin grammar school. Latin was still the backbone of the course, but it was now taught through the medium of English; Greek was frequently if not commonly offered; English grammar, rhetoric, declamation held an important place; history, geography, arithmetic, geometry, astronomy and the natural sciences also received some attention from the first. Another novel feature in American secondary education, which appeared with the rise of the academy, was the ever-increasing number of girls seeking admission into those schools. It was not long before a number of academies for girls were opened. To complete this brief retrospect upon American education at the close of the eighteenth century mention must be made again of the fact that there were then in existence nine colleges, founded between 1636 (Harvard) and 1770 (Dartmouth). During this period the work of the American college had been a faithful following of the studies pursued in like institutions on the other side of the Atlantic, especially at Cambridge, the purpose being to raise a body of learned men, especially ministers. Greek and oriental languages as a preparation for Biblical exegesis, logic, ethics, politics, "Divinity Catechetical," scholastic disputations, English composition and declamation, together with a smattering of arithmetic, geometry, astronomy, history and botany, constituted the work of all the American colleges down to the middle of the eighteenth century. Around that time, with the foundation of the Philadelphia Academy and a little later of Kings College, there appears a tendency to

[1] See Vol. II, p. 176.

introduce a little more science into the curriculum, but the complete breakdown of the old curriculum did not occur until a century later.

The French secondary schools, like those of all Catholic countries, were colleges affiliated with the Faculty of Arts of the universities, or institutions conducted France, by religious congregations, or again academies of the military type. Rollin's Traité des Etudes (q.v.) throws some light on the condition of French secondary education at the beginning of the eighteenth century, especially in the colleges affiliated with the universities. Of the congregational colleges the greater number and most flourishing by far were those conducted by the Society of Jesus.[1] The suppression of the Society occurring shortly after the middle of the century, and the subsequent closing of its colleges, was a great blow to secondary education. The place of the Jesuits was to some extent taken by the Oratorians, but they in turn were suppressed with the universities by the Revolution, and the whole educational system had to be organized anew.

In Germany the more common type of secondary school was still the gymnasium, but, though still essentially classical, its work had undergone a notable Germany. change under the influence of a movement started by Gesner (Johann Mathias, 1691-1761) at the newly established University of Göttingen, and known in the history of German education as new humanism. This new conception of classical studies controlled the aim and practices of the most influential German secondary schools and through them the ideals of the leading classes, even as late as the beginning of the present century. New humanism differed from fifteenth century humanism in this, that it stressed Greek instead of Latin culture. It insisted upon the study of the classics for the sake of their

[1] See Vol. II, ch. VI.

thought content, their ethical and aesthetic value. Gesner also recognized that the curriculum of the gymnasium, as it existed in his own time, was much too limited in scope. Next to the study of the classics he favored that of the mother tongue, modern languages, especially French, mathematics, natural science, history, and geography, but the actual modernizing of the classical course of study did not take place until the middle of the next century. The Ritter *akademien*, which had flourished in the seventeenth century, were now on the wane, but a new type of school had appeared, the real school, a product of Francke's work at Halle,[1] which was to win full recognition in the nineteenth century under various names.[2]

The universities were still, and would continue for many years to come, in the condition we found them at the close of the seventeenth century. Theology, law, medicine and arts, the latter here and there referred to as philosophy, were still the four university faculties. Their work and the spirit in which it was carried on were still the work and spirit of post-Renaissance and post-Reformation days. As noted before,[3] the only places where there was any sign of a departure from the traditional university work and spirit were Halle and Göttingen in Germany and to some extent Cambridge in England.

On the whole, after due allowance has been made for partisan exaggeration, for the educative influence of other

---

[1] See Vol. II, pp. 227 ff.

[2] The condition of the schools in France was typical of their condition in other Latin countries; schools in Switzerland, Austria-Hungary, Holland, Scandinavia were more or less in the same condition as in Germany. In Russia, just emerging from barbarism, Peter the Great, with the help of Westerners, had founded a few schools for the preparation of experts in the navy, the artillery and engineering corps. Poland had three universities and many secondary schools conducted by the Jesuits and Piarists. In both countries hardly any provision was made for the school education of the masses. Everywhere in Latin lands, as also in Poland and Russia, the Church had, of course, her own schools for the preparation of the clergy.

[3] See Vol. II, pp. 229 ff.

agencies than the schools and the conditions of eighteenth century life, it must be admitted that education was then far from what its friends would have wished it to be. Elementary schools were far too few and poorly equipped, their teachers poorly prepared and poorly paid, classroom work was of the most mechanical character, and the school reached only a small fraction of the population. No provision worth mentioning had been made so far for an adequate industrial preparation of the masses, there were no technical institutions, and the secondary schools and universities kept aloof from the realities and needs of the time. In short, reforms were sorely needed everywhere, and they were soon to be started in earnest. Unfortunately the spirit in which they were undertaken and carried out was too often a spirit of antagonism to the past, to tradition, to christianity, for no better reason than they were tradition, past, and christianity. Theories born of blind prejudice, blissful ignorance of the past and a shallow philosophy became the standard by which existing institutions should be judged and a new order of things established in their stead.

SOURCES

Barnard, H., American Journal of Education, contains many reprints of original documents either in toto or in part.
Dexter, E., History of Education in the United States, contains many references to original sources.
Home and Colonial School Society. Annual Reports.
Some of the books listed below also contain several references to sources.

REFERENCES

Allain, L'Abbé E., L'instruction primaire en France avant la Révolution.
Allen, W. O. B., and McClure, E., Two Hundred Years; History of the S. P. C. K., 1698-1898.
Barnard, H., English Pedagogy.
Barnard, H., German Teachers and Educators.
Bartley, G. C. T., The Schools for the People.
Cardwell, J. F., The Story of a Charity School.
Dittes, F., Geschichte der Erziehung und des Unterrichtes.
Field, Mrs. E. M., The child and his books.
Findlay, J. J., Arnold of Rugby.

Huxley, T., Lay Sermons.
Johnson, Clifton, Old Time Schools and Schoolbooks.
Lantoine, H., Histoire de l'enseignement Secondaire en France au XVIIme et au
    début du XVIIIme siècle.
Lecky, W. E. H., England in the Eighteenth Century.
Pascoe, C. G., Two hundred years of the S. P. G.
Paulsen, Friedrich, German Education, Past and Present.
Paulsen, Friedrich, The German Universities.
Scott, J. F., Historic Essays on Apprenticeship and Vocational Education.
Sydney, Wm. C., England and the English in the 18th Century.
Tuer, A. W., History of the Horn Book.
Tuer, A. W., Old Fashioned Children's Books.

CHAPTER III

THE ENLIGHTENMENT

THE EIGHTEENTH CENTURY HAS BEEN RE-
ferred to by its admirers as "the philosophical age,"
"the age of reason," "the age of nature," "the critical age,"
"the scientific age," "the pedagogical age," and what not.
None of those terms, taken singly, would do full justice to
all the propensities of the period, and some of them are decidedly pretentious. The eighteenth century "philosophers"
were fond of referring to their own time as "le siècle
éclairé," the "enlightened age," and it will be for that reason alone that we shall consider the eighteenth century
tendencies under the heading of Enlightenment.[1] Taken
literally, the term means the action of giving light, of dis-
pelling darkness, breaking the clouds which obscure the
sky; figuratively, from the Enlightenment
viewpoint, the sky to be enlightened is the
human mind, the clouds obscuring it are
the traditions and beliefs which the past
has bequeathed to us, and the light bearer, the cloud dis-
pelling sun, is reason; understand here by reason, the preconceived notions which the eighteenth century philosophers
entertained concerning man, society and nature. Reason,
enlightened reason, was declared to be our one safe guide
in life, the supreme arbiter in all things; religion, traditions, literature, art, science, philosophy, institutions must

The meaning
of the term.

[1] See Catholic Encyclopedia, art. "Illuminati," "Masonry," "Rationalism";
Brunetière, F., Etudes Critiques; Faguet, E., XVIIIᵉ siècle; Cambridge
Modern History, Vols. V, VIII; Lavisse et Rambaud, Histoire Générale,
Vols. VI, VII.

all appear at its bar and submit to its scrutiny. This "free thinking," it was asserted, is the surest road to happiness, because once enlightened, man will be free from the shackles which a superstitious past has put upon his conduct; he will be able to follow the unerring promptings of his own unerring nature, and having reached that stage of blissfulness, he will be in duty bound to work for the salvation of his brethren still groping in darkness.

The "philosophers" of the eighteenth century recognized a certain kinship of spirit between their own age and the radical humanists of the Renaissance, whom they hailed as their intellectual forbears, the first enlightened men of the Christian West. They might, for that matter, have proceeded one century further back; Froissart's *Chronicles* give us the picture of a feudal nobility which had indeed preserved all the fine panoply and trappings of chivalry, but had become withal not a wit less materialistic, skeptical, self-centered than the aristocrats of the eighteenth century salons. The "Defensor Pacis" of Marsilius of Padua (1270-1342), has been likened in some respects to Rousseau's *Social Contract*, and there is much in the nominalism of William of Ockham (1280?-1349) that would recommend itself to men like Locke and Hume.[1] Nor were Marsilius and Ockham isolated instances; the second, at least, had quite a following. Not all Ockhamists, of course, shared the extreme views of the master, but the very existence of "Ockhamism" shows that, as early as the fourteenth century, the current of Western thought had branched off into two streams, the main one running as before along the lines of Catholic doctrine, while the new current, after proceeding for some time close

The enlightenment originated in pre-Renaissance days

---

[1] William of Ockham has been described as the first Protestant. Shorn of the element of faith his philosophy would lead to materialism.

to the parent stream, withdrew farther and farther away
from it. The real parting of the ways came with the revival
of paganism in the fifteenth century. We
and developed have seen that the humanists were not, as a
through the rule, friendly to medieval learning.[1] Some
revival of of them tried to revive in all their pagan
pagan phi- originality the philosophical systems of an-
losophy, cient days. Gemistus Pletho, a Greek scholar
who had attended the Council of Ferrara-
Florence (1438-1445) as ambassador of Emperor John VIII,
founded a Platonic Academy at Florence. His fellow coun-
tryman, later Cardinal, Bessarion, succeeded him in the
government of the school, which he had to defend against
his compatriots, Gennadius, Theodorus, of Gaza, and Geor-
gius of Trebizond, who were then trying to win adherents
for the Lyceum.[2] Justus Lipsius (1547-1606) and Gaspar
Schoppe (born 1562) revived the doctrines of the Stoa, Gas-
sendi (1592-1655) those of Epicurus, while Pyrrhonism reappeared in the Essays of Michel de Montaigne (1533-1592).

Of a deeper significance than this revival of ancient philosophy, and a clearer symptom of the new orientation
philosophy was likely to take, were the great discoveries of
the latter fifteenth and the sixteenth centuries. A fever for
researches, discoveries, new theories, seems to have taken
hold of the men of the age. A curious product of this intellectual restlessness is seen in those theories,
the new phi- partially modeled after Neo Platonic doc-
losophies of trines, which go by the name of theosophy, a
nature strange medley of old superstitions, Christian beliefs, philosophy and experimental
science. In the study of nature the purpose of theosophy was
first to discover traces of the Great Mysterious Being whom
nature conceals and yet, in some ways, reveals to us. That

[1] See Vol. II, chs. II, III.
[2] See Vol. II, ch. III.

purpose, so the theosophist believed, could be achieved through some mysterious sesame, some secret doctrine, such as we find in Neo Platonism and the Jewish Cabala. But the theosophist was not satisfied with trying to fathom the Great Mystery; his greater ambition was to rule over nature, and he believed that he could control it through the secret arts of magic and astrology. Neo Platonism taught that the world is a hierarchy of divine forces, a grading of agencies in which the higher ones command and the lower ones obey. Hence, so argued the theosophist, in order to govern nature and fashion it according to his wishes, he must be united with the hierarchy of sidereal powers on which the earthly forces depend.

This enthusiasm for long discarded philosophical doctrines and wild theories may have been nothing else, on the part of some humanists, than a form of protest against the decadent philosophy of the schools, but there were others, like Leonardo Bruni, Lorenzo Valla, Angelo Poliziano, Pietro Pomponazzi,[1] who were in full sympathy with the spirit of pagan philosophy and would have it translated into practice. Life, so taught those neo pagans, was to be thought of as a perpetual festival, as a work of art, receiving meaning and value from what it can yield in wealth, knowledge, power, honor, comfort and pleasure. Christianity promises eternal life to the just man; why should not we try to fashion for ourselves, like the heroes of old, another ideal life in the Halls of Fame? Christian asceticism teaches us to despise the body, but is not a strong, healthy body the first prerequisite for the enjoyment of this life? And the second great prerequisite for happiness in this life is a well-developed mind, well stocked with the wisdom of the ancient sages, untrammeled by prejudice or tradition, ready to appreciate beauty under whatever form, conscious of its

[1] They all belonged to the fifteenth century.

own power to attain truth, with none of the medieval reliance upon authority.[1]

Greek philosophy had risen from speculation on the nature of the physical world to the study of the nature of man, and it had culminated in some sort of natural theology in the Alexandrian Period. The reverse process is shown in the evolution of modern philosophy. Starting from its opposition to Scholasticism it falls back upon the spiritualism of the Academy and Lyceum, then gradually sinks into physics. This trend downward has already been noticed in the theosophists; it becomes more evident in the doctrines of Francesco Patrizzi (1527-1597) and Bernardino Telesio (1508-1588), the latter the founder of the Accademia Telesiana of Naples, whose cosmological conceptions very closely approximate the naturalistic systems of the Ionian School. Telesio's writings were known to and influenced Giordano Bruno (1548-1600) and Francis Bacon (1567-1626), the two founders of the modern philosophy of nature. Bruno accepts unreservedly the heliocentric system and makes it the pivotal element in his metaphysics, a sort of naturalistic pantheism. Since the Universe is infinite, Bruno teaches, and since there cannot be two infinites, God must be identical with the Universe. God is neither the Creator nor the first mover, but the matter and soul of the world, not a transcendent and temporary cause, but the inner and permanent cause of things, a principle at once material and formal, producing, organizing and governing things from within. All beings whatsoever are both body and soul, and they reproduce in some particular form the God Universe. The cosmos is in a constant process of evolution, of which the human soul is the highest form. Tommaso Campanella (1568-1639), another representative of the Italian philosophy of nature, tried, but in vain, to reach some sort of a compromise between Pantheism and Catholic theology. God is absolute

[1] See bibliography of Vol. II, ch. II.

power, absolute knowledge, and absolute will or love. All created beings, not even excepting inert matter, participate in the absolute and reproduce its essential elements: power, knowledge and will. All created beings strive to return to the absolute and in that sense they are religious; religion is the universal, natural condition of all creation. With Francis Bacon (1561-1626) naturalism abandons what it calls a priori speculation in order to confine itself to the observation of nature, *i.e.,* physics. Philosophy affirms its complete independence from theology; philosophers, for a time at least, will profess to be naturalists in science and supernaturalists in religion. But the road is not a long one to travel from the exclusion of the spiritual from the domain of science to denying its very existence, witness Thomas Hobbes (1588-1677) and his materialistic metaphysics.[1]

Meanwhile free thinking had also asserted itself in the field of religion. Why could not we, who are versed in the study and interpretation of the ancient texts, study the Sacred Scriptures and the Fathers of the Church as we do Plato or the Pandects? Thus argued the radical humanists; and the Reformation. thus, two centuries later, were to argue the Encyclopedists. From this "freedom" of thought to an actual break with the Church the step was not a long one; it was taken by Luther and Calvin, both of whom, as we have seen,[2] were for some time on the best of terms with the humanists, in the belief that they were all serving a common cause. But the times were not propitious for "free" thinking; passion was running high and woe to him who dared, in the Protestant camp, avail himself of that freedom of thought proclaimed so loudly by the Reformation leaders. Michael Servetus had good cause to regret his trust in Calvin's liberalism.[3] Rabe-

---

[1] See Turner, W., History of Philosophy, pp. 422 ff.; Weber, A., History of Philosophy, pp. 300 ff.

[2] See Vol. II, ch. IV.

[3] See Erichsohn in Opera Calvini, Vol. LIX, pp. 533, 534.

lais escaped a similar fate in France only through a strict adherence to his motto, "As far as the stake exclusively." He was ever careful to cloak his paganized Christianity under a semblance of respect for the Sacred Scriptures and the authority of the Church. He was never loath to affirm his belief in a Creator and Lord of nature, the immortality of the soul, eternal rewards and punishments. Even so, his protectors in the court circle were more than once hard put to it to save him from going to the stake "inclusively."[1]

The stream of free thought was, for some time, forced to run under ground and we have to wait until the end of the sixteenth century before we see it reappear, not in a bold, assertive attitude to be sure, but in the garb of Montaigne's amiable skepticism. Outwardly the seventeenth century was christian enough, but signs were not wanting of a deep undercurrent of skepticism and negation which through the Reformation and Montaigne's skepticism connects the radical humanists with the Enlightenment. The rationalism, infidelity, materialism of the eighteenth century did not then lack either examples or outspoken teachers in the preceding age, but the impetus to the movement came from a new system of philosophy which very few men at the time, least of all its author, suspected of being so revolutionary in character. Seen from our vantage point, the philosophy of Descartes (1596-1650) throws much light on the intellectual movement which, originating in the Renaissance, culminates in the "scientific" culture of our own time. It shows us in a bold, clear, though somewhat abstract form, the purpose of the whole movement: to develop a purely rational, scientific conception of the universe, of life and its meaning, of man, his origin, destiny, and relations to his fellow men. Reason is to be the supreme arbiter of the true; authority, tradition, revelation are to be set aside whenever it is a question of reaching certitude; our one sure guide is the method of the

[1] See Lanson, G., Histoire de la Littérature Française, pp. 250 ff.

mathematician who is ever careful to hold fast to the thread connecting one truth with the next and the preceding. Through the use of this purely rationalistic method man can legitimately hope some day to grasp and explain every truth, however remote it might   Through appear at present. There is no limit to scien-   Cartesianism tific investigations and discoveries, no limit either to the material progress following the application of those discoveries; disease, even death, will be conquered, and man may hope some day to be the sole, unchallenged master of his own habitat; understand that he will substitute his own self to God. All that and more is contained in principle in Descartes' rationalism, but was not evident from the first. When Cartesianism appeared it was hailed by many, even leaders of the Gallican Church, as a new and sturdy ally of the Catholic faith. It was not until the close of the century, after the dogmatic assertions of Descartes had been proven untenable upon his own ground of systematic doubt, that the dangers to the faith, involved in his rationalism, became evident.[1]

One of the first philosophers to draw from Cartesianism conclusions that were undreamed of by its author was the Englishman, John Locke, (1632-1704) whom we may consider as the intellectual father of eighteenth century Enlightenment. Locke's philosophy came as a protest against what he calls the favorite method of the universities, of closing one's eyes, of stopping one's ears, of ignoring the real world. In his *Essay Concerning Human Understanding* he undertook to prove that all our ideas come to us from without. More explicitly, his purpose was to discover the origin of our ideas, to ascer-   and Locke tain the degree of evidence and extent of our knowledge, and to mark clearly the limits of human un-

[1] See Mahony, M., Cartesianism. For extended bibliography on Descartes and Cartesianism, see Ueberweg-Heinze, Gesch. d. Philos., and Baldwin, Dictionary of Philosophy and Psychology.

derstanding. There is no innate idea; all our knowledge is acquired. The soul is originally an empty tablet. Not a new conception this, but Locke has a way of his own to explain it. According to him our understanding is nothing else than a passive capacity to receive. Sensation and reflection are the efficient and only cause of our ideas. Sensation is the source of our knowledge of external objects; reflection, of our knowledge of internal facts. The so-called first notions, first principles, are a product of the materials supplied by experience, and all such first principles can be reduced to that of identity, which again is supplied by experience. The truth of the matter, Locke's view notwithstanding, is that sensation is the partial, material cause of knowledge, that abstraction, not reflection, is responsible for the appearance of ideas. Locke was fond of repeating the old psychological maxim, "Nihil est in intellectu quod prius non fuerit in sensu," "There is nothing in the mind which was not before in the senses," to which one of his correspondents once replied, "True, except the mind itself," *i.e.,* the faculty it possesses for elaborating the materials it receives, in other words, the power of analyzing, abstracting, comparing, generalizing, judging and reasoning. All that we may call reflection, but not in Locke's sense. Again it is doubtful whether all first principles can be reduced to that of identity, but surely the latter is not supplied by experience. Experience deals with particular facts; the only assertion we can make on its authority is that such or such a thing which is, is. The principle of identity, on the other hand, expresses an absolute, universal, necessary impossibility of contradiction which transcends experience.

Knowledge, says Locke, is "the perception of the connection of and agreement or disagreement and repugnance of our ideas." It is of three kinds: intuitive, the perception of the agreement of two ideas without the intervention of a third one; demonstrative, following the intervention of a third one; sensitive, the perception of finite things without us. Locke rates lowest the third kind of knowledge; yet he holds that our knowledge after all does not go beyond it, for whenever metaphysics attempts to go very far beyond it, it is confronted with insuperable difficulties. Locke's political and moral doctrines do not rise one whit above the trend of his theory of knowledge; they bear the stamp of an empiricism which must ultimately lead to a crude sensism, and that was Locke's main contribution to the eighteenth century.

To Locke's time belong the first noteworthy protagonists, in modern times, of a sort of "naturalistic" philosophy of religion, purporting to free religious thought from the control of authority. Its motto is "Believe in God and do your duty"; any positive religion, according to those deists, is but "a creation of cunning rulers and crafty priests to enslave mankind"; Christianity in its primitive form was an ideal expression of the universal, natural religion, but it has deteriorated through the accretion of positive elements. John Toland, Anthony Collins, Matthew Tindal, Thomas Chubb, Thomas Morgan, and Henry St. John Viscount Bollingbroke[1] were the leading exponents of this natural religion. To the same period belong a group of English moralists, who developed from Locke's ethical principles a new system of ethics independently both of religious and state authority. Thus for Shaftesbury (1671-1713)[2] the essence of morality lies in the proper balancing of the social and selfish impulses, and this balancing is achieved through what he calls the aesthetic sense, or power to perceive beauty, which he is careful to distin-

---

[1] All these men belonged to the late seventeenth and early eighteenth century; cf. Stephen Leslie, History of English Thought in the Eighteenth Century.
[2] Cf. Stephen Leslie, op. cit.

guish from the rational faculty. Such a balancing or harmony, we are told, is our one sure guaranty of happiness, and it constitutes virtue. Positive religion degrades man by its promises of eternal rewards for his virtuous acts. Virtue should be its own reward. first in England, So much for this lame stoicism. Francis Hutcheson (1694-1746)[1] removes the faculty of moral discrimination still further from reason; with him the "moral sense" is an instinctive tendency very akin to the desire of pleasing and helping others. For Joseph Butler (1692-1752)[2] conscience, the guide of our conduct, is an autonomous ruler, which must be obeyed no matter what the effect of our action might be upon ourselves or others. Adam Smith (1723-1790),[3] the author of the *Wealth of Nations*, traces the morality of our actions to the feeling of sympathy, a doctrine we shall have occasion to see at work in the Emile of Rousseau. In short, eighteenth century ethics does away with the traditional and only sure foundation of morality: obligation, duty to God, to one's fellows and to one's self; it breaks loose from any supernatural connection; it is based on the whims and material needs of the individual; the useful, the pleasant, the agreeable become synonymous with the virtuous.

It is this deistic, empirical trend of English thought during the latter part of the seventeenth and the early eighteenth century, which we may consider as the actual beginning of the Enlightenment. It has been very aptly characterized as a reaction against the religious fanaticism which had raged longest and fiercest in the British Isles. Many men turned away in disgust from those extremes of misguided religious fervor and went to the other extreme of denying the validity

[1] *Ibid.*, also Albee, History of English Utilitarianism.
[2] *Ibid.*
[3] *Ibid.*

of revealed truth which they began to assail in book and pamphlet. On the whole, however, the warfare remained confined within the circle of scholars, philosophers and theologians, and, for the time-being at least, had practically no influence beyond that circle.[1] later in France and other countries.

French Enlightenment, on the other hand, assumed from the very start an aggressive, proselytizing attitude, and, with astonishing rapidity, it won many adherents in all classes of society. The explanation of the success of this propaganda is not far to seek. The wars of Louis XIV and the ruinous splendor of the court of Versailles had considerably increased a burden of taxation which even before was heavy enough. There was much discontent throughout the kingdom. Men's minds naturally turned to examining and criticising a social and political system which, under different circumstances, might still have endured unnoticed for generations. Books and pamphlets began to appear in which were assailed the despotism and irresponsibility of the royal power, the suppression of the local liberties, the inequality of taxation, the drying up of the sources of national wealth, the large incomes and idleness of the privileged classes.[2] With characteristic ignorance of human nature and the lessons of history, the French "philosophers" set themselves to the task of remedying those evils with all kinds of newfangled theories and declamations on despotism, fanaticism, tolerance, liberty, equality, fraternity.

The first leading protagonists of the movement were

[1] In fact, a reaction against this wave of skepticism seems to have set in in England about 1750, freethinking being then mostly confined to the secrecy of the Masonic lodges. The first grand lodge had been opened in London in the early part of the century and the society had spread in a few years to every state in Europe, North America and East India. Its membership was mostly recruited from the upper classes and its aim was then, as it is now, to replace Christianity by some sort of humanitarian philosophy. Cf. Catholic Encyclopedia, art. "Masonry," with an extensive bibliography.

[2] See de Tocqueville, Sorel, Taine, *op. cit.*

Montesquieu (1689-1755) and Voltaire (1694-1778). Returning towards 1730 from a sojourn in England, they acquainted their countrymen with the English form of government, English attitude toward the press, freedom of thought, English progress in the sciences and the doctrines prevalent among English deists and empiricists. Locke's philosophy soon had many French followers, chief among them Condillac (1715-1780), the founder of absolute sensism. Locke had distinguished two sources of ideas: sensation and reflection; Condillac recognizes only one, making reflection a product of sensibility; in

It affected every phase of Western thought.

other words, all our ideas, without exception, are derived from the senses, especially touch. Condillac, however, is not an avowed materialist. He refuses to share Locke's view that matter can think, but his French followers were not slow in taking the final step, which some philosophers across the Channel had long since taken. John Toland (1670-1722) had taught that thought is a function of the brain just as taste is of the tongue. The doctrine was reproduced with some variations by a number of eighteenth century writers: the physician and naturalist, David Hartley (1705-1757); the theologian, philosopher, and naturalist, Joseph Priestley (1733-1804); in the *Testament de Jean Meslier*,[1] which Voltaire made public; by the physician, Julien Offroy de la Mettrie (1709-1751), one of the first avowed materialists in France; by Denis Diderot (1713-1784), Robinet (1723-1789), Charles de Bonnet (1720-1793), Helvetius (1715-1771), the mathematician, Dalembert (1717-1783), the Baron d'Holbach (1723-1789), the political economist, Turgot (1727-1781), and Condorcet (1743-1794); it was finally reproduced on the eve of the Revolution, by the physician Cabanis (1757-1808), who formulated the

---

[1] Published in 3 Vols., with a preface and biographical introduction, by R. Charles, Amsterdam, 1765.

principle of psychological materialism with a frankness that has seldom if ever been surpassed. The soul is nothing else than the body endowed with feeling. The body or matter thinks, feels, and wills. Physiology and psychology are one and the same science; man is a bundle of nerves; thought is the function of the brain just as digestion is the function of the stomach and the secretion of bile that of the liver. What men call intellectual and moral phenomena are nothing else than an expression of the properties of matter, of the laws governing the whole universe, the nature of things. It was also during this period that the evolutionistic conception of the universe, which had been familiar to ancient philosophy, reappeared in various forms, foreshadowing the theories of Lamarck and Darwin.

Not all the enlightened "philosophers" openly professed the crass materialism of a Cabanis, but there was a fairly unanimous agreement concerning the position of man in the universe. Man, it was held, had been wrongly placed on a sort of pedestal by Christianity; he should be returned to nature, understand physical nature, where he belongs, because man is first of all and essentially an animal endowed with senses and sensations. Is not sensation the origin of all our ideas and therefore of all institutions? Science, not religion, gives us the true explanation of man's nature, man's origin and destiny. Economics, politics, ethics, education are all adjuncts of the sciences dealing with nature to which man belongs. Let then religion relinquish to science the place of honor which superstition, ignorance, fanaticism had assigned to it. Let science, *i.e.,* reason, pure, untrammeled, universal, reign supreme and lead us on to progress and all the comforts of civilization, the one thing after all which counts in this life.

All the characteristics of the Enlightenment were not equally evident from the first, nor, for that matter, at any one of the stages in the evolution of the movement. During the first half of the eighteenth century it was essentially skeptical and rationalistic; its fundamental principle at this stage is reliance upon human understanding, unbounded faith in reason, which is proclaimed self-sufficient and the final arbiter in all things. In the name of reason the leaders of the movement wage a relentless warfare against traditions, revealed religion, its dogmas and rites, which they deride as so many forms of ignorance and superstition; they rebel against all authority, in Church, State, society, morals, which they look upon as tyranny of thought, government, social relations, conduct. And because of this exaltation of reason the early phase of the Enlightenment was intensely aristocratic. Its leaders' aim was to substitute an aristocracy of intellect and wealth for the existing one of birth, privilege and position. For the lower classes the "philosophers" had nothing but contempt. The intellectuality of the masses, it was held, was hardly above that of the savage, and therefore they were beyond the pale of "enlightened" society. Locke's *Thoughts on Education*, or, better still, Chesterfield's *Letters*,[1] fairly express the conception of education corresponding to that phase of the Enlightenment. Its finished product, the skeptical, heartless, licentious prig, whose education has been devoted to the mastery of the stilted forms of a most artificial society, has been made familiar to us by many a novel dealing with the eighteenth century society.

The other phase of the Enlightenment may be generally characterized as a sort of reaction against the preceding tendency; over and against the cold calculations of reason it sets the claims of sentiment, as a fuller and truer expression of our nature; the skepticism, infidelity, atheism of the "intellectuals" it would replace by some sort of "natural" religion, which would more or less exclude the supernatural elements of Christianity but accept the bulk of its

[1] See Monroe's Cyclopedia of Education, Vol. I, p. 596.

morality; for the government of the privileged few, it would substitute that of the masses for whom, at least in theory, it professed unbounded sympathy. Those two complementary tendencies of the Enlightenment could be referred to as "rationalistic" and "sentimental" respectively, and their character will be still better understood after a brief consideration of the personality and writings of their leading protagonists, Voltaire of the first, and Rousseau of the second. The latter's personality and creed, because of their deep influence upon nineteenth century education, will be treated at some length in a subsequent chapter.

A second rate, some critics even say a third rate, poet and novelist, a dry if lucid historian, hopelessly superficial whenever he ventures to dabble in philosophy or science, Voltaire is at his best as a   Voltaire. pamphleteer and epistolary writer, and, as such, he displays, indeed, dazzling intellectual gifts. Unfortunately his talent too often appears in the service of destruction, personal grudges, unsufferable vanity, selfishness, spite and vindictiveness, base flattery of the powers that be, whenever flattery can bring money or honor. Intellectually, Voltaire is shallow, lacking in depth and breadth of vision, lacking the sense of the mysterious, of the infinite; he is incapable of appreciating and admiring what is really noble, great and beautiful; he lacks the historical sense, the ability to live in the past, in sympathy with bygone civilizations, the ability to appreciate their contributions to the spiritual treasures of the present. But he was gifted with a clear, lucid, alert intellect, which could detect at a glance the one important point in a bewildering mass of details; he was a past master in the use of irony and in the art of clear, arresting exposition, of bringing within the grasp of the uninitiated what seemed to be the most abstruse problems of religion, or science, or philosophy. Voltaire's treatment of these questions never, of course, goes beneath the surface of things, but he gave to his shallow, fickle generation the illusion of understanding everything, and the satisfaction of being able, without much work, to discuss questions which had seemed to belong to the province of experts. Voltaire is sometimes referred to as an eighteenth century philosopher; that needs some explanation. Of a system of philosophy he has none to offer. What he has to offer is a certain view of life made up of irreverence, even contempt for all authority, malicious criticism of all its policies, and downright, if not outspoken, materialism. His vision is all of the material present; his desire for reforms in morality, politics, economics is limited to an increase in material comfort and pleasure, for, if there is one thing which Voltaire wishes to enjoy to the full, it is this life, and herein lies the secret of his hatred of Christianity. Because Christianity teaches self-restraint, self-sacrifice, Voltaire has sworn its destruction, which he did his best to achieve by teaching unbelief, by heaping ridicule upon its doctrines, its rites, and clergy.[1]

VOLTAIRE

The critical propensities of the Enlightenment, if nothing else, would have prompted its leaders to turn their attention to education, and our survey of eighteenth century schools showed us that their condition called for much deserved

[1] See Lanson, G., Histoire de la Littérature Française; Faguet, E., XVIIIe Siècle; Brunetière, F., Etudes critiques, Séries 1, 3, 4.

criticism. In spite of the progress of science, universities and secondary schools were still conducted along strictly scholastico-humanistic lines. Apart from the work done by some religious congregations, particularly the Brothers of the Christian schools, there was as yet no provision made for industrial preparation in the schools. There were no agricultural or commercial or technical schools to meet the growing demands of the trades and industries. Elementary schools were few and poorly equipped, their teachers poorly prepared, the scope of their work too limited. But the more weighty reason urging the "philosophers" to turn their attention to education was the desire to spread their principles and to reconstruct society upon a "rational foundation." There was no surer way, it was held, nor a more rapid one to realize that dream, than to take hold of the schools and instill the principles of "enlightened" culture into the mind of the young. Once a generation had been brought up in a "new atmosphere," the triumph of the Enlightenment, it was believed, would be assured. What this new atmosphere of the school should be was not very clear as yet. Some "philosophers," like the Frenchman Diderot, and many of his confrères of the Encyclopédie would have thrown all religious beliefs and dogmas overboard, whereas the "naturalists," following the lead of Rousseau, were in favor of some sort of a "natural religion."

The attitude of the Enlightenment towards religion,

The denial by Luther and his followers of the principle of authority in matters of religious dogma should logically have led Protestants to the same conclusions as those of the naturalistic school, but they recoiled from the consequences, and so we hear even Frederick II, the "philosopher-king," declare it necessary and wholesome that the schools lay the foundation of a rational and Christian education for "the fear of God, and other useful ends." Wherever the views of the Enlightenment prevailed, however, we find that all that is characteristic of Christianity has been suppressed and all denominations have been brought together under some hazy deistic notion, as in Basedow's Philanthropinum at Dessau. There, religious instruction was based on the principle that "we owe the All Father the service of a righteous conduct," and it was to be neither Catholic, nor Lutheran, nor Calvinistic, nor Jewish, nor Mohammedan, but respect the convictions of all denominations. Institutions of the philanthropinist type, however, were the exception at the close of the eighteenth century; German schools were still and would continue to be for a time Christian in spirit. No less conservative was the English attitude towards education. Even Locke, the leading exponent of the English Enlightenment, does not hesitate to write, concerning the beginnings of education, that "The Lord's Prayer, the Creed and the Ten Commandments, t'is necessary he (the young gentleman) should know perfectly by heart." Religion continued to hold its place in the English schools as it had in the past; only there was some relaxation of the old spirit of intolerance as we can see from the new text books used in the eighteenth century, and the fact that the Dissenters were allowed once more to conduct their own schools.

The attitude of the Enlightenment towards classical studies was a sort of compromise. There was felt a certain kinship of spirit between the new age and the radicalism of some of the sixteenth century humanists. Both groups of reformers were warring against medieval ideals and traditions; both welcomed the teachings of the wise men of Greece and Rome, both idealized the ancient republican forms of government, the Greek and Roman enthusiasm for liberty, and the pagan conception of life. There was this difference, however, between the Enlightenment and the humanists, that whereas the latter had devoted themselves wholeheartedly to the revival of classical studies, the former would more or less consider such studies a waste of time. Kant well expresses the attitude of the leaders of the Enlightenment when he says: "It is absurd to deem the ancient writers superior to the modern, as though the world were decadent and all modern things, therefore, inferior to the ancient."[1] Thus Diderot makes but scant provision for classical studies in his *Plan of a University*, Rousseau banishes them entirely from Emile's education, Dalembert derides them in the Encyclopédie; they teach us, he observes, "parler sans rien dire"[2] and are perfectly useless as means of intellectual improvement. Basedow (1723-1790), it is true, included Latin in the curriculum of his Philanthropinum, but merely, so he tells us, out of consideration for the wishes of his pupils' parents. The reason for this neglect of, even contempt for the traditional linguistic studies, is not far to seek. The trend of Enlightenment thought was utilitarian. Of what use could classical studies be in preparing the young to meet the exigencies of common, everyday life? What one needed was not a mastery of the niceties of expression, but a good stock of useful knowledge in the service of a keen, alert mind, and that could be far better achieved, it was declared, through science than through language. No radical changes, however, such as those suggested by the Enlightenment, took place in the work of the schools. Tradition had firmly intrenched classical studies in the curriculum, and they had, besides, sturdy and able defenders, such as Gesner (1691-1761) and Ernesti (1707-1781) in Germany, and Rollin (1661-1741) in France, who were fully aware of the value of the ancient languages in education. Then too, the neoclassicism which developed at the University of Göttingen about 1750, around Greek instead of Latin, neutralized, in

[1] See Willmann's edition of Kant's Pädagogik, Leipzig, 1873, p. 7.
[2] Encyclopédie, s. v. Collége.

Teutonic lands at least, the anti-classical influence of the Enlightenment. "The creations of the German classicists demonstrated that the ancient classics were not a heap of learned rubbish, but still a very vital element, and one that offered such educational and cultural opportunities as the age stood sorely in need of. . . . The poetry of Schiller and Goethe, which deals extensively with antique subjects, popularized the ideas and the mythology of the ancients and rendered them more familiar to the masses than they had been in the Renaissance period. By being introduced into the schools this poetry was a telling factor in favor of the classical studies. German literature, much more than English literature or the literature of any of the Latin peoples, is a sealed book to anyone unacquainted with the ancient classics."[1] Nevertheless, many classicists, such as Gesner of Göttingen,[2] were well aware of the limitations of the traditional secondary school course of study, and they were ready and willing to make concessions to the Encyclopedic tendency of the age, to reach some sort of a compromise between the narrow humanism of a Sturm and the realism of a Francke or Basedow. One of the chief defects of the old schools, it was admitted, was the neglect of the modern languages, particularly of the mother tongue, and it was suggested that they be added to the classical studies. More time, it was also suggested, should be allotted to history, geography and mathematics, which did not occupy in the classical course of study a position corresponding to their educational value.

Various considerations prompted the leaders of the Enlightenment to make ample provision for the sciences in their plan of education. Remarkable progress in science had been made since the days of Copernicus and Galileo and the

[1] Willmann-Kirsch, The Science of Education, Vol. I, p. 291.
[2] Cf. Gesner's Primae lineae isagoges in eruditionem universalem, 2 Vols., 1776 and 1786.

first applications of scientific discoveries to practical life
were just opening a new era in the industrial
life of the West. Science was fast becoming   the sciences,
a power to be reckoned with and the "phi-
losophers" intended to enlist it in the service of their cause,
all the more eagerly because they believed that science and
the Enlightenment were at war against a common enemy.
Is not science, like the Enlightenment, they argued, eminently rational? Is not man a product of nature, subject to
the laws of nature, an animal endowed with senses and
sensations, which are the sources of all our ideas and institutions? Let science then take the place of religion. Let science explain to man what he is, whence he comes, whither
he goes, what he should do or avoid doing. Science and the
scientist must be shown the greatest consideration. Henceforth the scientist will share with the artist and man of
letters the favors of the salons, which will now evince great
interest in laboratories, experiments, observation, from
which is expected a solution of the problems of the day.
Leading men of letters like Voltaire, assuming, it would
seem, that one can turn scientist overnight, try their hand
at all sorts of experiments, in the hope of adding the fame of
scientific discovery to their literary laurels. But science cannot achieve its mission of enlightenment in its present garb;
it must be popularized. Hitherto the scientist and scholar
had been satisfied with appealing to the select few, both in
subject matter and style of presentation. They must now
try to catch the ear of the general public by using the
vernacular instead of Latin, by offering matter of present
day interest and divesting their style of those technicalities
which would be understood only by the initiated. One of
the earliest and, from a literary viewpoint, most remarkable
illustrations of this new popular way of treating science was
the "Pluralité des Mondes." Its author, Bernard de Fontenelle (1657-1757), succeeded in achieving what might then

have seemed well-nigh impossible, to treat astronomy, a subject hitherto regarded as a closed book for the uninitiated, in a manner at once interesting and intelligible to all. The ladies of the salons could now read of astronomy with no more preparation and no greater concentration of attention than was needed for the reading of a novel. More remarkable still was the achievement of Buffon (1707-1788). His "Natural History" was at once a noteworthy contribution to French literature and the natural sciences of the time.

Thus brought into contact with the conditions of real, everyday life, science could not fail to be influenced by its demands. Scientific research assumed a more practical character. The scientist could no longer confine his interest to the advancement of science for its own sake, he must study the possible consequences of the advancement for the life of the people and their education. On the other hand, this popularizing and, to some extent, nationalizing of the sciences did not go without some disadvantages. The medieval unity and solidarity of intellectual life, which had been furthered by the Renaissance but greatly impaired by the Protestant Revolution, was now broken up, and it has happened since, again and again, that departments of learning have developed in one country independently of the progress made in other countries. Then too, the desire to cater to the general public, to give it the illusion that no question in science or philosophy is beyond its grasp, often led to the most superficial and therefore inaccurate treatment of the subject.

The popularizing of philosophy began with Locke. His reasoning out of simple problems appealed to all those who were, or thought they were, philosophically minded, but were scared by the depth or intricacies of the system of a Descartes or Spinoza, or Leibnitz. Locke had many imitators, especially in France, where self-styled philosophers of the world were always sure to find a ready audience in the

Paris salons. On the other hand, Locke's philosophy never thrived on German soil, and when German philosophy left the lecture halls for a time   philosophy. it never assumed the facile, easy-going atti-tude of English and French sensism, though probably exert-ing an even greater influence; Kant's philosophy especially stimulated and even aroused whole classes of the German nation.

On the whole, eighteenth century philosophy had a deep and far-reaching influence in the schools and out of the schools. Wherever Catholic influence did not prevail, it supplied the content of philosophical instruction, taking the place of the traditional course in philosophy, or what re-mained of it, and it was not long before it found its way into the lecture halls of Protestant theology and the newly founded State normal schools. Many "ministers of the gospel" and the instructors of prospective teachers, at the beginning of the nineteenth century, were men whose higher education had been steeped in rationalism. Little wonder, then, that in many quarters religion came to be looked upon as a mere adjunct of philosophy, at best a school subject of no greater value than grammar, or the classics, or mathematics. In Bacon's time modern philosophy had been satisfied with formulating a few suggestions as to method of instruction and making a plea for the recognition of the educational value of science. It now assumes the rôle of dictator and begins the building up of a science of educa-tion to its own image.

The tendency of the eighteenth century to bring knowl-edge out of the narrow confines of the schools or learned circles, and make it, if possible, the common property of the public in general, is also evident in the appearance of new encyclopedias. The series of works of this type begins with the publication in 1696 of the *Dictionnaire historique et critique*, of Pierre Bayle, a forerunner of the Enlightenment. The "Dictionnaire" is noteworthy not only for its rationalistic, anti-Christian animus, but also for a new method in the arrangement of materials. In previous encyclopedias the subjects had invariably been arranged according to some preconceived system.[1] Bayle used the alphabetical method, which was soon universally adopted because it made the contents of encyclopedias more easily accessible to all. By far the most pretentious achievement of the eighteenth century in this field was the *Encyclopédie ou Dictionnaire raisonne des sciences, des arts et des métiers*, edited by Diderot and Dalembert.

The encyclopedic tendency.

DALEMBERT

The original plan, a very modest one, had been to make Chambers' Encyclopedia (2 volumes, Dublin 1728) accessible to French readers. It was Diderot who saw the "philosophical" possibilities of the undertaking: to give a sort of panoramic view of the progress achieved all through the ages in the various branches of knowledge and their applications to life, to show what reason can do to better the intellectual and material conditions of the race, and in that wise to build up a monument that would be at once a storehouse of modern learning and "a battery of guns" against the spirit, beliefs, and institutions of the past. The plan of the work, outlined in Diderot's

---

[1] As *e.g.*, the "Origins" of St. Isidore, "On the Universe" of Rabanus Maurus, the "Speculum Majus" of Vincent of Beauvais; see Vol. I, pp. 85, 106, 175.

prospectus, and Dalembert's *Discours Préliminaire* is based on Bacon's conception of psychology. Human psychical powers are classed as memory, imagination and reason, to which corresponds, we are told, a threefold division in the sciences and arts. Memory is the principle of history because history is concerned with the past; poetry and the fine arts have their principle in the imagination which supplies sensuous images; science proper and philosophy have their principle in reason, whose function it is to pass judgment on things. The shallowness of this classification is at once evident; no science nor any one of the arts is the exclusive product of any single mental faculty, but the subjective character of the plan is a clear index of the nominalistic, Sophist-like trend of "enlightened" thought—no branch of knowledge, and therefore no school subject, has any value independently of the minds that conceive it. On the other hand, in at least two respects, the Encyclopédie deserves commendation: the generous allotment of space in its volumes to trades, industries, inventors, who are styled "the great benefactors of the race," and the historical treatment of the sciences, which afforded a constant means of criticism, by comparing successive stages of progress in the evolution of the subject.

Begun in 1751 the Encyclopédie was not completed until twenty-three years later, after a checkered career of official favor and disfavor. In its final form it comprised seventeen folio volumes of text and eleven volumes of illustrations. Additions were made as late as 1780. Avowedly, the Encyclopédie was intended to promote knowledge and learning, to increase the numbers of scholars, artists, lovers of science, to be for the educated man a compendium of all that is worth knowing, for the specialist a work of reference on all subjects outside his own particular field. All of which it was, or did, in some measure. But it was and did something else of far greater import: it was a rallying point for the "philosophers" whom it gathered into a party, the "Sainte Confédération contre le fanatisme et la tyrannie," as Cabanis called it; it was the "Summa" of rationalism and materialism, the compendium of enlightened opinions on all and sundry subjects. Similar in purpose and spirit, though far inferior in the treatment of their diversified subject were the many imitations of the French Encyclopédie which appeared, especially in Germany, in the latter part of the eighteenth century. The most famous of these popular cyclopedias was Basedow's *Elementary Work*[1] to which we shall have occasion to recur later.

Starting from the materialistic premise that man is essentially a product of physical nature, the eighteenth century "philosophers" undertook to revise the traditional conception of the socio-political sciences. We have seen that Locke, Condillac and their followers transformed psychology into mere sensism, that the "utilitarians" made of ethics an adjunct of the new science of economics. The reshaping of the traditional treatment of history was undertaken by Voltaire and Montesquieu.

The revision of the socio-political sciences.

The latter's *Considérations sur la Grandeur et la Décadence des Romains* is a sort of "philosophy of history." The term is of eighteenth century coinage, but it should not be understood to mean a new type of speculation. St. Augustine's *City of God* and nearer to us, Bossuet's *Discours sur l'Histoire Universelle*, to mention only two, are classics of this type of historical writing. The originality of Montesquieu's work lies in this, that he ignores the influ-

[1] In 1768 Basedow had made an appeal for financial assistance in certain educational reforms and particularly in the publication of a work on elementary education. Money poured in from all sides: from princes, nobles and commoners, from rich and poor alike, throughout Europe. The "Elementary Work" appeared in 1774, with its companion volume, the "Book of Method." The subject matter of the "Elementary Work" was illustrated by a number of plates published in a separate volume.

ence of Divine Providence and tries to explain the sequence of historical events as we would explain physical phenomena. Religion, which played such an important part in the life of the early Romans and the economic conditions of the Empire, one of the main causes of its fall in the West, are scarcely touched upon. What scientific value the book might otherwise retain is rendered nil by a lack of criticism of the sources of information and a mania for hasty generalizations in true Enlightenment style. No less typical of the spirit of the age and its conception of the treatment of history are Voltaire's *Essai sur l'Histoire générale*[1] and *Siècle de Louis XIV*. The general purpose of the author was to write a sort of history of civilization—this term also dates from the eighteenth century—or as Voltaire puts it, a history of the progress of mankind. Here, as in Montesquieu's *Considérations*, the directing influence of Divine Providence is eliminated from history. The past is explained through the action of fatal relations between successive events. This mechanistic conception of history was of itself sufficient to rob the author's account of civilization of all intellectual and ethical value. His anti-Christian animus, glaringly present all through the *Essay*, disqualifies it as a work of history. To Montesquieu the eighteenth century was also indebted for the popularizing of the political science but here again the author is handicapped by his philosophy. His *Esprit des Lois*, which is a sort of philosophy of law, is marred by the same defects as the *Considérations*: lack of criticism in the use of materials, overvaluation of the physical factor, and hasty generalizations. His definition of law: "the necessary relations resulting from the nature of things" warns us from the very start that the title of his work is a misnomer, that he will omit from his considerations the one essential factor in human activity: free will. At best, the *Esprit des*

---

[1] Essai sur l'Histoire générale, et sur les moeurs et l'esprit des nations depuis Charlemagne jusqu'à nos jours.

Lois is but an account of the physical factors that we should consider when trying to explain laws and constitutions and their influence upon the destinies of nations.

During the same period the Frenchman, Jacques Turgot (1727-1781), and the Englishman, Adam Smith (1723-1790), laid the foundations of a new science, economics, which until then had been treated as a branch of politics, but was destined, under the influence of the Industrial Revolution, to become one of the leading social sciences. The development of aesthetics into a distinct science also dates from the eighteenth century. In antiquity and modern times, as well, down to the middle of the eighteenth century, aesthetical criticism had been restricted to poetry and rhetoric. Plato's Symposium, which might have been developed into a science of aesthetics, is but the sketch of a general theory of art. Aristotle, Cicero, Horace, Quintilian, more recently the Frenchman Boileau among many others, were looked up to as guides in matters of aesthetic appreciation, but they all confine themselves to a consideration of literary production. During the second half of the eighteenth century aesthetic criticism was extended to other expressions of the beautiful, the history of art was studied quite extensively and an attempt was made to build up a science of aesthetics.[1] Winckelmann (1717-1768), Lessing (1729-1781), Herder (1744-1803), Goethe (1749-1832) in Germany, Diderot (1713-1784) in France, were the pioneers in this artistic movement, which was to add a new subject to the college and university course of study.

SOURCES

The works of the leaders of the movement, particularly Voltaire's Lettres and Dictionnaire Philosophique.

[1] Baumgarten, a disciple of Wolff, seems to have been the first to use the term in his "Aesthetics" (1750) to designate that branch of knowledge which has beauty as its goal, in contrast with logic, concerned with the true. Cf. Kant's use of the term as denoting the *a priori* principle of sensible experience and Hegel's "Aesthetik," the science of the fine arts.

REFERENCES

Higgs, Henry, The Physiocrats.

Kovalevsky, M., Die oekonomische Entwicklung Europas, trans. from Russian by Motzkin, L., 7 Vols.

Leslie, Stephen, History of English Thought in the Eighteenth Century; English Literature and Society.

Sorel, A., L'Europe et la Révolution française, Vol. I.

Taine, H., The Ancient Régime.

Tocqueville, Ch de, The State of Society in France before the Revolution of 1789.

Turner, W., History of Philosophy.

Weber, A History of Philosophy.

See also references appended to Ch. I.

CHAPTER IV

SCHOOL REFORMS

THE ONLY ATTEMPT AT A SCHOOL REFORM
in eighteenth century Latin Europe, before the French
Revolution, and an unmistakable sign of the trend of the
pedagogy, of the Enlightenment was the closing of the
Jesuit colleges and the expulsion of the members of the
Society from Latin countries. That was to be the first step,
especially in France, in a comprehensive scheme of the
"philosophers" to wreck the Church and de-christianize the
population. Says the Protestant historian Schoell: "The
Church had to be isolated; and to be isolated, it had to be
deprived of the help of that sacred phalanx which had
avowed itself to the defense of the Pontifical throne . . .
such was the real cause of the hatred meted out to that
Society."[1] Voltaire and his associates in the literary and
political world dreamt of nothing less than of doing away
with all revealed religion, of "crushing the
Infamous," as the leader of the movement
went on repeating, and since the Jesuits were
the more formidable enemies of the scheme
they were to be struck first. A campaign of
the vilest mendacity was organized and
carried on for years against the hated Order by the philosophers, who found useful and willing allies in the Jansenists,
Regalists and Febronians.[2] Then came the first blow. It was
delivered by Carvalho, better known as Pombal, who was

The expulsion
of the Jesuits
from
Portugal,

[1] Schoell, M., Cours d'histoire, XLIV.
[2] See Catholic Encyclopedia, art. "Jansenism," "Régale," "Febronianism."

then under Joseph I, the tyrant of Portugal. Under trumped up charges, without even a semblance of trial, the Jesuits in Portugal and its colonies were arrested and packed like cattle into small ships to be thrown on the shores of the Papal States. Their property had of course been confiscated. This happened in 1759. Pombal then proceeded to fill the place of the Jesuit institutions by schools of philosophy, chairs of rhetoric, history and literature, Greek schools, and elementary Latin schools. A bureau of education under the presidency of the Rector of the Coimbra University was to control all schools, and a special tax, "subsidio litterario," was levied to defray the expenses of the schools which thus became State institutions. Pombal's reforms, though inspired by the Enlightenment, did not contemplate anything beyond the establishment of a State Church and a State school system; when he discovered that the Jesuits were opposed to his plans, he simply treated them as he did his political adversaries; he put them in jail and finally expelled them from the country.[1] Choiseul, the French Prime Minister, and his enlightened confrères used a more urbane, more refined procedure than the Portuguese "butcher with an axe," but their purpose was far more radical and comprehensive. The licentious and weak Louis XV was terrorized into submission to the Parliament of France, Paris[2] which was then under the control of Gallicans and Jansenists, the sworn enemies of the Jesuits. Committees were appointed to examine and submit reports on the constitutions and publications of the Society. Eventually, a decree was issued declaring that the property of the Institute was to be confiscated, forbidding any subjects of the King to become Jesuits, or to attend any lecture given by the Jesuits, or to visit their houses, or to have any communication with them; the Jesuits themselves were forbid-

[1] See Schmid's Enzyklopädie, Vol. VI, p. 123.
[2] The name refers not to a political assembly but a court of justice.

den to write to each other. A second decree ordered the works of thirty-one leading Jesuits to be burned by the public executioner. Not even the semblance of a hearing had been allowed the accused in this travesty of justice. Similar decrees were issued by other parliaments in the kingdom, though it must be said to the credit of the French magistracy, that in spite of the tremendous pressure from above, the majority in favor of the decrees was slight in more than one case; some parliaments, like that of Artois, had even the courage to come out boldly in favor of the Jesuits and to proclaim "the sons of St. Ignatius as the most faithful subjects of the king of France and the surest guarantee of the morals of the people." In 1764 Choiseul, seconded by the king's mistress, Madame de Pompadour, succeeded in extorting the royal signature to a decree expelling six thousand Jesuits from France and her colonies. The exiles, however, were not without some consolation. Shortly after their expulsion Clement XIII issued his Bull "Apostolicum" in which he vindicated the character and the work of the Society in unmistakable terms, ". . . we . . . say and declare in the same form and in the same manner as has been heretofore said and declared, that the Institute of the Society of Jesus breathes in the very highest degree, piety and holiness both in the principal object which it has continually in view, which is none other than the defense and propagation of the Catholic Faith, and also in the means it employs for that end. Such is our experience of it up to the present day. It is this experience which has taught us how greatly the rule of the Society has formed up to our day defenders of the orthodox Faith and zealous missionaries who, animated by an invincible courage, dare a thousand dangers on land and sea to carry the light of the Gospel to savage and barbarous nations. . . . Let no one dare be rash enough to set himself against this my present approbative and confirmative Constitution lest he incur the wrath of God."[1]

Choiseul had cloaked the expulsion of the Jesuits from France with some pretension at legality. Aranda, the Spanish Prime Minister, and Tanucci, the Regent of the Kingdom of Naples,[2] then a dependency of the Spanish Crown, did not

Spain.

even bother themselves with this formality. On April 2, 1767, not a single reason being given for the measure, all Jesuits living on Spanish soil were gathered in the nearest port of embarkation for transfer to the Papal States; all their property had, of course, been confiscated. The same fate overtook a few months later the members of the Society in the Kingdom of the Two Sicilies and in Parma. All the while the saintly and courageous Clement XIII had steadfastly refused to heed the importunities, even the covert threats of schism, of the ambassadors of the Bourbon kings, who would be satisfied with nothing short of the suppression of the Society. The Brief of Suppression, "Dominus ac Redemptor," was wrung from the new Pope, Clement XIV, whose only purpose in granting it was to bring peace in the Church and avoid the schism with

The suppression of the Society.

which it was threatened from Paris, Madrid and Naples. The Pope did not pass judgment upon the charges made against the Order; he merely took notice of those charges and adopted an administrative measure called for—so he thought—by the conditions of the time.[3] in 1749, a few years before the final blow came, the Society conducted 669 colleges, and fully one half of its 22,589 members were en-

---

[1] See Catholic Encylopedia, art. "Society" for list of documents and special works dealing with the event.

[2] *Ibid.*

[3] Frederick II forbade the publication of the Brief of Suppression in Prussia as did Catherine II for Russia, and the Jesuits were for years in this rather incongruous position of being disbanded in Catholic lands and maintained in the dominions of a Protestant ruler and a Greek orthodox ruler.

gaged in teaching in secondary and higher institutions.[1]
Scant provision was made in the plans of the reformers to
fill the gap made in the ranks of the teaching body by the
banishment of thousands of highly trained teachers. When
the French Revolution broke out one generation later secondary and higher education had not yet recovered from
the blow.

The expulsion of the Jesuits, "the Revolution of 1762,"
was followed in France by a series of projects for radical

THE BASTILLE

educational reforms. First in chronological order comes
La Chalotais' *Essai d'éducation nationale*, published in 1763,
a year after the Emile. The author's rancorous diatribes
against existing conditions, particularly what he calls monastic, ultramontane influence in education, won for him the
distinction of being enthusiastically supported by the leaders
of the Enlightenment. For the rest, his Essai is a fairly accurate expression of the educational views of the age. The
study of the classics, as they were then taught, is pronounced to be a useless, profitless occupation resulting only
in "peopling seminaries, cloisters and the Latin colonies";

---

[1] Distributed in 41 provinces; besides, there were 61 novitiates, 24 professed
houses, 176 seminaries, 335 residences, 1542 churches and 273 foreign
missions.

this in many respects an echo of the Emile, minus the witchery of the style. The new purpose of the school should be to do away with "monastic, ultramontane education," a discipline "which seems intended only to debase the spirit"; the schools should rid themselves of those scholastic studies from which young men "form the habit of disputing and caviling" and they should do away as well with ascetic regulations "which set at defiance nature and health." School life is divided by La Chalotais into two periods, from five to ten years of age and from ten to seventeen. Utility is his criterion in the organization of the curriculum. The studies and other school activities for the first period should be reading, writing, dancing and music, historical narrations and geography, physical and mathematical recreations, the fables of LaFontaine, all of which children should commit to memory, walks, excursions, recreations. The program for the second period of school life should include French and Latin literature, with at least two foreign living languages, history, geography, mathematics and the natural sciences, criticism, logic, metaphysics, the art of invention and ethics. La Chalotais lays much stress on the study of the mother tongue and national literature; he also believes that a well educated man should know at least two modern languages, English and German in the case of the Frenchman.

French plans for school reform:

La Chalotais,

No serious difficulties, he thought, stood in the way of carrying out his plan; all that was necessary was an ample supply of books and teachers, but since competent elementary school teachers were as yet very few, all reliance for the time being should be put upon good text books. Once the king had approved the plan, the members of the learned academies could begin the work of preparing good text books, of which, in two years, there would be an abundant and excellent supply. La Chalotais has all the aristocratic prejudices of his own age concerning the masses; their education should not be carried too far, because forsooth that would estrange the laboring classes from their manual occupations.

The plan submitted to the Paris Parliament by Rolland (1734-1793), another thorough-going Gallican, Jansenist and religious baiter, is made up for the greater part of extracts from various sources.
Rolland,
He borrowed freely from La Chalotais' "Essai" and from the reports drawn up by the University of Paris at the request of the Parliament, but chiefly from Rollin's (1661-1741) *Traité des Etudes*, in which, so he tells us, "every teacher will find the true principles of education." His one noteworthy contribution to French educational literature of that age is a plan for the national organization of education. All teachers are to be lay teachers. There should be established a higher normal school or seminary for the preparation of prospective teachers. Admission to this institution was to be by competitive examination. In the drawing up of this plan Rolland freely borrowed from the Jesuit system of education. "Les parlementaires empruntaient aux Jésuites ce que l'institut des Jésuites avait d'excellent; l'unité et la suite dans les méthodes, la discipline et la hiérarchie."[1] Normal school students were to be divided into three classes, corresponding to the three grades of admission. Pedagogy was to be one of the subjects of instruction. Assignment to a position in any school could come only after graduation from the normal school; there were to be appointed inspectors or "visitors" whose duty it would be to examine the work of the schools at least once a year. Finally Paris was to become the centre of the national school system which would pass from the hands of the clergy into

---

[1] Compayré, G., Histoire critiques des doctrines de l'education en France, Vol. II, p. 273.

those of the State; all the provincial universities were to become mere dependencies of the University of Paris. A "bureau de correspondence" was to be the centre of educational administration.

Similar views are set forth by the economist Turgot (1727-1781) in his *Mémoires* to the king. Education is to be controlled by the State, to reach every part of the country, however remote from the   Turgot, centre, and to have civic, national, industrial purposes. Interesting as an index of the trend and spirit of those *Mémoires* is the reminder to the king that "his kingdom is of this world." Other plans for educational reforms in France rapidly succeeded one another in the closing years of the eighteenth century. They were all short lived and had little practical value; they are given here in outline as an expression of educational opinion in that phase of the Revolution during which they appeared.

Mention should be made first of all of the "Cahiers" of 1789, which can be considered as voicing French public opinion on the reforms to be   the Cahiers, accomplished in the kingdom. The following is an extract from the "Cahiers"[1] of the clergy of Blois.

". . . . . . We desire:
1. That public instruction should be absolutely gratuitous, as well in the universities as in the provincial schools;
2. That the provincial *collèges* shall be entrusted by preference to the corporations of the regular clergy;
. . . .
4. That in towns too small to support a *collège* there shall be at least one or more masters, according to the importance of the place, who shall be able to teach the principles of Latinity or the humanities, and that their salaries shall be sufficient to allow of absolutely gratuitous instruction;

[1] *I.e.*, instructions drawn up by each locality for its representatives; see Archives Parlementaires, Vol. II, pp. 373-378, trans. by Whitcomb.

5. That this instruction shall be under the supervision of the parish priests and municipal officers;

6. That each candidate seeking permission to teach shall be obliged to produce proofs of correct life and habits, and to give evidence of his capacity in an examination before the principal and professors of the nearest *collège*;

. . . .

8. That for the purpose of facilitating the education of girls, communities of religious women, whatever may be their institution, shall be obliged to open free public schools for girls under the supervision of the parish priests."

The views of Mirabeau (1749-1791), as set forth in his posthumous essay *Travail sur l'Education publique*[1] are remarkably free from the "philosophical" animus so common in eighteenth century literature of that kind. He is opposed to compulsory education which, he maintains, the State has not the right to impose upon its citizens. "Society," he says, "has not the right to prescribe instruction as a duty . . . public authority has not the right, with respect to the members of the social body, to go beyond the limits of watchfulness against injustice and of protection against violence." There should be complete liberty of teaching for both properly qualified laymen and clerics, but uniformity of school work and State centralization should be avoided. Over and above primary schools Mirabeau would establish colleges of literature with a single Lycée National in Paris wherein "a select number of French youth could complete their education."

Talleyrand (1758-1838) had been commissioned by the Constituent Assembly (1789-1791) to draw up a plan of education based upon the principles laid down in the Constitution of September 3, 1791. "Il sera créé et organisé une Instruction publique, commune à tous les citoyens, gratuite à l'égard des

_____

[1] Published by his friend, Cabanis, the full title runs as follows: "Travail sur l'Education publique trouvé dans les Papiers de Mirabeau l'aîné" (Paris, 1791).

parties d'enseignement indispensables pour tous les hommes
et dont les établissements seront distribués graduellement
dans un rapport combiné avec la division du royaume."[1]
Liberty, equality, fraternity shall be the motto of education
as it is of political life. There must be schools everywhere
and they should be accessible to all (*as though this was a
novelty*); there should be no privileges in instruction; everything is to be taught which can be taught; the "Declaration
of the Rights of Man" will be the new catechism of childhood and youth. To know, to love, to obey and perfect the
constitution is the duty of all citizens, which they must be
taught from early childhood. Talleyrand's report provided
for four grades of schools: the primary or "canton" school
to teach all that is necessary for everyone to know; the secondary or district school, to develop more fully the mental
faculties; the department school, to prepare for the learned
professions; "an institute" to be the capstone of the whole
system. The report lays particular stress on the teaching of
"universal morality"; read "morality" without any admixture of religious belief. Talleyrand's Report to the Constituent Assembly was followed a few months later by that
of Condorcet (1743-1794) to the Legislative
Assembly (1791-1792), the best illustration   Condorcet,
of the strong scientific and utilitarian bias of
the Enlightenment, of the dreamy vagaries of the Revolu-
tionists, and their shallow platitudes upon justice, liberty,
equality, progress and general brotherhood. His Report provides for five grades of schools; every village of one hundred
inhabitants is to have a primary school, and every city of
four thousand or more a secondary school. The program
of elementary studies should comprise the three R's and the

[1] "There will be established and organized a system of public instruction; it
will be common to all citizens and gratuitous with regard to those branches
of learning which are indispensable to all men; institutions of learning will
be gradually distributed throughout the kingdom according to a ratio corresponding to its divisions."

rudiments of surveying, building, economic geography, the useful arts and ethics; in the secondary school should be taught orthography, the history of France and neighboring countries, the elements of the mechanical arts, of commercial science and drawing, ethics, sociology, applied mathematics and natural history. There should be established one hundred and ten institutes in which will be taught the use-

CONDORCET

ful sciences, particularly mathematics and physics, with a smattering of Latin. The universities will be replaced by nine Lyceums and the capstone of the whole system will be the National Society of Arts and Sciences. The Report advocates the establishments of courses for adults on Sundays, "lay sermons to be given by the local teacher in e a c h community"; it stresses the importance of technical education, the diffusion of the knowl-

edge of the arts and crafts, the establishment of libraries and museums of the useful arts in all schools. For various reasons, some sound, some questionable, Condorcet is much in favor of identical education for the two sexes. His Report is typical of the spirit and visionary hopes of the Enlightenment; the past is ignored or sneered at; the educational value of science is extolled at the expense of language, religion is banished from the curriculum, in order to make room for instruction in "lay morality." The teaching body, exclusively lay of course, is granted practically complete autonomy, it becomes a sort of state within the State, but strangely enough Condorcet's plan makes no provision for the recruiting of this "Academic Church," for it is silent on the normal schools, beyond suggesting that the teachers in each grade be prepared in the next above.[1]

Under the National Convention (1792-1795), a host of plans, reports, decrees and laws on education succeeded one another posthaste, but very little of it all was actually carried out. Condorcet's report acknowledged the State's rights in matters of instruction, but it virtually left the education of the future citizen in the hands of the individual. The Convention closed the old schools, confiscated their property and asserted the supremacy of the State in all matters educational. The Lakanal Law of November 17, 1794, ordered the establishment of an elementary school for every one thousand inhabitants, with separate divisions for boys and girls, and providing instruction in reading and writing the French language, lessons on the Declaration of the Rights of Man and the Constitution, lessons in Republican morals, the rules of simple calculation and surveying, lessons in geography and the phenomena of nature, on heroic actions and songs of triumph. There were even extremists who were in favor of an absolute State monopoly and would have harnessed France with the Spartan system of education. Lepelletier Saint-Fargeau, an out and out Jacobin, prepared an educational bill in which we read: "Let us ordain that all children, girls as well as boys, girls from five to eleven, boys from five to twelve, shall be educated in common, at the expense of the State and shall receive, for six or seven years, the same education." The child, it is further asserted, is the property of the

Lakanal,

Lepelletier.

[1] See Barnard's Journal, Vol. XXII, pp. 562-563.

Republic, which must see to it that he will be fashioned to
its own image and likeness. Reading, writing, arithmetic,
elementary ethics and domestic science will form the course
of study of those Republican barracks, but there should also
be some manual labor. All children should be employed in
tilling the soil, and if there is not enough land attached to
the school for the purpose, let the children pick up and
scatter stones on the highways! Robespierre pronounced the
scheme to be the inspiration of the genius of humanity and
the historian, Michelet, writes of it in all seriousness as
something "admirable in spirit," a "revolution of childhood"![1]

Lakanal had advocated the foundation of a normal school.
The idea was adopted by the Convention and actually carried
out in 1795, its purpose being to supply professors for the
higher institutions, but it soon closed, a virtual failure as a
normal school. Napoleon reopened it in 1808 as a training
school for teachers in the higher secondary
schools, and as such it has ever since rendered great services to the country. Lakanal's
Report also recommended the establishment
of central or higher schools, one for every three hundred
thousand inhabitants. The first central schools were established in 1795, others were added in the following years,
and they continued, but without great success, till the law
of May 1, 1802, which suppressed them. The educational
work of the Convention was brought to a close by the Law
of October 27, 1795, which represents a reaction against the
radical trend of earlier days; it placed greater stress than
preceding laws on secondary and higher institutions, but
was less generous in its provisions for elementary education.
This Law of 1795, the only permanent contribution of the
period to elementary education, was but feebly administered
under the Directory (1795-1799), and Napoleon, who was

Actual
reforms.

[1] On the educational activities of the Convention read in Dictionnaire de
Pédagogie, art. "Convention."

master of France for the next sixteen years, was far more interested in secondary and higher institutions than in elementary schools. In the latter part of its history the Convention had decreed the foundation of many higher institutions of learning, most of which have persisted to this day: the Polytechnic School, the Conservatory of Arts, the Conservatory of Music, the Conservatory of Arts and Trades, the Museum of Natural History, new medical and veterinary schools, new military schools, the Museum of Archeological Monuments, the National Library, the Bureau of Longitudes. In all fairness to the past, however, it must be said that some of those institutions had existed under different names before the Revolution, and the Convention did nothing else than try to repair the damage it had wrought.

Among the German States the example of school reforms was set by Austria and Prussia, and they were at first mainly prompted, it seems, by economic and political reasons. It was hoped that the improved schools would supply the practical knowledge and technical skill which was indispensable for the improvement of the trades and industry, and thus increase the national wealth. Considerations of a higher order, however, were not entirely foreign to those reforms. The imperial and royal decrees on education again and again express the sovereign's interest in the spiritual as well as the material welfare of his subjects, and the conviction that a good education is conducive to both. In general the language of the decrees is remarkable for its moderation and a certain reverence for existing institutions, for the traditional trend of education, which one seeks in vain in the pronouncements of the Neapolitan or Portuguese or French reformers. It, none the less, remains true that here, as in the more revolutionary measures that were then carried out in Latin States, there is an over-estimation of the powers of the State to achieve a

School reforms in Prussia.

social transformation. Most eighteenth century reformers seem to have shared in the naïve belief that systems of education and other systems as well can be created or remodelled over night by a stroke of the pen.

The way had been paved for a school reform in Prussia by Francke's Institutions at Halle and similar ones founded or remodelled by his disciples.[1] Those schools supplied Protestant Germany with teachers and text books that spread the principles and practices of Pietistic pedagogy. One of the warmest supporters of this pedagogy was Frederick William I of Prussia (1713-1740) who was then reorganizing the whole administration of Prussia. He issued a number of decrees in which parents were strongly urged to send their children to school, sent commissioners around to provide school masters for the villages that had none as yet, started an endowment fund for the schools of East Prussia and set aside large tracts of land for the same purpose. His *Principia Regulativa* prescribing conditions for the building of schoolhouses, the support of the schoolmaster, tuition fees, and governmental supervision became the fundamental educational law of Prussia. Though his decrees failed to achieve a complete school reform, they prepared the way for further reorganization and they accustomed the people to the idea of State school supervision and State school support. Frederick William's work of organization was carried still further and in the same spirit by his son and successor, Frederick II. In 1740, 1741 and again in 1743 he issued "regulations concerning the support of schools in the villages of Prussia." New schools were to be established, teachers to be provided therefor, and it was ordered that "the existing school regulations and the arrangements made thereto should be permanent and that no change should be made under any pretext whatever."[2] In 1750 all the provincial Church Conventions, with the excep-

---

[1] See Vol. II, pp. 227 ff.
[2] See Barnard's Journal, Vol. XXII, pp. 861-877.

tion of that of Catholic districts, were centralized under the Berlin Consistory which became the agent of the central Government in the administration both of religion and education. The Seven Years' War interrupted the work of organizing the administration of the schools but as soon as peace was re-established that work was resumed. Frederick II entrusted a follower of the Halle movement, John Julius Hecker,[1] now a pastor in Berlin and counsellor for the Berlin Consistory, with the organization of the national school system. Hecker is the author of the General *Land Schule Reglement* (general school regulations for the rural schools) of 1763, whose purpose was "to banish from the country the ignorance which is so harmful in its effects and so great an obstacle to the spread of Christian ideas"; the legislator expressed the hope "that by improving the schools our subjects will be made morally better and industrially more efficient."[2] Two years later a similar set of regulations was drawn up for the schools of Catholic Silesia, a new province wrested by force of arms a few years previously from Austria. Those regulations constituted the first general School Code for the whole kingdom and they form the real foundation of the Prussian elementary school system.[3] The Code made education compulsory from the age of five to thirteen or fourteen, regulated the teaching of apprentices, Sunday and summer sessions, tuition fees, the requirements for teaching licenses, school schedules, text books to be used, the extent to which a teacher might ply his trade, the relations of schoolmaster and clergyman.

Before the introduction of the Prussian Code into Silesia the Augustinian Abbott, Johann Ignaz von Felbiger (1724-1788), had achieved a re-   Felbiger markable reform of the Catholic schools of that province. His interest in education was aroused by the

[1] See Vol. II, p. 227.
[2] See note 1.
[3] *Ibid.*

deplorable condition of the schools near his monastery at Sagan, which was mainly due, he realized, to the poor quality of the teachers in charge. To remedy the evil he published in 1761 his first school ordinance for the dependencies of the Monastery of Sagan, but his best results were achieved after he had been acquainted with the work of Hecker and Hahn in Berlin. He became an enthusiastic propagator of the latter's methods of instruction by initials and tables; the so-called tabular method consisted of tables presenting subjects in their various divisions which were displayed in the classroom as a help in maintaining discipline; the "initials" or alphabetical method on the other hand consisted in the use of initials as a help for recalling words, and it was thought that the method would stimulate curiosity and arouse an interest in the learning of spelling. Both methods were nothing more than teaching devices, of doubtful pedagogical value at that; they are however interesting to the student of the history of education as evidence of a desire, now beginning to spread among educators, to improve the methods of instruction. Felbiger published many textbooks, notably a new catechism; he founded a college or training school for teachers and at the request of the government of Silesia he issued a general school ordinance for the Catholic elementary schools of the province. His reforms attracted wide attention and in 1774 he was called to Vienna by the Empress Queen Maria Theresa to become Commissioner of Education. His first step was to draw up a general school ordinance which was issued the same year and is here reproduced in substance as the best illustration of the more conservative school reforms of the eighteenth century.

School reforms in Austria-Hungary

"Maria Theresa, etc. . . . .

"Having nothing more at heart than the true welfare of the countries which God has confided to us, and having always attentively considered whatever might contribute to this end, we have observed that the education of both sexes, the basis of the real happiness of nations, requires our special care. This very important object has all the more attracted our attention because the future destiny of man, the genius and thought of entire nations depend mainly on the good instruction and right training of children from the tenderest years. Such an object, however, can never be attained if the darkness of ignorance is not dispelled by well-regulated instruction and education, so that every individual can acquire knowledge according to his ability and condition. These necessary ends, the utility of which is generally acknowledged, we desire to reach by the following regulations for all schools in our kingdom and hereditary States."[1]

In each State of the monarchy there was to be established a school commission. There were to be three grades of schools, normal, principal and trivial. Each province was to possess a normal, *i.e.*, model school, each capital of a canton, a principal, *i.e.*, higher primary, school. Villages, towns, cities were to be provided with trivial, *i.e.*, primary schools, according to local needs. The establishment of schools, the course of study and methods to be used in each type of school were carefully regulated. The course of study in the "normal" school was intended to be introductory to higher and more specialized studies preparing for the trades and professions; it included religion, reading, writing, arithmetic, the mother tongue and the elements of Latin, geography and history, the principles of surveying and mechanics, the principles of economy, natural history, the history of the arts and trades. Courses in methodology and classroom management were also provided for prospective teachers. So far as circumstances would permit, the course of study of the principal school was to be the same as that of the normal school. Religion, reading, writing, and the elements of arithmetic were to be the subjects of instruction in the trivial schools, *i.e.*, the schools of small cities, boroughs and villages. The ordinance then considers the appointment of teachers, the books to be used, school attendance, school records and schedules. Magistrates are requested to see to it that parents

[1] See Barnard's Journal, Vol. XXII, pp. 879-884.

send their children to school. Provision is made for the instruction of orphans, continuation schools, the appointment and duties of school inspectors, examinations, reports, the promotion of teachers and their extra professional activities. Because of the suppression of the Society of Jesus the higher schools also had to be reorganized; the work was entrusted to the Piarists[1] who had taken over the Jesuit schools, and so long as Maria Theresa retained her hold on the government this work of reorganization was carried on in the spirit of moderation and respect for tradition which characterized all the reforms of the Empress. With the accession of Joseph II, however, there began an era of experiments which were prompted by the Enlightenment. In the course of a few years the new ruler succeeded in bringing chaos in the whole Austrian administration and alienating from his rule the population of Hungary and his Netherland possessions.[2]

The Prussian and Austrian school reforms aroused much interest in the other German States and the rivalry between the Governments spurred them on to the greatest efforts. The reform measures in Protestant States were as a rule patterned upon the Prussian school reforms, or on those of the more conservative among the Philanthropinists, whereas the Catholic States would commonly follow the example of Austria. Problems of education were discussed not only by professional educators like Hecker, Hahn, Basedow, but by leaders in all walks of life: eminent scholars like Gesner (1691-1761)[3] in Hanover, Ernesti (1707-1781)[4] in Saxony, eminent writers like Herder (1744-1803),[5] the founder of the normal school in Weimar, great statesmen

and other German lands.

[1] See Catholic Encyclopedia.
[2] See Krones, F., Handbuch der Geschichte Oesterreichs, Vol. IV, Bks. XIX, XX.
[3] An eminent philologist, one of the founders of new humanism in Germany and the author of "Primae lineae isagoges eruditionem universalem," a sort of cyclopedia for the benefit of prospective teachers.
[4] Another eminent philologist and founder of new humanism.
[5] See Paulsen, Fr. Geschichte des gelehrten Unterrichts, Vol. II.

like Frederick II and Maria Theresa, eminent churchmen like Felbiger, already mentioned, and Franz von Fürstenberg (1729-1810), Vicar-General of the Diocese of Münster, and the real founder of that diocese's school system. He modernized the gymnasium by giving more prominence to German, mathematics and the natural sciences; he improved facilities for the education of the clergy, obtained for the town of Münster its University in 1771, and founded a normal school which under the able direction of Bernhard Overberg (1754-1826), a saintly priest and leading educator of the time, soon became a model training school for Catholic countries.

It is in those eighteenth century school reforms that we must look for the beginnings of our own modern state school systems, *i.e.*, systems of schools supported and controlled by the state which must be understood to mean here not only the central government but the local civil authorities as well. This state control of the schools naturally implied the professional training of teachers and the determining of their rights and duties; eventually state control led to compulsory school attendance, i.e. laws making it mandatory upon parents who cannot provide for the instruction of their children at home, to send them to school until they have reached a certain age. Compulsory school attendance remained confined for some time to Prussia and a few other Protestant States. Catholic governments, as a rule, were at first satisfied with reminding parents of their duty to provide their children with a minimum of education without compelling them to send them to school. Nowhere as yet did the state assume a monopoly of education; private institutions were allowed to continue their work but they were made to comply with certain government regulations, the scope and stringency of which varied from country to country.[1]

The most salient feature in the reform of secondary and

[1] See chs. IX, XI.

higher education was the foundation of schools preparing for the trades and mechanical arts.[1] As noted elsewhere the appearance of these new institutions coincided with the beginning of the Industrial Revolution,[2] but there was of course more than a mere coincidence between those two facts. Another innovation in the field of secondary education which has already been mentioned,[3] was the Realschule which appeared first at Halle as one of the Institutions of Francke and his co-workers, and was transplanted later to Berlin by John Julius Hecker. Hecker's successors organized the school into three distinct courses: a pedagogium for higher learning; a school of art with courses in commerce, architecture, engineering, the fine arts, military science; a German or industrial school. The Realschule was not fully organized until a later period but its influence was felt at once in the work of other institutions. Many Latin schools gradually added modern subjects to their traditional course of study and new schools were founded, these of an intermediate type between the elementary school and the gymnasium or college, which offered only modern subjects. To this class belong most of the first girls' secondary schools. The more evident result of the school reform for the universities was the loss to the state of their medieval autonomy in matters of administration, or of teaching, or both. A few additions were made to their courses of study: lectures on economics, aesthetics, pedagogy, the historical and natural sciences, the introduction of laboratory methods in the faculty of medicine. The modernizing of the universities, however, was to be the work of the nineteenth century.[4]

---

[1] See chs. IX, XI.

[2] *Ibid.*

[3] See Vol. II, p. 228.

[4] School reforms were also attempted in Poland, Russia, Sweden, Denmark. Laws were passed by the Polish Diet (1783-1790) to organize a whole system of Public Instruction in the country, but the Partition of Poland put an end to the reforms.

Under the influence of the French intellectual leaders, Voltaire, Diderot, Rousseau, later under that of Austria, Catherine II made extensive plans

SOURCES

On the suppression of the Society of Jesus the original sources of information are of course the Vatican archives and the archives of the Society; on school reforms, the school laws of the different countries and the school plans mentioned above.

Barnard's American Journal of Education also contains many extracts from various sources.

REFERENCES

Allain, E., L'instruction publique en France avant la Révolution; l'oeuvre scolaire de la Révolution.
Barnard, H., German Teachers and Educators.
Dittes, F., Geschichte der Erziehung.
Hippeau, C., L'instruction publique en France pendant la Révolution.
Lantoine, H., Histoire de l'enseignement secondaire.
Liard, L., L'enseignement supérieur en France.
Paulsen, F., Geschichte des Gelehrten Unterrichtes.
Schmid, K., Geschichte der Erziehung.

for the organization of a complete system of Public Schools in Russia. She even secured the aid of Jankovicz de Mirievo, who had been an associate of Felbiger, to assist the commission in charge of the school organization. Scant practical result, however, followed the attempt. (cf. Rousseau's considérations sur le gouvernement de Pologne, ch. 4, and Diderot's Plan d'une université.)

CHAPTER V

NATURALISM[1]

AS A MODERN REVIVAL OF THE PAGAN WOR-
ship of nature, both human and subhuman, naturalism
had its first devotees among the radical humanists of the
fifteenth century; Giordano Bruno, Francis Bacon, Thomas
Hobbes, Spinoza, John Locke were its leading sponsors in
the philosophy of the sixteenth and seventeenth centuries;
Rousseau's writings popularized it among the theorists, men
of letters, artists, of the late eighteenth and early nineteenth
century. Around 1850 naturalism began to assert itself in
science, art, literature, philosophy, morality, education. Its
better known protagonists were then Comte, Renan, Taine
in France, J. Stuart Mill, Darwin, Huxley, Spencer in England, Strauss and Haeckel in Germany, and Lombroso in
Italy. Zola might be taken as the representative of an extreme type of it in literature. Materialism, pantheism, posi-
tivism, evolutionism, modernism, realism genre Balzac and
Flaubert, those and kindred terms, all express some variation of the doctrine with its
possible applications to psychology, ethics,
economics and politics, literature and art,
religion and education.

What is
Naturalism?

What then is naturalism?

Let it be remarked to begin with that it could hardly be
described as a special system of philosophy, like Platonism,
Stoicism or Cartesianism; rather is it a certain viewpoint or
tendency common to many systems which otherwise would

[1] Cf. ch. III.

seem to be antagonistic to one another. And it must be noticed further, as the above listed terms would suggest, that naturalism does not in every instance stand committed to one identical set of doctrines. Some "naturalists" profess a belief in the existence of a Creator, others ignore or deny it outright; some see nothing else in the whole universe than a gigantic machine, set into motion by physical forces, subject to none but mechanical laws; others admit a dualism of mind and matter, explaining that material and psychical phenomena are parallel manifestations of one fundamental, underlying principle. But amidst the diversity of opinions there is one central idea concerning which there seems to be fairly unanimous agreement. It is this: that nature is the source of all that exists; hence whenever we attempt to explain anything we should do it in terms of nature. Faith, sound philosophy, common sense tell us: Man is above nature; there is a difference in kind, not of degree, between him and the brute, an abyss between matter and spirit. Naturalism, on the other hand, teaches: the difference between man and the animal is accessory; both are a product of the same fundamental forces, through a slow process of evolution, under the influence of laws that are necessary and eternal. In due course of time vegetation sprang from inorganic matter, animal life from vegetable life, man from the higher animals, and all our present day civilization from a primitive natural state. The traditional conception of nature, according to which it is founded upon a pre-ordained plan, must be rejected as a mere figment of the imagination. The whole universe, such as it is today, man and society included, is nothing else than the product of blind forces acting upon matter. From those premises there follow a number of important conclusions Consequences for the sciences, philosophy, religion, art, for science, literature, morality, education. Heretofore the natural sciences had been more or less relegated into

the background, but since nature, insofar as we are concerned, is the only reality, it follows that the sciences of
nature should come to the front, that their methods, observation, experimentation, induction are the true, unerring methods; that progress can be achieved only through a study of
the natural sciences and an application of their discoveries.
The immortality of the soul, a supernatural life, faith, revelation, are mere deceptions. Religion has failed
religion,   to explain and it will never explain the
riddle of life. "Upon science alone shall we
be able henceforth to found a creed; science alone will be
able to solve for us those eternal riddles for which human
nature imperatively demands an answer."[1] No less radical
is the view of naturalism concerning philosophy, the traditional conception of man and his relation to society, of art,
literature, history, education. Philosophy, it
philosophy,   holds, at best can be an accessory of science,
natural science of course. What the latter
cannot explain, the former a fortiori cannot; philosophy is
the field of the unknowable; all that we have a right to say
concerning its subject matter is: I do not know (agnosticism). Man, according to naturalistic science, is but one of
the products of the forces that have been at work in nature
from time immemorial. He is but a higher animal. What
tradition tells us to call his spiritual life is merely one of the
aspects of his organic life, itself subject to the laws of physics,
chemistry and mechanics. Thought is a function of the
brain; a concept is a transformed sensation, free will an illusion; man's behavior, in whatever sense we take it, is determined by his antecedents and surroundings. Ethics is no
longer to be considered as the science of what ought to be,
but of what is useful to the individual and the community
he happens to live in, and that means that morality is rela-

[1] Renan, E., L'Avenir de la Science.

tive; its standards vary with individual, nature, time, surrounding conditions. Society is looked upon
as a vast organism of which every individual   society.
is a cell. No new conception this.[1] What is
peculiar in the naturalistic use of the simile is that the personality of the individual is submerged; the one reality here
as in nature is the whole organism. Society, not the individual, comes first, and he who would understand and explain present and past social conditions can do it only
through a consideration of physical, biological, economic
factors, the prime movers of any society. Art, literature,
philosophy, religion, law, customs, traditions, political and
social events, are all ultimately reducible to climatic and
racial conditions.

Enlightening on the naturalistic conception of history and
civilization are Gobineau's *Essai sur l'inégalité des races
humaines* and Taine's *Philosophie de l'Art* and *Histoire de
la Littérature Anglaise*. And if we care to see naturalism
actually at work in the domain of literature we have but to
turn to the literary output of the second half of the nineteenth century. Perhaps Zola's works would be typical in the
case, and he went, besides, into the trouble of giving us a
theory of the "naturalistic" novel, *Le Roman expérimental*.[2]
The best known and most influential exposition of the
naturalistic conception of education in the nineteenth century was probably that given by Herbert Spencer (1820-
1903) in his "Education, Intellectual, Moral, Physical" to
which we shall later return. At present we must for a brief
while consider the prototype and chief inspiration of modern
naturalistic education: Rousseau and his doctrine of the
natural state.

Of the man Rousseau we have a lifelike, if not very edify-

[1] See Willmann-Kirsch, The Science of Education, Vol. I, pp. 7 ff.
[2] See Brunetière, F., Le Roman Naturaliste; Doumic, R., Portraits d'écrivains.

ing picture in the *Confessions,* in which the author recounts in his fascinating style and with a wealth of details all the incidents of a life that was "natural" indeed. Jean-Jacques Rousseau was born at Geneva in 1712, the son of a clockmaker of French, Calvinistic ancestry. The death of his mother, when he was

Rousseau.

ROUSSEAU HERBORIZING

still very young, left him in charge of a careless father and over-indulgent or indifferent relatives. Of sound, solid training in early life he had next to nothing. He was early taught how to read but was allowed to devote most of his time to the unrestricted reading of romances. After a brief stay as a boarder at a country parsonage he was apprenticed to a Genevan engraver who, it appears, was over-free with the rod, to which the boy retaliated by stealing his master's apples and asparagus. One evening, upon returning to the city from a day of frolic in the country, the lad Rousseau found the gates of Geneva shut before him. That, he thought, was a sure sign of God's will. He turned his back on his native city and for the next fifteen years he led a vagrant, aimless life through Savoy, Piedmont, the south of France, Switzerland—he even made a trip to Paris—now lackey, now mountebank, now teacher of music for which he seems to have had a considerable talent; he even began to study for the priesthood, and whenever he felt the pinch of need he would fall back upon the generosity of a Madame de Warens who had been instrumental in his shortlived conversion to Catholicism. But this period of his life had at least one merit; it developed and strengthened his knowledge and love of nature, and it stored his mind with that natural imagery which was to be such an important element in all his writings. At the age of thirty he went to Paris to seek his fortunes there; he secured a position as secretary to the French ambassador to Venice, but his incurable spirit of independence soon sent him back to Paris. It was about this time that he met Thérèse Levasseur, a poor, hardworking girl, whom he soon made his wife in all but the name. She bore him five children, all of whom were remorselessly sent to the Foundling Asylum immediately after their birth, never to be seen again by their parents. Rousseau's literary fame began with an essay which was published in 1749 on the following question proposed by the Academy of Dijon, as the subject of the following year's prize essay: Has the Progress of the Arts and Sciences Contributed to Corrupt or to Purify Morals? His answer in the negative won for him the prize and the recognition of the literary world as a rising man.

He made many friends among the fashionable world and the Encyclopedists. His opera, *Le Devin du Village* and his comedy *Narcisse* were produced with success. In 1753 his second *Discourse* on the *Origin of Inequality among Men* added to his reputation and carried his thought still further in the direction of his conception of the natural state, which he developed at length a few years later in the *New Héloïse,* the *Social Contract* and the *Emile.* Except for the suffering of a diseased imagination Rousseau's life so far had been a quiet one, but no sooner did the *Emile* appear than it raised a storm; the book was burned at the stake both in Paris and

Geneva and orders were issued to arrest its obnoxious author. The next eight years found him a fugitive in various places in France, Switzerland, England. Tired at last of wandering, and feeling that he might with safety return to Paris, he repaired thither in July 1770 and here he passed the next eight years living a very simple life on a meager income which he eked out by copying music. His *Dialogues*, his *Rêveries* and some other minor works belong to that period; his *Confessions* had been published during his wandering years. His fame was now world-wide. He could feel himself surrounded by the sympathy and admiration of thousands, but he was not happy. He suffered a good deal from bodily ailments, his morbid mind was haunted by all kinds of gloomy forebodings. In 1777 he accepted the invitation of the Marquis de Girardin to come and live at Ermenonville and there he died a few months later in 1778. The rumor was that he had committed suicide, but the fact has never been substantiated.

Such was the life of the patriarch of modern naturalism, related here at some length because it reveals the soul and character of the man as few writers' lives have ever done; also because it supplies the best explanation of his theories. For if there is one conclusion that forces itself upon the impartial student of Rousseau's life and writings it is this: that his theories on the natural state are nothing else at bottom than a sort of justification for the "natural life" that he lived.

In his second letter to de Malesherbes,[1] Rousseau tells us that his Discourses on the *Sciences and Arts* and the *Inequality among Men* together with the *Emile* form a single whole. He might have cited the whole list of his writings, because they all form a "single whole," centering around the same thought, developing Rousseau's doctrine of the natural state, in society, economics, politics, the family, edu-

[1] Director general of the Librairie, *i.e.*, censor.

cation, art and literature. That, however, should not convey
the impression of a well-reasoned-out system, for if there is
one thing conspicuous in Rousseau's writings it is the lack
of well ordered thinking. What thinking he did, like his
acting, was done under the influence of passion. He was essentially a man of feeling, of desires and impulses, and what
he voices more than anything else in his works is a craving
for an easy-going life without obligations of any kind, an
ardent desire for all kinds of half animal pleasures to be
obtained with the least possible amount of exertion. Whatever would interfere with the sort of life he was craving for
finds no mercy under his pen.

"Everything is well as it comes from the hands of the
Author of things; everything degenerates in the hands of
man." Such is the opening sentence of the *Emile*, the thesis
which Rousseau develops in one form or
another in all his writings, the doctrine of   The doctrine
the goodness of the natural state. Man is   of the natural
good, essentially good in that state. How   state.
could it be otherwise since there are as yet
no rules, no laws, no morality, all creations of society? In
all that he does in that state man is merely prompted by his
instincts which are all good, he is seeking the satisfaction of
his own desires, he means harm to no one. Corruption,
misery, unhappiness begin when reason steps in to take the
place of instinct, to multiply our needs, to add artificial
pleasures to those suggested by nature, to create privileges,
to make unnatural provisions for the future. This unhappy
state of affairs is the work of society whose fundamental de-
fect is inequality: inequality in power, rank, honors, comfort,
opportunities for leisure and self-improvement, all of which
flow naturally from inequality in property. Society is essentially bad, so its progress can only be from bad to worse.
But one of the surest signs of social progress is the advance-

ment of learning and the fine arts. In every country, in
every age, belles-lettres, fine arts and the sciences are in a
close alliance with wealth and luxury, the privilege of the
few, a sure sign of social inequality and social decay. And
of all types of literature the one most closely related to a
high degree of civilization is the drama, which has for its
object the picture of social conditions, social relations, and
thus teaches, perhaps unconsciously, all the vices inherent in
a civilization that has reached a high degree of perfection.
Such is the gist of Rousseau's essays on the *Sciences and
Arts,* on the *Inequality among Men* and his *Letter on the
Theatre.* And the conclusion to be drawn from essays and
letter is the same, viz., that we should restore in us and
society the state of nature. But it does not mean that we
should go back to the condition of the savage; that would
be impossible and unadvisable. Impossible, because nature
does not know regression; unadvisable, because with all his
faults and vices civilized man is in some respects far superior
to the savage. His mental faculties are better developed, his
sentiments more refined, his intellectual horizon much
wider, his aspirations loftier—precious possessions all these,
which we should endeavor to keep and combine with primitive goodness, liberty, happiness.

The return to the natural state, the work of reconstruction, should be individual and social, its instruments being
education, family life and a new covenant in political, economic and social relations. Nature is good and society is
bad. Let us then in education heed the voice of the first and
shun the influence of the other. The body, the senses should
be developed, strengthened, trained, and so should the instincts. Reason should not be appealed to too early; it should
await the summons of nature. Need, experience, have been
the great teachers of mankind, so they should be of the
child. Nature knows nothing of moral codes, of revealed

religion; they should then have no place in a scheme of natural education. Literature is a sign of social corruption, banish it from the course of study, at least, until such time as the student is mature enough to detect and reject corruption, to retain and appreciate what is really beautiful. This process of individual reconstruction, of which the first instrument is education, can and will go on in family life if the relations which it entails between husband and wife before and after marriage are based on nature, if frankness, truth, liberty determine relations between the two partners. But the benefits of this individual reconstruction of men and women in family life will extend far beyond the limits of the family circle. It will be one of the means of social reconstruction, for the family is the "most ancient of societies," the "first model of all political societies." Society, however, will not regain its primeval simplicity and usefulness unless it returns to its fundamental principle, its "raison d'être," the good, welfare, happiness of all its members.

Prior to the establishment of any civil, political society, all men were equal and free. They have, all of them, voluntarily relinquished that liberty to the state, they all have voluntarily subjected their will to the will of the community, not for the benefit of a few privileged individuals but for the benefit of the whole community, that each one of its members may enjoy the greatest sum of freedom, comfort, happiness, compatible with the welfare of the other members of the community. For that purpose, and none other, has a social contract been entered into between government and governed. To the extent that a government remains true to that contract, to that extent only is it legitimate. At the top of his system Rousseau places God, who is ever present in everyone of us, who inspires and sustains us in our striving after the good.

But where shall we find the man of nature, the prototype

of individual and social reconstruction? Rousseau leaves us no doubt on that point. That man whom society may have suppressed elsewhere is still living in his person, oppressed, it is true, but none the less present in what a boundless pride prompted Rousseau to consider as the simplicity, sincerity, naturalness of the primitive man. As it has already been re-marked, Rousseau has left us an interesting picture of such a man in his *Confessions*. There poses before us a sensuous, intensely selfish individual, a born enemy of any kind of re-straint, a hater of society and the forms which it imposes upon its members to make possible social intercourse, for which his own education, or rather lack of education, has not fitted him, a creature of instinct, of feeling, incapable of following any other rule than the promptings of his own selfish nature. Allied with those rather repulsive traits in Rousseau's character we find a deep love of sub-human na-ture; he never was so happy as when he could live in the country, in close communion with its beauties which at times would send him into a sort of ecstasy. And we also find in him a deep, generous sympathy for the down-trodden, suffering masses of eighteenth century France, at least insofar as it entailed nothing else than a flow of elo-quence.

In thus baring before us the nakedness of his rather repul-sive ego, Rousseau reveals the first great source of his doc-trines, viz., his own intensely emotional, impulsive nature. His Genevan origins and the very life that he lived would suggest a second source of inspiration of those doctrines. The fact that he was born a Calvinist and lived for some time in Geneva, under a republican form of government might to some extent account for his doctrine of the sovereignty of the people, the equality of all before the law, the election of all state officers. His free, vagrant life, in the most pic-turesque surroundings, the long, aimless hikes on the high

roads of Savoy and southeastern France, the daily uncer-
tainty as to one's shelter or meal for the night, must have
deepened his sense of independence and his love for nature.
But there were still other influences at work in the shaping
of his doctrines. His omnivorous reading supplied him with
elements which it would not be difficult to trace to their
origin: poets, historians, philosophers, theorists of every description, in antiquity and modern times. From Montaigne[1]
especially, and still more from Locke,[2] to whom he freely
acknowledges his indebtedness, Rousseau received his inspiration for many of the principles he develops in the
Emile. His naturalism, as we have noted before, can be
traced through French sensism to the Englishman's philosophical creed. Like Locke he is very insistent upon physical
education, training in sense perception, appealing to the
child's natural curiosity, making learning as easy and
pleasurable as possible, educating morally through the discipline of consequences, but whereas Locke carefully tempers
his naturalism with an appeal to authority, Rousseau, true
to his own rebellious nature, would have nothing to do with
it. Other influences, nearer home and more potent still,
aided Rousseau in the formulation of his theories. He was
for years a personal friend of Diderot, Condillac, in fact
most of the "philosophers." The former was, like Rousseau,
at war with society and an apostle of the new gospel "back
to nature." From the latter, the leader of French sensism,
Rousseau may have received the leading principles of the
learning process, as it appears in the *Emile*: that the process
should have its starting point in experience, in sense impression, that the child should be guided and not told. It would
be a gross error, indeed, to credit Rousseau with the discovery of all the strange, novel theories which he develops

[1] See Vol. II, p. 206.
[2] See Vol. II, p. 210.

on society, government, marriage, education. His rôle was far more modest, though a very telling one at that: to lend to the creed of his age the magic of a rhetoric which carried conviction with many.

A brief analysis of the *Emile* will help us reach a still clearer notion of Rousseau's educational opinions, and form a still more correct estimate of his real con-

The Emile or education according to nature.

tributions to modern educational theory. The *Emile* is a sort of pedagogical novel woven around Emile, an orphan boy and the son of wealthy parents, whose education has been entrusted to Rousseau. The very title of the book, with its sub-title *Education According to Nature* is a promise of a novel treatment of education. It tells us, if titles means anything, that the author is primarily interested in the child and a process of education suggested by the child's nature. The book is divided into five parts. The last and least important deals with Sophie, the prospective wife of Emile; the other four treat of the kind of education Emile should receive in each of the four main periods of pre-adult life: infancy and early childhood, childhood, boyhood and youth. Rousseau's philosophy of education, a faithful mirror of his philosophy of life, amounts to this. The end of life is happiness and happiness consists in the sensuous enjoyment of each moment as it passes, without any plan or thought of the future, or effort, or consideration for others. All aspirations to, and striving after a higher, better life, all self-restraint, self-control, self-sacrifice are a folly. This enjoyment of the present is the birthright of everyone of us. Parents and teachers have no right to deprive the child of the "pleasure of living now" under the pretense that through discipline, self-control, they prepare for a happier life in the future. Whatever interferes with life in the present is an evil.

Education, we are told, comes to us from nature, from man and from things. The internal development of our faculties and organs is the work of nature. The use we are told to make of this devel-   The threefold opment is the work of man. The acquisi-   nature of tions of our own experience, through the   education. objects that affect us, is the education of things. Education by nature does not depend on us; education through things depends on us only in some respects. We are in control only of the second mode of education, which should conform to the other two if we are to achieve anything worthwhile. Or again: Emile will have two teachers: nature and Rousseau. By nature is meant first, the animals, plants, inanimate objects with which Emile will come into contact; second and chiefly, the boy's native capacities. Rousseau's policy as a teacher will be, in the main, one of noninterference: to remove, so far as it can be done, whatever may hamper the work of the great teacher, nature. And since nature never uses authority but resistance it follows that authority should be banished from education.

But what is human nature? Rousseau's answer is in keeping with his conceptions of life: the sum total of man's instinctive, spontaneous tendencies before they are altered by reflection. Hence educa-   Human nature. tion should always conform to those instinctive, spontaneous tendencies. Comment is unnecessary upon this primitive, animal-like conception of human nature. None the less, much of what the author says concerning the early life of the child, a protest against the practice of his own time, is deserving of commendation. The mother should be, he tells us, the nurse of her own child, not only on physical but on moral grounds as well. The child should be allowed complete freedom of movement, be scantily clad, go barefoot, be inured to heat, cold, hunger and thirst. The influence of Montaigne and Locke is here evident. Emile's

life and education from five to twelve years of age will continue to be what it has been in infancy and
Education   early childhood. He will be allowed to grow
from birth to   and develop in complete freedom, will be
twelve years   encouraged to play to his heart's content,
of age   in fact will spend most of his time outdoors,
running and frolicking around; he will
be accustomed to be left alone and in the dark; he will be
brought into fearless contact with his surroundings. In this
wise he will not only develop a strong, sturdy body, but
will acquire a goodly stock of first-hand knowledge concerning sub-human nature. More important still, his senses
will be trained and Rousseau has a few interesting remarks
to make in this respect. Of what is commonly referred to as
intellectual and moral education, Emile will have none. In
Rousseau's own phraseology his education must and will be
negative; he must be free to come and go as he pleases, there
should be no systematic instruction on religious, or moral,
or any other subject. Yet, for all that, Rousseau claims that
Emile's intellectual and moral education has not been
neglected. The sense training he has received, and the hap-
hazard knowledge he has acquired through play and his
roamings through the fields and woods, have provided an
intellectual equipment which is, we are told, far superior to
anything the school might offer. Emile has never heard his
tutor say, "do this," "don't do that," but the discipline of
the natural consequences of his doings has supplied a training far better, so Rousseau pretends to believe, than the so-
called moral habits. Emile will receive no spanking for
wilfully spilling his milk, or breaking a windowpane in his
bedroom in a fit of anger; he will go without
should be   milk and be exposed to the consequences of
negative.   a mid-winter draught, because, forsooth, that
is nature's way of dealing with law-break-
ers. On the injury, physical and moral, which the disci-

pline of consequences may inflict upon the child, or boy, or young man, Rousseau is silent, nor does he seem to realize that the child will often fail to see the relation of cause and effect between his wrongdoing and its consequences, and thus miss the lesson it should convey. But even assuming that the relation will be clear to the child in every case, the result of such training would not be morality but utility; the child would not learn to do good and shun evil but to do what is likely to bring useful, pleasant consequences and to avoid what is likely to have harmful results.

At the age of twelve Emile is hardly anything else than a little animal, with a strong, healthy body, highly developed instincts, well trained senses; he does not know what authority is, or school life; he has never felt any restraint except that imposed upon him by necessity, but he is anxious to learn, and he has a great surplus energy that should be turned to useful purposes. Now then, says Rousseau, is the time to begin his intellectual education. Its motto will be "interest and utility." Emile will learn only those subjects in which he is interested or may prove of practical value in later life. Emile is wealthy, but his wealth may fail him some day; against such a day he should and will learn a trade, and with it acquire a measure of consideration for the laboring classes. He will study geography, astronomy, the natural sciences, which have a certain practical value in life, but he will not study those subjects in books; far better is the method of actual observation of one's surroundings, of the heavens, and the method of experimentation. There are far too many books and most of them are useless when they are not harmful. There is one book, however, that Emile will read and read over again: Robinson Crusoe, the book of the man of nature, of the model to be set before the boy. In Robinson's company Emile will learn what it really matters for him to learn, and

Education from twelve to fifteen

his reasoning powers will constantly be called upon to solve little practical problems which better than anything else will develop a sound practical judgment.

At the age of fifteen or therabout the social feelings show signs of rapid development, a warning to the tutor that Emile's education enters now into a new *and fifteen* phase. Thus far he has lived a solitary life; *to twenty.* he should now share the society of his fellow beings; now should begin his social and moral education which is to be founded not on the "unnatural" sense of duty but on sympathy for one's fellows. If the teacher will see to it that the sympathy of his charge goes to people who are worthy of genuine sympathy, everything, so Rousseau assumes, will be for the best. At last Emile reaches his twentieth year. The tutor's work is now nearly completed. One day the young man is wondering at the origin and the cause of the natural beauty that surrounds him, on a glorious morning in the country. He is told there is a God and that is all his religious education.

Stripped of its rhetoric and sophistries the Emile boils down to the following principles which *Summing up.* had been lost sight of in eighteenth century education:

1. That education is first of all for the benefit of the child, not for the sake of any conception, however hallowed, of the function of the teacher, or the curriculum, or the school;

2. That the child should be treated as a child, not like a miniature adult, as it was so common in the eighteenth century;

3. That education should so far as possible provide first-hand contact with the child's physical environment;

4. That education is not some kind of artificial procedure, but a process of growth and development determined, partly at least, by a corresponding process of physical and psychical growth and development in the child;

5. That the method of instruction should be based upon the psychological development of the child;

6. That education should be a practical preparation for life.

Always bearing in mind that Rousseau was the mouthpiece of tendencies current in his own time, it is no exaggeration to say that few men have had on modern thought an influence comparable to his. Kant's philosophy drew its chief inspiration from Rousseau, and the creed of the "Vicaire Savoyard" has remained to this day the religion of millions whose faith is a matter of mere emotion instead of settled convictions. In art, and especially in literature, Rousseau's influence was paramount during the two generations following his own time. Bernardin de St. Pierre, Chateaubriand, Madame de Stael, Lamartine, Musset, Victor Hugo, George Sand,[1] were his literary disciples, and his influence was not limited to France; abundant evidence of it could easily be gathered in the literature of England, Germany, Italy, Scandinavia, Russia. In fact the whole romantic movement, with its fondness for the picturesque, the rural, its morbid pathos, its display of insincere virtue and vague religious sentimentalism, its rebellion against the conventional, was to a great extent a product of

HUXLEY

Rousseau's teaching. To speak of his influence on politics and economics is almost superfluous. No single man contributed more than he did to the French Revolution; its most radical leaders were all his avowed disciples; socialism claims him and rightly as its patriarch, and the language of the Declaration of Independence shows that even the sober-minded, practical framers of the American Constitution did not escape his influence.

We are here chiefly concerned, however, with Rousseau's

[1] All of them more or less representatives of romanticism in the latter part of the eighteenth or in the nineteenth century.

influence on education which will be described at some length in this and subsequent sections of this volume. Let it be said at present that, beginning with the eighteenth century Philanthropinists, through Pestalozzi, Herbart, Froebel, Spencer and a host of other educational theorists and teachers, that influence spread for good or evil to the whole Western world.

It is in the work of Basedow (1723-1790) and his fellow Philanthropinists that we find the first practical application of Rousseau's doctrines to school work. In his "Address to Philanthropists and Men of Property on Schools and Studies and their Influence on the Public Weal," Basedow made an appeal for financial aid, in order to be able to establish a large publishing house and a training school for teachers to be connected with "An immense school for the race and humanity." He began to realize his great project with the publication of his *Elementary Work*, a sort of popular encyclopedia and an imitation, though a pale one, of Comenius' *Orbis Pictus*.[1] In the *Philanthropinum*,[2] or Elementary Institute, he founded at Dessau, Basedow tried to apply his own interpretation of the doctrine of education according to nature, already formulated in his Book of Method, the chief features of which were the following:

The Philanthropinists.

1. Children to be treated as children, not as miniature adults;
2. Play and physical training to be recognized as normal activities of school life;
3. The learning of a trade for social and economic reasons;
4. The use of the vernacular as the means of classroom intercourse;
5. Languages to be taught through the natural, i.e., conversational method;
6. A religious but non-sectarian atmosphere.

Basedow's ambition was to enlist the aid of the State for his plans, and he repeatedly petitioned the Governments to

[1] See Vol. II, p. 218.
[2] See Barnard's Journal, Vol. V, pp. 487-520, for a full account of the institution.

establish some sort of State control of education. He also was eager, in fact all Philanthropinists were, to secure the interest of the masses in educational reforms. Their educational writings were generally addressed to the people at large, and they at least succeeded in winning over to their cause the interest of the middle class. Most active and conspicuous in this work of educational propaganda were Campe (1746-1818)[1] and Salzman (1744-1811). The Philanthropinums, however, were shortlived; with the exception of Salzman's school at Schnepfenthal[2] none survived the eighteenth century, but they had at least achieved one purpose: to give the governments an opportunity to inaugurate school reforms.

The adepts of the doctrine of education according to nature have been legion since Rousseau's time. Most of them, following the lead of Pestalozzi, Herbart and Froebel, have tried to reach some sort of compromise between tradition and the doctrines of the Genevan reformer. In many instances the spirit of naturalism has even been ignored entirely, and the application of the doctrine has been confined to the province of methodology; appeal to the senses, the use of observation, the laboratory, visits to museums, excursions into the country, as so many means of awakening the dormant powers of the child. There is however, a rather important group of educational theorists and teachers who not only have made the whole of Rousseau's gospel their own, but have even outdistanced his radicalism. The best known representative of   Spencer
this "integral" naturalism in education is
Herbert Spencer (1820-1903) an English philosopher and

---

[1] A rather prolific writer, the author of "Robinson der Jüngere," the model of the famous "Swiss Family Robinson."

[2] It celebrated its one-hundredth anniversary in 1884; Carl Ritter, the founder of modern geographical study was one of its pupils and one of its first teachers was Guss Muths, the founder of the German system of gymnastic education.

publicist, whose influence has been paramount in many educational circles of the English-speaking countries. Spencer's views on nature, man and life, are set forth in his *System of Synthetic Philosophy* or *Principles of Biology, Psychology, Sociology, Ethics and General Principles.* His educational creed, a corollary of his philosophy, is formulated in *Education, Intellectual, Moral, Physical,* a book consisting of four essays, each of which appeared at first as a magazine article. Spencer's philosophy can be summed up in the word "agnosticism"; we know nothing, nor can we

HERBERT SPENCER

prove anything of a hereafter; so far as we can ascertain, human life is all of this world, it begins and ends in nature. Let us then see what man is, and examine the conditions under which man has to live this earthly, "natural" life which, so far as one can see, is all that he can hope for. Man is primarily a living organism, an animal endowed with senses, and therefore the first and most essential prerequisite for the individual's success in life, for the nation's prosperity and welfare, is that man be a good animal, healthy, sturdy, endowed with a strong nervous system and well developed, keen senses. Human life is made up of certain activities which, according to Spencer, can be classed as follows, in the order of their importance: activities related to preservation of life and health; vocational activities, related to earning a living; domestic activities, related to family life and the rearing of children; social and political activities related to citizenship; leisure activities, related to the gratification of the tastes and feelings. The purpose of education, which can be formulated as a preparation for all those ac·

tivities, for complete living, demands both knowledge and training. What knowledge then answers best the purpose of education? What knowledge is of most worth? For centuries the child had been taught that man is created to the image and likeness of God, that man's first duty is to know Him, to love Him and to serve Him, in order to be happy in this life and the next; that the only knowledge which really counts is that which concerns our Lord and Creator, our origin and destiny, and the road thereto. Rubbish, says Spencer. Man is a product of nature, belongs to nature, lives and will entirely vanish in nature. The knowledge that he needs in preparing himself for the life he is to live is supplied by the sciences that deal with nature.

What knowledge is of most worth?

He needs a knowledge of biology, physiology and hygiene because such knowledge is essential for the preservation of life and health; of mathematics, physics, chemistry, biology, in order to be able to eke out a living under existing conditions of industrial life; family life and the rearing of children demand for their proper functioning a knowledge of biology, hygiene, psychology and ethics; political and social activities, a knowledge of the sciences of history, economics and politics. Last and least, man needs a knowledge of music, aesthetics and literature which belong to the leisure part of life and therefore should occupy a corresponding position in the curriculum. It is hardly necessary to remark that Spencer's conception of psychology, ethics, economics, politics, history, even art and literature, is in keeping with the naturalistic trend of his philosophy. His psychology and ethics are nothing else than some kind of "transcendental physiology." Thought life is brain life; conscience, duty, free will, moral responsibility, supernatural sanctions he ignores; his ethics is concerned with the intellectual development, physical well-being, material comfort and prosperity of the individual and the race. Historical events, economic, social and political conditions, art and literature, are so many manifestations of the hidden forces constantly at work in nature. A knowledge of the natural sciences is therefore a prerequisite for the understanding of past and present conditions of the race, the problems that face it, even for the enjoyment of art and literature.

In his treatment of method and training Spencer has nothing new to offer. He merely reiterates in his own way the principles formulated by Rousseau and Pestalozzi. The great teacher is nature; the ideal method is the method of nature. In teaching we should proceed from the simple to the complex, from the concrete to the abstract, from the empirical to the rational. And here we probably have Spencer's best contribution to modern educational theory and practice: the popularizing of Pestalozzi's didactic precepts in English-speaking countries. When dealing with moral training Spencer repeats Rousseau's doctrine of natural punishments. Parents and teachers should consider themselves as "the servants and disciples of nature." Their interference in the work of education should be reduced to a minimum. The discipline of the natural consequences of one's acts is the one true moral discipline.

Such, in brief outline, is the system of studies and discipline which naturalism, in the person of one of its leading representatives, would have foisted upon parent and school. Needless to say that, with the possible exception of Bolshevist Russia, Spencer's program has never been put to the test, though some features of it, such as the stressing of the sciences and care for the physical well-being of the child, have had some influence on school practice during the last two generations. Parents there may be who would watch with interest the application of "naturalistic" principles in the rearing of their neighbor's child, but they would most certainly think twice before attempting it on their own offspring. The rooted sanity of mankind recoils from a system of pedagogy which would degrade human nature, which sneers at what man instinctively considers as the greatest achievements of the race, the most precious part of the common inheritance. Education is a work of nature indeed, but not in the sense naturalism would have us think of it, for if there is one truth concerning this vital question, that is made plain by everyday experience, common sense, the wisdom and practice of the race, it is this: that education is first and last a work of authority.

SOURCES

A complete list of sources even if limited to modern times would be a long one. If restricted to strictly educational writings it would include:

Basedow, J. B., Elementarwerk and Methodenbuch.
Campe, J. H., Robinson der Jüngere and Theorophon.
Rousseau, J. J., Emile.
Salzmann, C. G., Conrad Kiefer.
Spencer, H., Education.

REFERENCES

Barnard, H., American Journal of Education.
Barnard, H., German Teachers and Educators.
Card, Mercier, Les Origines de la Psychologie Contemporaine.
Chesterton, G. K., Orthodoxy.
Davidson, T., Rousseau and Education according to Nature.
Eymieu, A., Le naturalisme devant la Science.
Messer, A., Natur und Geist.
Willmann, O., Geschichte der Idealismus.

CHAPTER VI

THE IMPROVEMENT OF METHOD

MUCH AS THE EIGHTEENTH CENTURY HAD accomplished in modifying educational ideals, improving educational methods and content, organizing schools, it dwindles into insignificance when compared with the educational activities of the last one hundred and twenty years. For convenience and clarity's sake, we consider those activities under the following headings taken up in this order:

Naturalism, or the spread of the spirit of the Enlightenment, which is treated in the preceding chapter;

The improvement of the methods of instruction;

Nationalism and socialism and the building up of national school systems;

The Industrial Revolution and its influence upon the schools;

Catholic education.

This survey of educational theory and practice in the nineteenth and twentieth centuries will close, by way of summing up, with a short description of the modern educational system in its present-day condition. That arrangement should not convey the impression of a chronological sequence in the above-mentioned movements: they were all taking place at the same time, though not proceeding at the same pace, and many of the men whose names are usually connected with one movement might as well be cited as leading representatives in another field.

Our survey of school reforms in the eighteenth century

has shown us the recognition, on the part of some educators at least, of the shortcomings of the methodology then in use in elementary schools, and a desire to improve it. Felbiger in Austria, Hecker and Hahn in Berlin, Overberg in Westphalia, the Philanthropinists in various parts of Germany, were all interested in the problem. Its solution, however, so far as the problem can be solved with any degree of finality, was achieved in the nineteenth century; of the many names associated with it in the first half of the century those of Pestalozzi, Herbart, and Froebel are the most commonly mentioned.

PESTALOZZI

Johann Heinrich Pestalozzi (1746-1827), a Swiss, and one of the leading educationists of modern times, spent a lifetime in an attempt to adapt Rousseau's doctrine of education according to nature to classroom work. His *Journal of a Father* is a record of his observations, experiments and experiences in the education of his son according to Rousseau's principles. It was a pioneer effort in experimental pedagogy which led Pestalozzi to modify some of the views of the Genevan dreamer. At the time he was thus experimenting on his son he had begun to develop ideas on the education of the children of the poor from the industrial standpoint. It was Pestalozzi's firm belief that the employer

Pestalozzi's work,

should be responsible for the education of his young employees. The children he employed on his farm at Neuhof were taught reading, writing, and the elements of arithmetic. With this there was combined for the boys practice in the processes of small farming, for the girls needlework, domestic work and gardening.[1] Financial difficulties compelled Pestalozzi to give up the experiments and for the next eighteen years he was engaged in literary activity. It was during this period that appeared *Leonard and Gertrude,* the best known of his writings, a sort of educational novel in which the author tries to show how social regeneration is possible through home and school education. In 1798 Pestalozzi resumed his pedagogical experiments with great success in an orphan asylum at Stanz, and a little later, with the aid of devoted, self-sacrificing, able colleagues, at Burgdorf, where his work attracted the attention of teachers in his homeland and abroad. It was here that he published *How Gertrude Teaches Her Children,* which contains the best exposition from his pen of his educational principles and practices. In 1805 Pestalozzi's Institution, now world famous, was transferred to Yverdun, where it remained until its end in 1825.

main
writings,

None of Pestalozzi's writings contains a clear, definite, systematic exposition of his theories. Such an account is to be sought in the outlines of his disciples, especially Morf.[2]

purpose,

Social regeneration, the betterment of the masses, physical, intellectual and moral, is the ultimate purpose assigned to education by Pestalozzi. To the achievement of that purpose the teach-

---

[1] This principle of combining industrial training with intellectual education, chiefly on social and economic grounds, had already been applied in some of the schools of the Christian Brothers, in connection with the English Charity Schools and in the Philanthropinums; it was strongly advocated by Rousseau in the Emile and in Pestalozzi's time received further and wider application in Fellenberg's Institutions.

[2] Morf, H., Zur Biographie Pestalozzi's.

er's work will contribute insofar as it leads to the natural, progressive, harmonious development of all the powers and faculties of the child. Instruction at its best can do no more than assist nature. "In the newborn child are hidden those faculties which are to be unfolded during life. The individual and separate organs of his being form themselves gradually into unison and build up humanity to the image of God. The education of man is a purely moral result. It is not the educator who puts new powers and faculties into man, and imparts to him the breath of life. He only takes care that no untoward influence shall disturb nature's march of development. The moral, intellectual and practical powers of man must be nurtured within himself and not from artificial substitutes. Thus, faith must be cultivated by our own act of believing, not by reasoning about faith; love by our own act of loving, not by fine words about love; thought by our own act of thinking, not by merely appropriating the thoughts of other men; and knowledge by our own investigations, not by endless talk about the results of arts and science."[1]

The Philanthropist Fischer, one of Pestalozzi's friends, thus sums up Pestalozzianism: to give the mind an intensive, not merely an extensive culture; to connect all instruction with language study; to start in all mental operations from fundamental data, mother ideas; to simplify the mechanism of instruction and   principles, study; to popularize science.[2] Morf, one of Pestalozzi's co-workers, has condensed the master's pedagogy in the following principles:

1. Intuition (i.e., observation) is the foundation of instruction.
2. Language should be connected with instruction.
3. The time for learning is not the time for judging and criticising.
4. In each branch, instruction should begin with the simplest ele-

[1] How Gertrude Teaches, p. 20.
[2] See first letter to Gesner in "How Gertrude Teaches."

ments, and progress by degrees while following the development of the child, that is to say, through a series of steps psychologically connected.

5. We should dwell long enough on each point of our teaching to enable the pupil to gain a complete mastery of it.

6. Teaching should follow the order of natural development, not that of synthetic exposition.

7. The individuality of the child is sacred.

8. The chief end of elementary instruction is not to impart knowledge and talents to the learner, but to develop and increase the forces of his intelligence.

9. To knowledge should be joined power; to theoretical knowledge practical skill.

10. The relations between master and pupil especially as to discipline should be based upon and ruled by love.

11. Instruction should be subordinated to the higher purpose of education.[1]

A full exposition and criticism of the above principles would require much more space than we dispose of here. Such as they are, even in their concise, aphoristic form, if taken together, they give us a fairly good idea of what Pestalozzi was trying to achieve through his pedagogical experiments, what he was wont to refer to as the "psychologizing" of education.

A favorite idea of Pestalozzi, and one in which he took great pride as a novelty in educational practice, is that language, form and number are the three instruments of all education. It seems strange, let it be remarked in passing, that he should have been unaware of the fact that from time immemorial, language, number and form have been the foundation of education and were used as such for thousands of years before Pestalozzi. Another favorite idea of Pestalozzi was that there should be a radical change in the character of the relations between teacher and pupil, which, he believed, should be those existing between parent and child. Writing of his work at Stanz, he says: "I was con-

[1] See Morf, H., Zur Biographie Pestalozzi's.

vinced that my heart would change the condition of my children, just as quickly as the sun of Spring would re-animate the earth benumbed by Winter," and again, "I was everything to my children. I was alone with them from morning till night. . . . Their hands were in my hands. Their eyes were fixed on my eyes."

Pestalozzi's main purpose, however, his most absorbing interest, was to improve the methods then used in the teaching of the elementary school subjects. It was his firm conviction that the methods of   leading instruction could be made so simple and   interest, mechanical that they might be employed to good purpose by the most ordinary teacher and by the most ignorant f a t h e r and mother. "I believe, he tells us, that we must not dream of making prog-ress in the instruction of the people so long as we have not found the forms of instruction w h i c h make of the teacher, at least so far as the comple-tion of the elementary studies is concerned, the simple mechanical instru-ment of a method which owes its result to the na-ture of its processes, and not to the ability of the one who uses it." He at-tached a special impor-tance to the object lesson, which, after the French, he calls intuition, and he has left us an account of a little classroom incident which led him to realize its value in teaching. One

ZELLER AND HIS PUPILS

day, while he was giving to his class a long description of what was to be observed in a drawing in which there appeared a representation of a window, he noticed that one of the children, instead of looking at the picture, was examining the classroom windows with the greatest attention. Here, thought Pestalozzi, was a sure sign of the method to be employed. Hereafter he would use the objects themselves and resort to their representations only when it could not be helped. The working out of the application of this principle of sense appeal to the teaching of the elementary school branches is probably the one lasting contribution of Pestalozzi to pedagogy. His purpose was to introduce the child to a knowledge of his immediate surroundings and to develop in him the power of observation, but he seems to have failed to realize that sense perception is but the beginning of intellectual growth, and the application of even the best of pedagogical principles may be carried to a point where instruction becomes puerile. It was not an idle sarcasm on the part of one of his critics to remark that Pestalozzi spent far too much time in trying to convince his class that they have one nose located somewhere in the middle of their face between the two eyes.

The schools at Burgdorf and Yverdun attracted the attention of teachers, philosophers and statesmen in every part of Europe and even America.[1] Visitors influence. flocked to those places in order to see for themselves the new venture in the domain of education. The innovator's influence was felt first most deeply in German lands, especially in Prussia. That country had suffered a crushing defeat at the hands of Napoleon in 1806. Her leaders saw in Pestalozzi's plan for the education of the masses a means of national regeneration. Prussian teachers were sent to Yverdun and the work of the Prussian

[1] See Griscom, J., A Year in Europe, Vol. I, pp. 415-420; Woodbridge, Wm. C., American Annals of Education and Instruction, Vol. VII, p. 14.

schools was reorganized along the lines of Pestalozzian pedagogy. Prussia's leadership of the German States in the War of Liberation in 1813 was, partly at least, the fruit of her educational regeneration. The influence of Pestalozzianism on the French schools came indirectly through the work of Victor Cousin (1792-1867), while he was Minister of Public Instruction. In 1835 he issued his *Report on the Condition of Public Instruction in Prussia,* which described the remarkable improvement in Prussian elementary school work as a result of the adoption of Pestalozzian principles and methods. In France and German lands the influence of Pestalozzianism extended to the whole field of education, aim, spirit, content and method. In England and the United States, on the other hand, it was at first limited to the Pestalozzian use of the object lesson, which was introduced in England by Charles Mayo (1792-1846) and his sister Elizabeth (1793-1865); in the United States by Joseph Neef, one of Pestalozzi's assistants, who had been invited by a Philadelphia philanthropist to open a school there.[1] The innovation, however, attracted little attention at that time among American teachers, and it was not until a generation later that Pestalozzianism began to make any headway in the United States, through the efforts of Horace Mann (1796-1859) and Henry Barnard (1811-1900), and especially through the Oswego movement. Edward A. Sheldon, the superintendent of schools at Oswego, New York, had been acquainted with Pestalozzi's methods as used in England and Canada. He introduced those methods in his schools and he organized for the same purpose a training class for teachers which became a State Normal School in 1866 and for a generation provided most of the experts to teach methods. Like the Mayo schools, the Oswego system has been severely criticized for its over-emphasis on the me-

[1] See Monroe, W. S., Pestalozzian Movement, chs. III-VI.

chanical side of instruction, thus missing the real spirit and
purpose of the Pestalozzian reform.

Two fellow countrymen of Pestalozzi, von Fellenberg and
Girard, whose fame was more or less overshadowed by that
of Pestalozzi, also made important contribu-
Fellenberg   tions to the school reform of the early
and industrial   nineteenth century. Phillip Emmanuel von
education.   Fellenberg (1771-1844), a wealthy Swiss
landowner and philanthropist, conducted
for years at Hofwyl a great educational establishment. In
1804 he founded a Charity
school which a few years
later developed into an
agricultural school, in
1807 the Literary Institution or Academy in which
the children of nobles and
gentry were to be re-
ceived, and in 1827 a
"real" intermediate or
practical school for the
children of the middle
class; in 1823 his wife had
founded a school for poor
girls, which was under
the charge of one of her

FELLENBERG

daughters. The most sig-
nificant feature in the
work of the schools was the provision for manual activity,
which Fellenberg regarded as the necessary complement
of sense perception and object teaching so much emphasized by Pestalozzi. The chief occupation was agriculture,
which for the poor children was decidedly vocational,
whereas for the pupils in the Literary Institution, who
might some day have estates of their own, the purpose

of the work was to give some preparation for the intelligent management of farming. A printing establishment, shops for the manufacture and repair of agricultural implements, the making and mending of clothes and footwear, were in due course of time added to the schools. The subjects taught in the lower schools were reading, writing, arithmetic, drawing, singing, natural history, geography, history, geometry and mensuration, botany, and agriculture; the more promising pupils were promoted to the higher schools and trained as teachers. The curriculum of the Literary Institution retained the classics, but it also emphasized the modern languages, science, drawing and music. Physical exercises and military drills were an important part of the school work, but what Fellenberg emphasized above all else was religion and moral education.

The institution at Hofwyl became almost as famous internationally as Pestalozzi's at Yverdun. The industrial work it suggested as a means of extending educational opportunity to the poor, the defective, the delinquent gradually became a feature of elementary school work at home and abroad. Every Swiss Canton soon had its farm school, in which classroom instruction occupied only a few hours of the day, the remainder of the day being devoted to work in the field, or garden, or some indoor craft. Reform schools, orphanages, and later on the continuation schools everywhere gradually adopted the plan suggested by the Pestalozzi-Fellenberg experiments: industrial training of some kind in the school, preparing for a period of apprenticeship. Striking examples of the value, for a certain class of boys and girls, of this combination of vocational training with the traditional elementary school subjects, was the "House of Redemption" of Hamburg, the George Edmundson School at Queenswood Hall, Hampshire, and the Battersea Training Establishment. In the United States there sprang up during the second quarter of the nineteenth century a number of secondary and higher institutions where the "manual labor" feature was an integral part of the school curriculum. The purpose of the addition was both economic and educational; to enable students to earn their way through school and to secure physical exercise for the youth under the strain of intellectual work. Gradually, however, the economic aspect of this industrial system was given up as impracticable and the educational purpose of the scheme was taken care of by athletics. The introduction of the Pestalozzi-Fellenberg training in American institutions for delinquents and defectives, to replace contract labor and factory work, did not take place until the close of the nineteenth century. More recent still is the organization of industrial training as an integral part of the public school system.

Girard, Jean Baptiste (1765-1850), better known as Père Girard, was a member of the Franciscan Order. In 1804 he was called to Freiburg, his native city, to **Père Girard.** organize public education. He made school attendance compulsory, organized school administration, insisted on the adoption of good text books and methods, and lacking assistants, introduced the monitorial system, avoiding, so far as possible, the abuse of mere memoriter work. The school he personally conducted grew in a few years from forty pupils at the start to four hundred, and attracted many foreigners. Though differing from Pestalozzi on several important points, he had the greatest admiration for his work and ability, and tried to put his theories into practice so far as possible. He accepted Pestalozzi's theory of harmonious development, but severely criticized his emphasis on the intellectual at the expense of the moral and religious aspects of education. A little incident which occurred in the course of a visit he paid to the establishment at Yverdun deserves to be related here, because of the light it throws on the difference between his and Pestalozzi's opinions on the immediate aim of education. "I made the remark," says Girard, "to my old friend Pestalozzi, that too much time was devoted to mathematics in his establishment and that I feared the result of this on the education that was given. Whereupon he replied to me with spirit, as was his manner: 'That is because I wish my children to believe nothing which cannot be illustrated as clearly to them as that 2 and 2 make 4.' My reply, in the same strain, was: 'In that case, if I had thirty sons, I would not entrust one of them to you, because it would be impossible for you to demonstrate to him, as you can, that 2 and 2 make 4, that I am his father and that I have a right to his obedience.'" In all his works, but particularly in the chief one, *"The vernacular tongue to the young as a means of intellectual, moral and religious development,"* Girard stresses the point, that the ultimate end of education is ethico-religious, *i.e.,* to make men better.

Pestalozzi's one great ambition was to supply a psychological basis for classroom methods of instruction, but his investigations never carried him beyond the first stage, sense perception. His work was taken up at this point by Johann Friedrich Herbart (1776-1841) a German philosopher, educator and educational theorist, whose work and career are in several ways the very antithesis of the Swiss reformer's. Pestalozzi's early training and schooling had been of a rather desultory, disjointed character; he was by temperament and he remained all through life an incorrigible sentimentalist, a visionary whose positions were always somewhat vague, based upon sympathetic insight, a sort of intuitive knowledge of child nature, rather than a clear, scientific vision of the problem facing him; his work was confined to the elementary stage in school life and his emphasis upon sense perception led him to a like emphasis upon nature study, geography, drawing, oral compositions, mental arithmetic and gymnastics.

Herbart, was gifted with a clear, keen intellect, and he

had the benefit of a good, systematic training, first at home
under the direct supervision of his mother,
Herbart.   a woman of more than ordinary ability, and
later at the gymnasium of Oldenburg and
the University of Jena, where he was an enthusiastic student
of Greek, mathematics, and philosophy. Before taking his
degree he became tutor to the sons of the Governor of Inter-
laken, Switzerland, and his observations of these children
became the basis of much of his later educational theories.
While in Switzerland Herbart also became acquainted with
the work and writings of Pestalozzi and after his return to
Germany did much to popularize the "new education," with
which he then was in full sympathy. For several years he
lectured on philosophy and pedagogy at the University of
Göttingen and in 1809 was appointed professor of philosophy at the University of Koenigsberg, which had been
made famous by Immanuel Kant (1724-1804). While there
he established his pedagogical seminary and a practice
school connected with it; the work of the student teachers
in this practice school was supervised by the professor and
then criticised for the benefit of the whole class in the seminar. Most of those student teachers—the first Herbartians—
eventually became principals and inspectors, and through
their influence classroom work in German schools was
greatly improved.

Herbart's doctrines are set forth in a number of pedagogical writings, chief of which are: *The Aesthetic Presentation
of the Universe, The Science of Education,*
His chief   and *The Outlines of Educational Doctrine.*
writings,   The full import of those doctrines, however,
can be grasped only in the light of Herbart's
philosophy and particularly his psychology. Herbart rejects
the traditional view of a soul endowed with certain native
faculties or powers. For this he substitutes a simple soul
possessing but one faculty: that of entering, through the
nervous system, into relations with its surroundings, from

which it receives presentations, impressions, and since, according to Herbart, we know nothing of the nature of this simple soul, our only concern should be with the series or mass of presentations that reach it through the nervous system. The whole spiritual life, so the theory goes, is nothing else than the outcome of the interactions, combinations, permutations of those presentations, or, to use the Herbartian phrase, the result of the process of apperception, which can be briefly described in some such way as this. The first sensation or impression yields   conception of no knowledge; it sinks into the subcon-   psychical life, scious self, there to be awakened by the next impression which it modifies and partially fuses with. This compound state in turn sinks into subconsciousness, where it is aroused by the next presentation, and so the process goes on, each new reception modifying "the apperceiving mass" and being in turn modified by it. In this wise is the mind built up of the ideas it has received; the facility and completeness of the assimilation of any new presentation depends on what has preceded it; an entirely new idea has no chance of being taken in because there is nothing

HERBART

ing in the mind to receive it. It is thus of paramount importance for the normal growth and development of intellectual life, that the materials of instruction be well selected, well presented and co-ordinated, that the teacher be familiar with his subject matter and possess an adequate knowledge of each pupil's capacities for education, his apperceiving masses and physical nature. More vital still, according to Herbart's theory, is the influence of instruction on conduct. Knowledge, we are told, begets interest which leads to new knowledge and which in turn arouses new interests. Thus both knowledge and interest constantly react upon each other. The chief function of the teacher should be to develop in his pupils "a many-sided interest" of the right kind, through the proper presentation of appropriate subject matter. For in this wise he can determine not only what his pupils should see and learn but what they should desire and will. All actions spring out of the "circle of

of the educa-
tional aim

thought," made up of presentations, ideas, interests, desires, volitions, conduct. Knowledge is the cornerstone of character; "Knowledge is virtue," is the gist and burden of Herbartian pedagogy, even more thoroughly than it was of Socrates' teaching, for Herbart conceives the soul as being nothing else than a sort of meeting place for the presentations flowing in upon us from without; out of their interaction our whole psychological life is fashioned; there are no psychological faculties that change those presentations into images, concepts, judgments, volitions; particularly, there is no free will. The will and its character, weak or strong, good or bad, are, like the intellect, the ultimate resultants of presentations. As a man knows, so he will act. Knowledge is the essential prerequisite of virtue, just as ignorance is the main factor in vice.

The ultimate end of education, Herbart tells us, is the formation of a good moral character, and

and the means
to achieve it:

that, insofar as the school is concerned, is achieved through government, training and instruction. Government is concerned with the conditions under which the instructive process must function in order to be effective; it maintains order, keeps the child busy, secures his obedience. Training concerns itself with the discipline of the will, but since willing is the outcome of knowing, it follows that instruction is the central factor in education. Not all instruction, however, is conducive to this end; mere information, the storing of facts, will never result in the formation of a good moral character. Instruction is educative, it leads to a good moral character:

when it develops in the child an abiding interest in his environment;
when it secures the attention of the pupil and has enlisted his hearty co-operation in the work on hand;
when the matter to be assimilated and the method of instruction are well adapted to the learner's capacity;
when the teaching process is arranged into a series of well-graded steps;
when all the items of knowledge are well correlated, so that there will be presented to the mind a unified view of the world.

Virtue, the ultimate purpose of instruction, says Herbart in substance, can only be attained through another and nearer aim, interest, "many-sided interest." In the development of the doctrine of many-sided interest with its related topics, we have Herbart's most important contribution to the theory of education. We commonly think of interest as a means to a proximate end, an incentive to study. We know that children are interested in their own experiences, that they take delight in relating what they have seen, or heard, or done, in collecting all kinds of odds and ends, in doing sundry little tasks, and we try to enlist those interests of the child in the service of classroom work, of composition, of arithmetic, of science, of observation. Herbart sometimes uses the term interest in this sense, but he also and more commonly refers to it in another sense that is essentially his own. "The word interest," he says, "stands in general for that kind of mental activity which it is the business of instruction to incite. Mere information does not suffice; for this we think of as a supply or store of facts, which a person might possess or lack, and still remain the same being. But he who lays hold of his information, and reaches out for more, takes an interest in it. Since, however, this mental activity is varied, we need to add that further determination supplied by the term many-sidedness."[1] The teacher's aim then should be to develop in his pupils this kind of interest. Thus in teaching national history his aim should be to develop in the class an abiding interest in the achievements of the nation, in teaching language an interest in the nation's literary achievements, in teaching religion an interest in eternal salvation. From that viewpoint Herbart divided interest into two classes: those arising from a knowledge of nature, and those arising from the association with our fellow-beings. Interests of the first class might be empirical, the outcome of sense experience; they might be speculative, resulting from speculation on the nature of the object, or again aesthetic, from a contemplation of its beauty. Interests of the second class might relate to individuals, or the community as a whole, or one's destiny. Many-sided interest as the immediate aim of instruction demands that no one kind of interests be unduly emphasized at the expense of the others. Aside from native capacity, which the school cannot create, the arousing of interests depends on the nature of the subject matter and the methods of instruction.

Corresponding to this two-fold division of interests, there are two main classes of subjects, historical, including language, literature and history, and scientific, including mathematics and the natural sciences. Many-sidedness of interest demands that all those branches be adequately represented in the curriculum and that instruction in all of them be of service to the child in moral and especially in social growth.

[1] Outlines, p. 44.

It should help him find his place and function in the world, it should form his disposition toward men and things, it should give him insight into ethical relations. Many-sided interest cannot be achieved at once. There must be, to start with, a store of ideas which, before school life, the child has acquired through experience and social intercourse. Instruction supplements this acquired knowledge, the apperceiving ideas, by supplying the proper kind of presentations. Should the teacher discover that there are wanting some apperceiving ideas he should, before attention, proceeding any further, make an effort to supply them, for the apperception of any new knowledge presupposes some old knowledge with which it must be connected, and the connecting link, the bridge so to speak, which connects old and new knowledge is attention.

Herbart considers attention as being of two kinds, involuntary or spontaneous and voluntary. The former, he holds, might be primitive, depending upon the strength of the sense impressions, and apperceiving, which presupposes primitive and "takes place through the reproduction of previously acquired ideas and their union with the new elements."[1] It is this latter kind of attention which, according to Herbart, should be mainly appealed to in the teaching-learning process, for which he outlined the following formal steps: clearness, association, system and method, which his followers developed still further into the series, preparation, statement of aim, presentation, association or comparison, generalization and application. The purpose of preparation is to ascertain whether the necessary apperceiving ideas are actually present in the learner's mind; the statement of the aim of the lesson focuses the attention of the class on the work on hand and arouses their interest; presentation and association introduce the new facts, showing at the same time their relation to one another and to

[1] Outlines, p. 63.

the old knowledge; generalization crystallizes into a concept what has been so far dealt with analytically, and application, so to speak, impresses it upon the mind through abundant practice. It is unfortunate that the terminology used is suggestive not so much of "steps" in apperception by the pupil as of "steps" in instruction by the teacher. Some such terms as reception, comprehension and application would, it seems, better answer the purpose, but the Herbartian terminology is well in keeping with the trend of the master's pedagogy to emphasize the teacher's function. It is doubtful, however, whether it was Herbart's intention to attach to the formal steps the importance which has been given them by his followers, whether he did not consider them as some sort of pedagogical device to help young teachers, not as a cure all for existing ills in classroom methodology.

apperception,

The materials of instruction, says Herbart, should be well correlated in order to present a unified world view to the child's consciousness and thus forestall the danger of a scattered many-sidedness of interest. This idea was elaborated by some of his followers into various schemes of concentration or co-ordination of studies. Concentration means unification of the curriculum around one central core study which is supposed to possess, for the time being, the greatest educative value, whereas co-ordination of studies means that, instead of one, there are two or three or more cores, *e.g.,* the mother tongue, history, geography, arithmetic, all groups being connected at some point with one another. Some followers of Herbart developed the idea of the correlation of studies still further into a culture epoch theory, a pedagogical application of the so-called recapitulation theory, according to which the individual, in his physical development from the embryo to the adult, recapitulates the main stages of development that took place in the evolu-

correlation of materials.

tion of the species. The theory also assumes that mental processes are but special manifestations of physical nature, and it claims further that in the course of its intellectual development the race went through the following stages: intuitive or presentative, during which knowledge was chiefly acquired through the instincts and sense perception; representative or imaginative, when the acquisition of knowledge depended upon memory and imagination; logical, when further progress was depending upon the use of reason. Hence, it is claimed, to conform to the proper order of development of the child: we should, at each stage in this development, take our materials of instruction from the corresponding stage in the evolution of the race; we should take the order of development of the instincts as an index in the presentation of subject matter; we should let every instinct have its "fling" at the time it is strongest, lest it re-appear later in a distorted form.

To illustrate the application of these pronouncements.— In the teaching of religion the child should first be treated as a little heathen offering up animal sacrifices, then as a Jewish child, then as a Christian. Let it be said, as a concluding remark, that those vagaries were never taken very seriously in curriculum instruction.

Herbart's pedagogy at first received comparatively little attention, but in the latter nineteenth century there developed at Leipzig and Jena two remarkable centers of Herbartianism which exerted a widespread influence particularly in Germany and the United States. Tuiskon Ziller (1817-1881) was the leader of the movement at Leipzig, and Karl Volkmar Stoy (1815-1885), later on Wilhelm Rein (1847-1915), at Jena. At both universities were established pedagogical seminars and practice schools for the study, theoretical and practical, of Herbart's principles which were treated quite independently by all three leaders. Instead of limiting the application of the doctrine to the secondary school, as their master had, they determined to extend it to the elementary school. Ziller developed the principle of the correlation of studies into that of concentration, using as a core history and literature which he considered as best fitted to reveal the moral universe to the child's mind, and he organized along those lines the eight grades of the elementary school. To Ziller is also due the elaboration of the culture epoch theory referred to above. The work of Stoy and Rein, eminently practical, at Jena, made that University the great center of Herbartianism to which flocked many students both from Germany and the United States, who became the missionaries of the doctrine in those countries. The National Herbart Society, which was founded in 1892 by some of those Jena students and became later the National Society for the Study of Education, was probably the first concrete evidence of a noteworthy Herbartian movement in the United States. By the end of the nineteenth century most of the normal schools had been won to its principles, and the teachers they sent out brought them into thousands of classrooms. As a result of the acceptance of those principles there has been a marked change of attitude towards the selection of materials of instruction and their organization. Greater emphasis was placed on the teaching of history and literature, regarded now as the two subjects best fitted for the development of moral character. From a few hours of American history in the upper grades, taught with the sole aim of developing patriotism, the course of study was extended to the lower grades, including, besides American history, some phases of ancient, medieval and modern European history; the purpose was now, not so much the development of patriotism, as the understanding of social life. In literature the scope of the course was also enlarged and its purpose somewhat changed. Instead of the study of brief extracts from literary productions with the

stressing of oral expression, the tendency since 1890 has
been to give more attention to the development of the aesthetic sense, through the reading of whole poems and stories,
which would also give a wider acquaintance with the complete range of literary production. Other evidences of the
influence of Herbartian principles in the United States are
the general adoption of the "method whole" or formal steps
by the normal schools, the discussions concerning the respective merits of interest and effort, and the efforts made to
apply the principle of the correlation of studies. Aside from
a few attempts at concentration, like Colonel Parker's (1831-
1902) with the sciences, especially geography, as a central
subject, or John Dewey's (1859-   ) around the social and
industrial activities, the application of the principle in the
United States has assumed the form of co-ordination, such
as inter-relating the work in arithmetic with construction
work, or geography, or history and civics. It must also be
noted that with its emphasis upon the importance of instruction, the need of sound methods of teaching based upon
a knowledge of the ways the mind functions, Herbartianism
has contributed much to enhance the teacher's position in
the process of education and his professional preparation.

    In all these contributions of Herbart to the theory and
practice of education there is much that is noteworthy and
valuable, but there are also some features to which serious
objections must be made. His ethical aim reduces itself in
the last analysis to a selfish culture of the ego. His conception of the soul, if carried to its logical conclusion, his
protest to the contrary notwithstanding, leads to a determinism no less rigid than that of the English associationists,
or, for that matter, the naturalism of some of his followers.
Further, as pointed out long ago by Aristotle in his criticism
of the Plato-Socratic doctrine, knowledge is not virtue, neither is interest, however many-sided it may be. Interest and
culture, if they are of the right kind, are, of course, ethi-

cally helpful, and it cannot be doubted that the moral quality of the ideas on which the child's mind is fed exerts a real influence on the will, but virtue is essentially a quality of the will, the outcome of repeated acts of self-control, self-denial, of repeated efforts in a line that is not usually that of Herbartian interest.

To Friedrich Wilhelm August Froebel (1782-1852) who, like Herbart, was a disciple of Pestalozzi, we are indebted for further important contributions to the theory and practice of education. He was born at Oberweissbach, a village in Thuringia, the son of the Lutheran pastor of a large parish, who had little time and it seems little disposition to take a hand in the education of this retiring, dreamy, introspective boy, and left him to the control of a harsh step-mother. Froebel's remembrance of his early childhood was, on the whole, an unhappy one, and it may account for his later emphasis upon sympathy as the true relation between the teacher and child. When ten years of age he was taken in charge by a maternal uncle who treated him very kindly and sent him to school, but he seems to have then displayed little interest in or capacity for formal school work. At the age of fifteen he was apprenticed to a forester and for the next sixteen years was engaged in a variety of occupations, forester, student, teacher at Frankfort and Yverdun, soldier in the war against Napoleon, curator in a museum of minerology. The two years he had spent at the University of Jena in an atmosphere of idealistic philosophy, romanticism, revolutionary theories in science,[1] left a deep impression on Froebel's mind. Finally in 1816 at the age of thirty-four, with five nephews as students, and the assistance of his war friends, Langenthal and Middendorff, he opened a school

Froebel

---

[1] In the closing years of the eighteenth and opening years of the nineteenth century Jena became a center for the dissemination of the theories of Kant; Fichter, Schelling, Hegel were among its prominent teachers; Goethe and Schiller were also connected with this university.

at Griesheim, later transferred to Keilhau, when the number of pupils increased. The school was conducted along Pestalozzian lines, but even then there was an emphasis on the application of the principle of self-activity through play. and his experiments. While at Keilhau Froebel published his *Education of Man*, his most important pedagogical writing, and the best exposition of the principles underlying his work. Financial

FROEBEL

difficulties compelled him to give up the Keilhau venture and from 1832 to 1837 he occupied various positions as teacher in Switzerland. Returning to Germany, he established at Blankenburg, in the Thuringian F o r e s t, a school for children between the ages of three and seven, which he eventually christened "kindergarten."[1] The institution was a great success from an educational viewpoint, and many teachers came to Blankenburg to study the new system of education, but again financial difficulties compelled Froebel to close his school after it had been in existence for seven years. During the next five years he traveled in Germany, lecturing with great success upon his system, especially before groups of mothers and women teachers. Kindergartens were opened in several cities by enthusiastic followers. It was during this period that he had the good fortune of securing the friendship of the baroness Bertha von Marenholtz-

[1] *I.e.*, gardens in which children are the unfolding plants.

Bülow, who did more than anybody else to spread Froebel's
ideas, both in Germany and abroad. The success of the
kindergarten seemed now secured. Unfortunately the Prussian Government, confusing Froebel's doctrines with those
of a socialist nephew of his, ordered the closing of all kindergartens in Prussia. Froebel never recovered from that
blow and died a year later.

The *Education of Man* opens with the statement: "In all
things there lives and reigns an eternal law. . . ." To those
that have faith this "law has been and is
His
philosophy of
education
announced with equal clearness and distinct-
ness in nature (the external), in the spirit
(the internal) and in life, which unites the
two. This all-pervading law is necessarily
based on an all-pervading, energetic, living, self-conscious,
and hence Eternal Unity. . . . This Unity is God. All things
have come from the Divine Unity, from God, and have
their origin in the Divine Unity, in God alone. . . . All
things live and have their being in and through the Divine
Unity, in and through God. . . . The divine effluence that
lives in each thing is the essence of each thing." This somewhat pantheistic creed is the groundwork of Froebel's
theory. The aim of education is more or less then the full
realization in the child, in the youth, in man and woman
of this all-pervading law of unity; in Froebel's own phraseology, to lead man "as a thinking, intelligent being, growing
into self-consciousness, to a pure and unsullied, conscious
and free representation of the inner law of divine unity, and
in teaching him ways and means thereto." Like Rousseau,
from whose works he received much of his inspiration, he
assumes the original soundness and wholeness of man and
therefore condemns "prescriptive, categorical, interfering"
education, because it must of necessity hinder, even destroy,
the realization of divine unity in the individual. Teaching

or education should become active, mandatory, only when natural development has been marred.

The law of unity is manifested in nature as a whole and in every aspect of it, in the human race, in the life of every individual, and every stage of his development from birth to death. And that implies, as a corollary, the law of continuity, of progressive development from the lower to the higher forms of reality in nature, from the lower to the higher periods of culture in the history of the race, from the lower to the higher stages in the development of the individual. Infancy, childhood, boyhood, girlhood, adolescence, maturity, and old age should be regarded as particular manifestations of the law of unity, but in view of the unity of human life they should never be thought of as independent of one another; each one of the stages, through a process of progressive development, is the resultant of the preceding and the promise of the next one; thus, *e.g.,* childhood should be treated as such, yet we must keep in mind that it was prepared by infancy and will in time prepare boyhood. The laws of unity and connectedness have further applications in the arrangement of the course of study, in the co-ordination of all the activities of school life, in fact, of all the educational agencies. All studies, all activities should help one another in making clear the manifold, yet unified, manifestations of the divine effluence. Development, the realization of the peculiar, personal form of humanity that lies and lives at birth in every individual, is the aim assigned to education. And because nature is good it should not be interfered with but allowed to expand, unfold itself freely. Education should be a "passive following"; the development of the individual is to be brought about through a free expression of his instincts and impulses, for "the eternal, divine principle, as such, demands and requires free self-activity and self-determination on the part of man, the being created for freedom in the image of God." Self-creative activity then, activity determined by one's instincts, desires, impulses, not merely by suggestions or instruction from parents and teachers, is to be the method of education. But motor activity as a means of natural development is not to function in isolation, as recommended by Rousseau; that would result in an unsocial, *i.e.,* unnatural, education, for man is by nature a social being; a full realization of self must come through a process of socialization, through participation in the intellectual life surrounding the child.

The kindergarten was the concrete expression of Froebel's principles of motor activity, creativeness, and social co-operation leading to a natural unfolding of
applied in the   the child's personality. Since play is the
kindergarten.   primary form of child activity, the kindergarten is based on the play instinct, and the expressions of the instinct most commonly used are song, gesture and construction, with the aid of language by the child as a further means of expression. The means of self-expression, so far as this is possible, should co-operate with one another. A story told by the teacher, *e.g.,* would be interpreted by the children in song, gestures, and paper or cardboard construction. In Froebel's plan the materials for use in the kindergarten were supplied by the *Mother Play and Nursery Songs,* the gifts and occupations. Mother Play is a little book of fifty songs, each illustrated with a picture and descriptive of some simple nursery game such as "hide and seek" or an imitation of some trade, like the carpenter's. "The gifts" consist of materials which do not change in form through use: balls of various colors, a sphere, cubes and cylinders, a cube divided into eight equal parts, divided in various ways, thin "tablets," sticks and rings. The exercises afforded by the gifts develop in the child ideas of color, material, motion, relation of parts to the whole and to one another, an interest in form and number, and a remarkable ingenuity in creativeness. The "occupations" consist of ma-

terials which change through use: paper, sand, clay, wood and other materials. Their use in Froebel's plan was to come after that of the gifts which were to supply the more fundamental ideas that would be expressed in all sorts of ways through the materials of the occupations.

After Froebel's death the kindergarten spread rapidly over Europe outside of Germany. As remarked before, its leading apostle was the Baroness von Bülow (1810- 1893). Having failed to obtain the removal of the ban on the kindergarten in Prussia, she turned to foreign lands, visiting nearly every nation in Europe, writing, lecturing, forming committees to carry on the propaganda. A few years after the death of the reformer, kindergartens, training schools, journals devoted to the movement, had been established in practically every land, the only noteworthy exception being Germany, where for a long time there remained serious hostility to the kindergarten idea. In some countries, as in England and France, the new institutions fused with an older one established for the caring of infants. Practically everywhere Froebelian principles received official recognition in the teaching of the State normal schools, though in many countries the kindergarten was at first and has remained to this day an entirely or partially voluntary institution.

Froebel's influence.

The United States is probably the country where the kindergarten, both as a private and public institution, has been most popular. The Germans who emigrated after the revolutionary days of 1848 brought it with them to their new fatherland. The first one seems to have been founded by Mrs. Carl Schurz in 1855 at Watertown, Wisconsin, and the earliest one for English speaking children in 1868 at Boston, through the efforts of Miss Elizabeth P. Peabody, an enthusiastic propagandist of Froebelianism in the United States. In 1878 a similar institution was established in New York by Maria Bölte, who had studied the system under

Froebel's widow. In a few years munificent foundations had been made for the support of private kindergartens, and there were many flourishing in various parts of the country. Gradually the kindergarten was incorporated into the school system of many American cities. The first and most remarkable establishment of the kind was founded in 1873 in St. Louis through the efforts of Miss Blow and Dr. William P. Harris, Superintendent of the City Schools. During the following decade other American cities followed the example of St. Louis, and there were also founded many journals, magazines and associations devoted to the spread of the movement.

Froebel's influence has not been limited to the establishment of the kindergarten. His principle of development through self-activity has been carried to the elementary and even the high school and college. The recognition of the educational value of play in all the stages of school life, not only for the physical welfare of the individual, but for his intellectual and moral training as well, is, to a great extent, the result of Froebel's insistence upon the value of play as an educational agency. To Froebel should also go a large measure of the credit for the introduction of manual training into the curriculum on purely educational grounds. Rousseau advocated it for economic and social reasons, Pestalozzi used it in his pedagogical experiments as a means to develop sense perception and acquire knowledge. Froebel on the other hand, as we see it in the kindergarten, insisted upon manual occupations as a form of expression of ideas, as a means of developing creativeness in the child, and furthermore his plan included practically all the schemes that have since been resorted to. Finland was the first country to carry manual occupations, as a means of intellectual development instead of industrial preparation, from the kindergarten into elementary school, and through the influence of the Finnish system the Swedish sloyd, in turn. which had been started as a means of reviving dormant industries, adopted the general educational aim. From Finland and Sweden the use of manual occupations as agencies in general education gradually extended to other European countries. In the United States the manual training movement was prompted by the Russian exhibit of manual occupations in the Centennial Exposition of 1876 at Philadelphia. Limited at first to the high schools, manual training rapidly extended to the elementary schools; today, in one form or another, it is part of the course of studies of practically all public schools.

Antonio Rosmini-Serbati (1797-1855), the founder of the Institute of Charity, was the author of a plan of education which greatly resembles Froebel's though developed in entire ignorance of the views   Rosmini. and work of the German reformer. It is expounded in the *Ruling Principle of Method*, a fragment of a more comprehensive but unfinished work which was to comprise five books and offer a method for the whole educational process. The ruling principle of method is thus stated by Rosmini: "present to the mind of the child (and that applies to man in general), first, the objects which belong to the first order of cognitions; then those which belong to the second; then those which belong to the third, and so on successively, taking care never to leave the child to a cognition of the second order without having ascertained that his mind has grasped those of the first order relative to it, and the same with regard to cognitions of the third, fourth and other higher orders."[1] Rosmini explains at some length, not only what is to be understood by cognitions of various orders, but the whole conception of psychic processes upon which his system of education is based; in fact, his work might properly be termed a treatise on genetic or educational psychology. Like Froebel, he stresses the

[1] Ruling Principle of Method, p. 40.

educative value of the child's surroundings, of the atmosphere in which it grows, the importance of activity, and particularly of play, as the most natural means of mental growth and development in the child.

Contemporaneously with Froebel and Rosmini, Joseph Jacotot (1770-1840), a French educator, for some time professor of the French language and literature

Jacotot.   at the University of Louvain, achieved some degree of success in his treatment of the problems of method. His principles of teaching and learning are set forth in his *Enseignement Universel* and the attention they attracted was probably due in no small measure to the paradoxical form in which they are stated, *e.g.,* "everyone can teach," "everyone can be his own instructor," "all is in all." In keeping with the last principle he prescribed that the student should know some subject thoroughly and refer all further studies to that, in the belief that all knowledge is so related that once we have gained a full grasp of any subject we can easily connect it with all the other subjects.

The principle of mental development through manual occupations has been applied since Froebel's time in a number of plans more or less at variance with

Montessori.   that of the German reformer. Two of those new methodological ventures, the Montessori and the Dewey plans, should receive some consideration because of the wide attention they first drew upon themselves. Maria Montessori (1870-   ) gained recognition as director of the State Orthophrenic school in Rome and her success in the teaching of feeble-minded children induced her to apply her methods to the training of the normal child. Like Rousseau and Froebel, she holds that nature is fundamentally good and therefore she demands complete freedom for the child; all education that is worthwhile, she maintains, should be "auto-education" and in practice she adheres to that principle even more fully than the Froe-belians. The child is allowed to choose whatever occupation interests him and to work at the solution of his little problems so long as it does not interfere with the work of others. It is claimed by its author that her plan has a thoroughly scientific foundation. Careful records are kept of the child's physical condition, its surroundings and antecedents. Some scientists, however, question the soundness of many of the statements in Dr. Montessori's *Method of Scientific Pedagogy*, and many pedagogues are of the opinion that her didactic apparatus devised for the training of the senses is better suited to mental defectives than to normal children. It is also pointed out that the work of the Montessori school lacks the social motive and is not likely to develop the imagination and the feelings. Dr. Montessori's methods have proved most successful in the teaching of the 3-R's and particularly of penmanship.

The social motive which is lacking in the Montessori school is the keynote of John Dewey's (1859-   ) educational theory, as it was of the experiment he conducted from 1886 to 1903 in a school at-   Dewey tached to the University of Chicago. Dewey starts from the premise that "the school cannot be a preparation for life except as it reproduces the typical conditions of social life." The typical conditions of social life, he believes, are determined in our own day by the industrial activities in which people engage; hence such activities should have a prominent place in the curriculum. He evolved his Chicago plan along the lines of shop work, cooking, weaving, sewing and other industrial activities, which were used in this school for liberalizing purposes rather than for technical preparation. Instruction in reading, writing, arithmetic was connected with the school industrial activities, so that the child, realizing their necessity in everyday life, would become interested in those school subjects. The plan, it has been claimed, provided a wider, more varied and fruitful appreciation of the two Froebelian principles of motor activity and social participation than the traditional Froebelian scheme.

Dewey's doctrines are set forth in a number of articles, monographs and books on philosophical and educational subjects. His pedagogy, a sort of corollary of his view of life, is a combination of pragmatism, socialism and materialism. "If ideas, meanings, conceptions, notions, theories, systems, are instrumental to an active reorganization of a given environment, to a removal of some specific trouble and perplexity, then the test of their validity and value lies in accomplishing this work. . . . By their fruits shall you know them. That which guides us truly is true. . . . The hypothesis that works is the true one."[1] Statements of this kind abound in Dewey's writings, making it plain that he is a true disciple of William James, and a radical one at that. Truth as such does not interest him. The worth of any belief or theory or system of philosophy is not to be sought in its validity, but in its practical value; it is not to be determined by an appeal to reason, but by the test of experience. The experimental method, he claims, is the only method worth using, and its application is not limited to the laboratory, it extends to all activities and situations in life. No thought, or theory, or system, should be accepted which has not stood the "trial by service rendered."

and the socialization of education.

No less thorough-going is Dewey's venture into social naturalism, and it is soon forced upon the reader of Dewey's writings. "The conception of growth as merely a means of reaching something which is superior to growth and beyond it, is a survival of theories of the universe as being essentially static. These theories have been expelled by the progress of

[1] Reconstruction in Philosophy, pp. 156-157.

science from our notion of nature."[1] "All morals based on the study of human nature instead of upon disregard for it would find the facts of man continuous with those of the rest of nature and would thereby ally ethics with physics and biology. . . ."[2] The genuinely moral person is one, then, in whom the habit of regarding all capacities and habits from a social standpoint is formed and active."[3] The list of quotations could be continued ad infinitum.

Modern life, according to Dewey, is characterized by three revolutions of which the school has just begun to take cognizance: an intellectual revolution, achieved by the progress of modern science, an industrial revolution, the work of modern technique and a socio-political revolution, which is the crowning consequence of the other two, and the one revolution of real concern to the school today. In other words, using another of Dewey's phrases, there should be "a complete socialization of education" and that calls for a radical reconstruction of educational principles, a radical departure from the traditional education, its aims, principles, methods, subject matter, the building up of a school system which will take activity as its motto—understand, physical, industrial activity—since that is the keynote of modern life. The only country to boast of such a system today is Bolshevist Russia, which has developed it by elaborating Marxist theories. Communistic teachers, influenced by Russia, have tried, particularly in Germany, to introduce something very akin to it, what they call a complete union of education with material production, a school becoming a sort of miniature factory, through which, so it is hoped, industrial civilization would be controlled.[4] To what extent

---

[1] Aims and Ideals, in Encyclopedia and Dictionary of Education (London, Pitman, 1921).
[2] Human Nature and Conduct, p. 12.
[3] Dewey and Tufts, Ethics, p. 301.
[4] See Educational Yearbook, 1924 and 1925, Part II. (International Institute of Teachers College, Columbia University.)

John Dewey is in sympathy with such experiments, naturally we do not know.

Aside from the institutions established for the deaf and the blind, little interest had been shown before the last quarter of the nineteenth century in the education of abnormal children. A school for such children—the first one to be established, it seems—was founded in 1816 at Salzburgh in Austria, but the experiment having proved unsuccessful the institution was closed in 1835. Gallaudet (1787-1851) tried to educate such children at Hartford in 1820. Edouard Seguin (1812-1880),[1] "The Apostle of the Idiot," began in 1837 a lifelong study of the training of the abnormal child, and he may be considered as the real pioneer in this kind of education. A few institutions for the study and training of the feeble-minded were founded in the following years in Switzerland and England; in the United States we find a class for idiots in the Boston Blind Asylum in 1848, and in 1851 was founded the Massachusetts Institute for Idiotic and Feebleminded Youth. All these schools or classes were special institutions, asylums like those for the blind or deaf mute, receiving children directly without their having passed through the common school.[2]

Seguin and the education of the abnormal child.

It is only in the last fifty years that a widespread interest has been manifested in children attending the common school, who intellectually are decidedly below the level of the class to which their age would normally assign them. Such children, evidently, hamper the normal work of the class, derive little if any benefit from their presence in the school, and it was held that they should be segregated and formed into special classes, receiving an instruction adapted

[1] See Seguin, E., Idiocy and Its Treatment by the Physiological Method.
[2] Most western nations now have institutions both public and private for the training of intellectual and moral defectives.

to their mental capacity. The first of such special classes were organized in Germany at Halle in 1863, at Dresden in 1867, and gradually in other cities in the succeeding years; Switzerland followed suit in 1881; then came England in 1892, Holland in 1896. In the last thirty years, largely as the result of the work of the French psychologist, Alfred Binet (1857-1911), this movement has become general, and it has gained immensely in its scope. Starting from an interest in abnormal or rather subnormal children, the original movement has widened into one affecting the whole school system and society as well. It has enlisted the services of psychologists, physicians, criminologists, lawyers and business men, as well as teachers. It has led to numberless studies and statistics, the foundation of clinics, vocational guidance departments, and countless devices to ascertain the aptitudes of children and adults as well.

Attempts have been made, especially in the United States, to measure variations in intellect, character and conduct, classroom and school results, with the same general technique that prevails in the natural sciences. Facts are gathered, analyzed and carefully recorded; exact measurements are made, "laws" and "equations" have been worked out to replace guess-work in estimating results and scales have been devised for the measurement of the results of instruction. Such scales are now available for several school subjects, especially arithmetic, spelling, penmanship, English composition and drawing. Accurate information concerning the school history of each pupil is now kept in many localities, making it possible to take statistics after a definite and uniform plan and make "surveys" which bring out the relative efficiency of different school systems, their organization and administration, their curricula and methods of teaching. There is as yet no sign of abating in this enthusiasm for, one is tempted to say, the worship of the mechanics

Tests and measurements.

of education. Educational psychologists, with the aid of educational or psychological laboratories and experimental schools, are busy the world over trying to discover new-fangled devices that would enable everybody to acquire an education at a discount. Interest along those lines seems to center now around the so-called psychology of special subjects, psychology of arithmetic, psychology of spelling, etc. Not a year passes without its crop of new plans or systems or experiments, whose originality may range from some comparatively innocuous innovation like the Dalton or Winnetka plans or project method, to such wild ventures as the laissez-faire community school of Hamburg.[1] Of late there has been much discussion around the activity school of Dewey of which Kerschensteiner in Germany, and Findley in England, have been the chief protagonists, and the so-called "integrated instruction" a new plan of instruction of German origin it seems, dispensing with time schedule and the division of the curriculum into subjects. The last

The "new education." word, by way of novelty, seems to belong at present to the "new education" more properly styled "the new school" with several National Associations more or less loosely organized into an International Association (La Ligue Internationale pour l'Education Nouvelle), with an International Bureau, and holding a congress every two years. Before the World War there were about eighty "new schools" in Europe, some of which disappeared during the War to be replaced by others later. Representatives of the new pedagogy are the Leitz Schools in Germany, the Glarisegg Institution in German Switzerland, the Doctor Decroly School in Brussels, and the Institut J. J. Rousseau in French Switzerland. The new schools have a maximum program

[1] See literature on "The New Education Movement"; cf. Educational Yearbook, 1924, pp. 599 ff. (International Institute of Teachers College, Columbia University.)

of thirty points, at least thirteen of which should be realized by any school expecting to be classed as "new," and a minimum program to be realized by all and formulated as follows: "The new school is a home boarding school, located in the country in which the personal experiences of the child furnish the starting point of (1) intellectual education, including manual activities, and (2) moral education through the practice of self-government by the pupils." We shall conclude this survey of the movement for the improvement of school methodology with a brief account of what seems to be its outstanding contribution to the cause of education: the spread of the normal school idea.

As noted before, prior to 1750, scant attention was given to the professional training of lay elementary school teachers. In 1684 St. Jean Baptiste de LaSalle founded the first normal school for lay teachers in France, and a few years later Francke's Teachers Seminary was opened at Halle. In 1747 Johann Julius Hecker, one of Francke's students and teachers, established in Berlin a private Teachers Seminary, which in 1753 became a national institution. A few other normal schools were founded during the next few years, both in Prussia and the other German states. We noted before the efforts of von Felbiger for the training of teachers in the Hapsburg dominions and those of von Fürstenberg in Westphalia. In the organization of public instruction in Denmark in 1789 provision was made for the establishment of normal schools, and the National Convention in France decreed the foundation of a Superior Normal School which was reorganized by Napoleon a few years later. On the whole, however, the elementary school teacher training movement was contemporary with and the consequence of the spread of Pestalozzianism in the first decades of the nineteenth century. Pestalozzian instruction called for a serious preparation of the prospective teacher: he must possess an extensive knowledge of the subjects to be taught; he must be able to interest the class and hold it under control; he must be able to keep in mind the essential points in the lesson, to raise questions and elicit answers in their proper sequence, thus leading the class along to the desired conclusions; in short, he must be able to stand on his own feet and teach, and that, aside from native ability, called for a serious preparation. The first European state to take up in earnest the question of the elementary school teacher training was Prussia; by 1840 it possessed thirty-eight Teachers' Seminaries, as normal schools are commonly called by the Germans; the other German states quickly followed the lead of Prussia. In France normal schools for the training of lay teachers were comparatively few until 1870, but after the Franco-Prussian War their number grew rapidly; today there is a normal school for men and one for women in each one of the departments into which the country is divided for administrative purposes. In the United States the normal school idea did not make any headway worth mentioning until after 1870, though a few State normal schools had been founded before that time, the first one at Lexington, Massachusetts, in 1839. In England, during the first decades of the nineteenth century, the only training prospective teachers received was that given by the Bell and Lancastrian Societies to their monitors, the pupils who were to assist the actual teacher in the conduct of classroom work. Later on the country came to depend upon the pupil-teacher system, an arrangement by which promising pupils were apprenticed for a number of years to a master who agreed to give them instruction in secondary school subjects and the art of teaching, in return for their help in the classroom. A few training colleges were established to which prospective teachers might go after completing their period of apprenticeship. Further progress has been made in England in recent years chiefly as a consequence of the World War. During the last two generations the normal school movement has spread through the world and it is an integral of the state school system in practically every civilized country.

SOURCES

A bibliography of the sources and references bearing on this phase of education would be interminable. Only the more important works will be mentioned.
Dewey, J., School and Society.
Froebel, F. W., The Education of Man.
Herbart, J., The Science of Education; Outlines of Educational Doctrine.
Pestalozzi, J., Leonard and Gertrude; How Gertrude Teaches Her Children.
Rosmini, A., The Ruling Principle of Method Applied to Education.

REFERENCES

Barnard, H., American Journal of Education.
De Garmo, C., Herbart and the Herbartians.
Graves, F. P., Great Educators of Three Centuries.
Guimps, R. de, Pestalozzi, His Aim and Work.
Krüsi, H., Pestalozzi, His Life, Work and Influence.
McMurry, C. A., The Elements of General Method.
Marenholtz-Bülow, B. von, The Child and Child Nature.
Monroe, W., The Pestalozzian Movement in the United States.
Monroe, J. P., The Educational Ideal.
Payne, J., Froebel and the Kindergarten.
Quick, R., Educational Reformers.

GERTRUDE DESCRIBING THE MISERY OF HER FAMILY

CHAPTER VII

THE INDUSTRIAL REVOLUTION

A LITTLE OVER A CENTURY AGO PEOPLE STILL
tilled the land, manufactured and transported goods,
traveled or communicated with one another very much in
the same way as they had in the days of Charlemagne, or
for that matter in those of Pericles or Khufu. Man, or
horse, or ox, the wind, the running stream,
Economic life or waterfall were still the chief sources of
in the eight- power. People moved about but little be-
eenth cause travel was slow, insecure and expen-
century. sive. A trip from Philadelphia to Boston, or
from Paris to Lyons was an event in the life
of the average eighteenth century man and he often thought
it prudent to make his will before starting. "King George,"
as Huxley remarks, "could send a message from London to
York no faster than King John might have done."[1] It took
a ship over a month to reach New York or Boston from the
nearest European port, several months to go by boat from
England to Asia, and four days by the stage coach to go
from London to York, a distance of 188 miles. Whether in
town or country, the home was still the center of industrial
activity, in which all the members of the domestic community had their share. Simple living with hard and con-
tinual labor was the rule for all, and children were apprenticed to it at an early age. Farm machinery was still of the
simplest kind; hand labor with the help of a team of horses

[1] Huxley, T. H., Methods and Results, Essay II, London, 1893.

or oxen performed all the operations of plowing, sowing, reaping, harvesting and threshing; the grain was ground at the neighboring water mill or windmill. This "domestic system" was also the rule in the making of finished articles of all kinds. The artisan's home was his shop in which were carried on the various phases of the craft by the master, his family and assistants.

The change from those time honored conditions of material life of a century ago to the conditions under which we live today is known as the Industrial Revolution. It was preceded, accompanied and chiefly caused by the remarkable progress achieved in the field of physical science in the sixteenth and following centuries. Says Huxley again of the early stage of this scientific movement: "In the early decades of the seventeenth century, the men of the Renaissance could show that they had already put out to good interest the treasure bequeathed to them by the Greeks. They had produced the astronomical system of Copernicus, with Kepler's great additions; the astronomical discoveries and the physical investigations of Galileo; the mechanics of Stevinus and the *De Magnete* of Gilbert; the anatomy of the great French and Italian schools, and the physiology of Harvey. In Italy, which had succeeded Greece in the hegemony of the scientific world, the Accademia dei Lyncei and sundry other such associations for the investigation of nature, the models of all subsequent academies and scientific studies had been founded. . . . The progress of science, during the first century after Bacon's death, by no means verified his sanguine prediction of the fruits which it would yield. For, though the revived and renewed study of nature had spread and grown to an extent which surpassed reasonable expectation, the practical results, the 'good to men's estate,' were at

The Industrial Revolution brought about by progress in

first, by no means evident. Sixty years after Bacon's death Newton had crowned the long labors of the astronomers and the physicists by co-ordinating the phenomena of molar motion throughout the visible universe into a vast system; but the Principia helped no man to either wealth or comfort. Descartes, Newton and Leibnitz had opened new worlds to the mathematician, but the acquisitions of their genius enriched only man's ideal estate. Descartes had laid the foundations of rational cosmogony and of physiological psychology; Boyle had produced models of experimentation in various branches of physics and chemistry; Pascal and Torricelli had weighed the air; Malpighi and Grew, Ray and Willoughby had done work of no less importance in the biological sciences; but weaving and spinning were carried on with the old appliances; nobody could travel faster by sea or by land than at any previous time in the world's history . . . metals were worked from their ores by immemorial rule of thumb. . . . The utmost skill of our mechanicians did not go beyond the production of a coarse watch."[1]

The outstanding feature of scientific research and discoveries in the last two hundred years is its practical character. Heretofore scientists had been satisfied with increasing man's knowledge of his natural surroundings, without concerning themselves with the possible use of their discoveries in practical, everyday life. With the eighteenth century begin the applications of science to transportation, industry, commerce, agriculture, home life, which were to revolutionize man's relations to his physical and social environment. In the following rapid survey of the Industrial Revolution we shall first consider the more important steps in the advancement of science since the seventeenth century and then the practical applications made of scientific discoveries.

[1] Huxley, T. H., Methods and Results, Essay II, London, 1893.

Chemistry had freed itself from alchemy but it was still in its infancy at the beginning of the eighteenth century. The real founder of modern chemistry was Antoine Laurent Lavoisier (1743-1794); be- chemistry, cause of his unremitting use of the balance in analysis he has been rightly called "the founder of quantitative chemistry." It was by this method that he proved that when metals are burned in air the resulting sub-

stances weigh more than did the metal; and that if burnt in a closed space the loss in weight of the air equals the gain in weight of the metal. By repeating with greater precision the experiments of his predecessors he was led to several important discoveries, chief among them that of oxygen and hydrogen. A most brilliant man of science, Lavoisier continued to do remarkable work to the very end of his life. A few days before his death he was carrying on impor-

LAVOISIER

tant researches and had every reason to hope that he was on the eve of another epoch making discovery when he was brought before the Revolutionary Tribunal and sentenced to death as a suspicious character. His request that he be granted a few days respite to complete his researches was met with the retort that "the Republic one and indivisible had no longer any need of chemists."

In the nineteenth century chemistry received a powerful

impetus through the establishment of laboratories in the universities. Justus von Liebieg (1803-1873), the founder of agricultural chemistry, was the pioneer in this movement at Giessen. New "elements" were discovered in the composition of matter and new theories were advanced to explain their relations; though serviceable for the time being those theories were severely criticised by some scientists and have since been partly replaced by other theories which better harmonize with discoveries made not only in the field of chemistry but in other sciences as well, physics, mineralogy, physiology, and mathematics. To this close co-operation among the natural sciences must be ascribed much of their advance in the nineteenth and present century.

The modern science of acoustics dates from Galileo (1564-1642). He showed how vibrations causing sound may be made visible, and how to measure the relative length of sound waves by scraping a brass plate with a chisel, thereby making dust on the plate take up positions in parallel lines. By placing a clock in a vacuum Hawksbee (?-1713) proved in 1705 that air is the real intermediary of sound. The studies, experimental and mathematical of physics, Newton (1642-1727), Euler (1707-1783) and Sauveur (1653-1715) brought acoustics to the point where it was taken up by Chladni (1756-1827) who laid the foundations upon which Helmholtz (1821-1894) and Tyndall (1820-1893) built up the science of acoustics such as we have it today. Among other branches of physics in which Galileo was interested may be mentioned the expansion of physical bodies by heat, but his contributions to the subject did not go beyond a few suggestive remarks. To Joseph Black (1728-1799), of Edinburgh, belongs the honor of having made the researches which paved the way for the modern study of heat and enabled Watt (1736-1819) to persevere and push to completion his discoveries in steam engineering. The idea that heat is not a substance but a mode of molecular motion had arisen in the seventeenth century, but it remained for Benjamin Thompson, Count Rumford (1753-1814) to give it a solid experimental basis.

Epoch making in the study of heat were the researches of Sadi Carnot (1796-1832), Julius Robert von Mayer (1814-1878), J. P. Joule (1818-1889), the founders of the science of thermodynamics. Modern scientific researches on light started with the great work of Newton (1642-1727) and Huygens (1629-1695); they continued in the eighteenth with the invention of achromatic (free from color) lenses leading to the construction of achromatic telescope objectives, but further progress in our knowledge of light was not made until the early nineteenth century. Huygens had supported for light a theory analogous to that admitted today for sound, *i.e.*, a wave theory; Newton, on the other hand, had accepted an emission theory analogous to that first advanced in explanation of heat, and it was still the accepted theory a century after the death of Newton. Huygens' wave theory was revised and definitely established by Thomas Young (1773-1829) and Augustus Fresnel (1788-1827), while the spectrum of Newton was being subjected to a closer study by a number of scientists, among them Gustav Kirchhoff (1824-1887) and Robert Bunsen (1811-1899) through whose work spectrum analysis was finally established as a means of detecting the presence of chemical constituents in sources of light.

Perhaps the most brilliant and far-reaching discoveries of the last two centuries were those made in the field of electricity and magnetism. Until about the middle of the eighteenth century William   especially
Gilbert (1540-1603) was the only important   electricity,
contributor to our knowledge of this branch
of the physical sciences. With the second half of the eight-

eenth century begins a period of rapid progress with which are connected the names of Benjamin Franklin (1706-1790), Galvani (1737-1798), Volta (1745-1827), and a little later the still greater names of Oersted (1771-1851), Ampère (1775-1836), Faraday (1791-1867), Maxwell (1831-1879), Helmholtz (1821-1894), Herz (1857-1894), Roentgen (1845-1923). The researches and experiments of those eminent scientists not only made evident the close relation of electricity and magnetism to heat and light but led to a number of inventions, the use of which is just as common today as was the wheelbarrow or the windmill one hundred years ago.

Modern mathematics had been the first of the exact sciences to reach the period of maturity with the calculus of Newton and Leibnitz. The main features of its subsequent history are the elaboration of the calculus into the form it has today and its applications to mechanics, physics, chemistry, astronomy. Among the leading mathematicians of this period in the evolution of the science are Maclaurin (1698-1746) of Scotland, the three Bernouillis (1654-1782) and Euler (1707-1783) of Switzerland, Lagrange (1736-1813) of Italy, Clairaut (1713-1765), Dalembert (1717-1783), Laplace (1749-1827), Monge (1746-1818), Cauchy (1789-1857), Poincaré (1854-1912) of France, Gauss (1777-1855), Riemann (1820-1866) of Germany. To the labors of some of those eminent specialists we owe among other things the present form of our college and university mathematics. A remarkable feature of this period in the history of mathematics is the critical revision of previously accepted axioms which has led to a non-Euclidean geometry. Another characteristic which has already been pointed out is the wide application of mathematics even to branches of knowledge which two centuries ago were supposed to admit of no

in mathematics,

and mechanics.

mathematical measurements. The sciences which have mostly benefited from the progress in mathematics were, of course, physics and mechanics, the latter being now considered by some as a branch of the other two.

The eighteenth century saw important progress in biological science, though the subject known today under that name was still undifferentiated, and like zoölogy, botany and geology still considered a branch of natural philosophy. The researches of physicists and chemists had shown that the four elements of the Greeks were no elements at all. Air had been proved to be a mixture of various elements and compounds; fire, long a mystery, was now regarded as a luminous center of intense chemical change; water had been

LINNAEUS

shown to be a compound of hydrogen and oxygen gases, which could be restored to a liquid condition by bringing these two gases together at high temperatures. The earth, however, though no longer regarded as one of the four elements, was still a puzzle to scientists in respect to its origin both as a whole and as to its parts. Astronomy had proved the planetary character of the earth, but it had not as yet suggested for it any natural origin, and it was silent as to the sources and

Progress in the biological and related sciences.

history of the earth's crust. A few, isolated suggestions, concerning the earth's prehistoric past had been made in the sixteenth and seventeeth centuries, but the beginnings of a geological science date only from the second half of the eighteenth century. Then it was that learned circles began to evince a real interest in the study of rocks and fossils. To that early period in the history of geology also belongs the foundation of the first school of mines of which we have a record, that of Freiberg in Saxony. As in the other natural sciences the nineteenth century saw rapid progress in geology and its sister science, palaeontology. As early as the forties those sciences had been given substantially the form they have today by the researches and fruitful hypotheses of Lyell (1797-1875), Agassiz (1807-1875) and Cuvier (1769-1832), among many others; the origins of what is known today as anthropology date from the same period.

A notable advance was made in the field of zoölogy and botany through the researches of the French naturalist, Buffon (1707-1788), and the Swede, Linnaeus (1707-1778). Buffon's special contribution to those sciences was a remarkable work on *Natural History* in several volumes, which abound in admirable descriptions and original views on geological transformation. Linnaeus' great service to science was his insistence on the importance of the careful observation of likeness and difference. His procedure in classification, however, was proved to be artificial and it was soon replaced by a more natural one suggested by B. de Jussieu (1699-1766) and worked out by his nephew A. de Jussieu (1748-1836). In 1801 appeared Lamarck's work *On the Organization of Living Bodies* which is considered a landmark in the history of biology and of the doctrine of organic evolution. In this work and in his *Philosophie Zoologique* Lamarck (1744-1829) suggests the substitution, for the notion of special creation, of the idea of gradual development or evolution. Systematic zoölogy and comparative anatomy were remarkably advanced by Cuvier (1769-1832) who, however, clung to the theory of special creation, while Geoffroy St. Hilaire (1799-1853), another comparative anatomist, favored Lamarck's theory. The seventeenth century had been rich in physiological and anatomical discoveries due to the genius of Vesalius (1514-1564), Harvey (1578-1657), Kircher (1601-1680) and Malpighi (1628-1699), the founder of comparative physiology, due also to the use of a new and valuable instrument, the compound microscope. To the work of these men in the seventeenth century was added that of Haller (1707-1777), Bonnet (1720-1793), Hunter (1728-1793) in the eighteenth, and far more important in the nineteenth that of Johannes Müller (1801-1858) and Claude Bernard (1813-1878), who

BUFFON

were not only eminent research workers but also great teachers. Because of its imperfections, in respect especially to spherical and chromatic aberrations, the compound microscope was often inferior for use to the best simple microscope. It was not until about 1835 that the compound microscope became the admirable instrument it is today through the accumulated improvements of many workers. Almost immediately there followed a number of important discoveries, the most remarkable of which were those of Pasteur (1822-1895). By the use of the microscope combined with new and ingenious methods of cultivation he proved beyond a doubt that yeast is the agent of alcoholic fermentation and that other microbes are the agents of other familiar fermentations, putrefaction, decay and certain diseases. This germ theory of fermentation and disease was confirmed by other conclusive experiments made by Robert Koch (1843-1910), in 1876, and it is responsible for the

use today of antiseptic and aseptic surgery, one of the greatest triumphs of nineteenth century science. The name of Pasteur is also inseparably linked with one of the liveliest scientific disputes of the nineteenth century, around the question of the beginnings of individual life. "Omne vivum ex ovo" was the motto of those who held that living things come only from antecedent life and for that r e a s o n w e r e known as biogenists. Opposed to them were the abiogenists who believed in spontaneous generation, *i.e.*, in the origin of living things from lifeless or non-living matter. The question was attacked by Pasteur and he showed that all the evidence advanced by the advocates of spontaneous generation was due to defective technique, for when such defects were removed no evidence remained of the generation of life from lifeless matter.

Between 1842 and 1846 appeared a revolutionary work

entitled *Vestiges of Creation* by an anonymous author, which aroused both intense interest and strong criticism. The work is now known to have been written by an Edinburgh editor, Robert Chambers, who preferred to remain unknown in order not to injure the interests of his patrons by making public the heterodoxy of his own views on the origin of the earth. The excitement had hardly subsided when another work, more revolutionary still, appeared, *The Origin of Species* of Charles Darwin (1809-1882), in which the author suggested the theory of organic evolution, *i.e.*, of the gradual development   The theory of of all existing species from a few original   evolution. ones. Darwin's theory reproduced with some variations the views advanced before him by Buffon, Lamarck and Geoffroy St. Hilaire, among others. Darwin's explanation of the origin of species, natural selection and the survival of the fittest, has now been rejected as inadequate, but the fact remains that his book deeply stirred the scientific world and contributed much to render popular the idea of evolution, though the explanation of the process of evolution is far from being uniform and often suffers from the serious, unscientific error of confusing fact and fancy. With remarkable success the idea of evolution has also been applied to history, linguistics and art, with more doubtful results to ethics and the new science of sociology. This very rapid survey of the scientific movement in the last two centuries would not be complete without a passing mention, at least, of the many voyages, explorations and expeditions which have been undertaken for the sole and specific purpose of the improvement of "natural" knowledge. The result of those explorations has been to throw much new light upon the configuration of the earth, its climates and the nature of its soil, the wealth and variety of its resources in minerals, plants and animals, its inhabitants, their racial characteristics, modes of life and capacities for self-improvement. Similar expeditions were made to the seats of ancient civilizations with astounding results for our knowledge of the past of the race.

As late as the beginning of the eighteenth century Latin was, with but few exceptions, the language of science; one of the consequences of this use of Latin was that interest in scientific discoveries remained confined within a narrow circle; scholars and scientists were satisfied with seeing their books in the hands of the learned few. In the course of the century the national languages gradually supplanted Latin in scientific intercourse as they had already supplanted it in public life, diplomacy and literature. Though the change was bound to take place at some time or other in the course of the development of the national languages, it was probably hastened by the eighteenth century tendency to make knowledge a common property of the masses, which necessitated not only a change in language but one in method of treatment. Writers on scientific subjects would now be guided, not so much by the nature of the subject they treated, as they would be by the scientific preparation or lack of it in the reader. Whatever may have been the disadvantages of this popularizing of the sciences, the advantages to the general public, science and education, are obvious: scientific research, which had been viewed askance by many, as a sort of queer, suspicious pastime, was shown to bear an intimate relationship to the life and material welfare of the people; men learned to take a saner, more intelligent view of their natural surroundings, and those facts could not fail, in due course of time, to have a healthy influence upon education.

Latin replaced by the vernacular in scientific relations.

As it was to be expected this undreamed of development of the natural sciences, and still more the new theories built upon it by some of its votaries, had an echo in all depart-

ments of knowledge, even in those which hitherto had seemed furthest removed from the pale of natural science. Before the eighteenth century psychology was everywhere treated as a branch of philosophy, closely related to biology, metaphysics and theology. Observation, introspection, and physiological evidence were   The new
used in the treatment of psychological ques-   psychology,
tions, but the method was mainly deductive
and the arguments metaphysical. The departure from this traditional conception of psychology began with Locke's *Essay on the Human Understanding* (1690), to which can be traced the marked empirical bent of psychology during the last two hundred years. Outside of Catholic circles the term "psychology" is today commonly confined to the positivist science of the phenomena of the mind directly observable through introspection and experimentation. All questions concerning the nature or destiny of the soul are pronounced to belong, beyond the scope of the science of psychology, to some branch of speculation that one may call metaphysics or ontology of the human mind. In fact most non-Catholic books on the subject do not even mention such questions, and the impression such books convey is that the soul, in the Christian sense of the term, is a non-entity. The progress made in physiology during the last seventy-five years has stimulated a closer study of the relation between nervous and mental processes, resulting in the building up of the science known today as physiological psychology which in turn has given rise to experimental psychology, the "New Psychology," as its more enthusiastic supporters sometimes style it. This new school seeks to secure for psychology a place among the exact sciences. Laboratories have been set up with ingenious apparatus to measure the varying intensity of sensations, the delicacy of sense organs, the "reaction time" or rapidity of the response of a mental process to stimulation. Memory and the higher mental activities have

also been subjected to various experiments. So far, however, the outlook for notable progress along those lines is not very bright. Psychological research has also extended, with varying degrees of success, to other fields and given rise to new departments of psychology or even entirely new sciences: comparative psychology including animal psychology, child psychology, the psychology of adolescence, race psychology, psychiatry or the science of mental diseases, behavioristic psychology, psycho-analysis. Of particular interest to the educator is genetic psychology which traces the various mental processes of the adult to their earliest manifestations in infancy, and tries to determine what is the product of experience and acquired habits, and what is the immediate outcome of original capacities.

No less startling than that of psychology has been the transformation of non-Catholic ethics. Eighteenth century philosophers like Shaftesbury, Hutcheson, ethics, especially Kant, had made familiar in certain quarters the notion that ethics and morality are independent of external authority, that of religion in particular. Auguste Comte (1798-1857) and his followers made the common good of mankind the end and criterion of moral conduct. The evolutionists tried to show that, just as man has evolved from the brute, so morality has evolved from "animal ethics" and become more and more refined with the progress of evolution; hence there can be no question of a fixed ethical standard, except perhaps utility, for the individual and the group. Of the same purport, though on somewhat different grounds, is the ethical teaching of Relativism and Pragmatism. Countries, we are told, differ from one another at any given time, conditions in the same country change in the course of time, men differ from one another and they too are individually subject to change, and so are their views of the norms of morality; that is true and good at any given time which experience proves to be useful for the time being; an unchangeable norm of morality is something impossible. On the border line of this ethical chaos appear out and out cynics like Max Nordau (1849-1923), Max Stirner (1806-1856),[1] Friedrich Nietzsche (1844-1900), who tell us that moral precepts are all nothing else than "conventional lies," that that alone is good "which serves my own interest," that "all morality is one long and audacious deception." All those ethical views, whether moderate or extreme, have this one common feature, that they exclude all consideration of religion, a widely spread tendency today, not only in the speculative treatment of ethics but in the teaching of morality as well.

To the scientific trend of intellectual life in this, our own age, must also be partly ascribed new conceptions of history, politics, scholastic philosophy and the appearance of a host of new social sciences, not the least of which is the science of education. and other social sciences. The scope of this work does not permit of dealing with all those new or renovated subjects beyond a passing remark concerning those in which we are here directly interested, viz., history, neo-scholasticism and the science of education; the last two are dealt with in other sections of this volume.[2] History is now treated from new points of view. Historians no longer confine themselves to the description of battles and sieges, relating the lives of kings, generals and statesmen, or explaining treaties and constitutions; they also try to explain how social and economic forces affect the lives of nations. And there is also a marked tendency to treat history according to the canons of a more exacting method than heretofore. Expeditions have been organized to study the remains of ancient civilizations; the contents of archives are carefully classified, catalogued and indexed; special schools and university

[1] Pseud. of Kaspar Schmidt.
[2] See chs. VIII and X.

departments have been established to give students of history the technical training which the scientific treatment of the subject requires.[1] Passing now to a brief consideration of the economic and social consequences of scientific progress, let it be remarked to begin with that it was only in the last one hundred and fifty years or so that inventions were made, in the main, as a direct consequence of scientific investigations. Before the nineteenth century inventions were mostly made without special scientific knowledge and frequently by persons who possessed skill rather than knowledge. They were brought about apparently more by accident and the practical needs of the age or country than through scientific insight. Yet, if we knew all the facts in every case, we would probably see every invention as the logical consequence of other inventions and science, already existing. That is, of course, a moot question, but whatever may have been in former times the bearing of science upon progress in the arts, the fact is that in the last one hundred and fifty years the great inventions have been made in the laboratory. Science which formerly stood aloof from practical life has become the servant of men's material needs which it even tries to anticipate. Man's wonderful material progress in the last four or five generations has come from his ability to control his environment and use it for his material comfort.

Antiquity and the Middle Ages used chiefly the power of men and animals and to some extent that of the winds and water. The first addition to those sources of power was made through the invention of gun-powder, known by the Chinese, it seems, a long time before its use in the West, in or around the fourteenth century. The manufacture of gun-powder marks the beginning of the manufacture of chemical power. Power from fuel begins with Newcomen

[1] See Bernheim, E., Lehrbuch der historischen methode; and Langlois, Ch., and Seignobos, Ch., Introduction to the Study of History.

(1663-1729), Watt (1736-1819) and the steam engine in the eighteenth century, though unsuccessful attempts had been made before to utilize heat as a source of power. To the same period belongs the invention of the "spinning jenny," the "water frame," the "mule," the "power loom" and "cotton gin"[1] which gave a powerful impetus to the weaving industry in England. Inventions rapidly followed one another in the nineteenth century, the greater number and more important ones by far before 1850; Fulton's steamboat in 1807, Stephenson's locomotive in 1829, the achromatic microscope around 1835; illuminating gas had already been introduced in 1792 by William Murdock but it was not perfected until 1802; friction matches were in use in 1827, the first sewing machine was patented in 1830, but the most important elements of the modern machine of American origin appeared only around 1846. The effect of sunlight on silver chloride had been observed by eighteenth century chemists, though the first photograph seems to have been made in 1802 by Wedgwood who could not, however, fix his prints; photography dates really from 1839 and commonly is connected with the name of Daguerre (1789-1851). Wells (1815-1848), a dentist of Hartford, Connecticut, first introduced anaesthesia in surgical operations in 1834, and to Helmholtz (1821-1894) we are indebted for the ophthalmoscope which was used for the first time in 1851; india rubber which had been noticed in use among the inhabitants of Haiti by the companions of Columbus was not adapted to industrial purposes until 1839. At about the same time the first telegraph line between two cities was established between Baltimore and Washington, and the first trans-Atlantic cable was laid in 1858. The telephone followed a few years later; wireless telegraphy and wireless telephone are of more recent date; electric light be-

The applications of scientific discoveries

[1] See bibliography appended to this chapter.

came of practical utility in 1880, and a few years previous to that Edison had invented the phonograph. The preserving of food by canning was first introduced in the British Navy in 1816, but like cold storage it became common only in the second half of the nineteenth century. In 1876 appeared the first successful rival of the steam engine, the internal combustion engine which is used today in motors of all kinds. The dyestuff industry has been revolutionized by the use of aniline first obtained from indigo in 1826, and the "age of steel" was ushered in by the discovery of the Bessemer process in 1856. Agriculture has shared with industry and commerce the material benefits of scientific discoveries. An era of improved agricultural implements began around 1850; one of its main results has been the opening of vast tracts of land which might otherwise have remained unproductive.

The effects of the application of all those discoveries to matters that immediately touch upon the life of man were so many and far reaching that the conditions *and their* under which men still lived at the close of *results.* the eighteenth century were radically changed in the course of the following century. As it was remarked before, it is this transformation that is commonly called the Industrial Revolution. The change began in England around 1770 with the appearance of the steam engine, the spinning jenny, spinning frame, and power loom; in scarcely half a century the Revolution was an accomplished fact. In the United States the change began around 1810 in the northeastern part of the country and it was complete throughout the land at the outbreak of the Civil War. Of more recent date has been the transformation in the other parts of the American continent. On the European continent the Revolution did not begin until after the Napoleonic Wars, with France in the lead from 1820 to 1870, then Germany after the Franco-Prussian War. In the last few decades the Industrial Revolution has even invaded the ancient civilizations of the East; Japan is already as much "industrialized" as either America or Europe, and the process of transformation is now going on in China, India, Indo-China, Persia, Afghanistan; even the darkest parts of Africa are now feeling the effects of the Revolution, the nature and the extent of which we shall now examine a little more in detail, the better to understand and appreciate later its influence upon education.

Formerly people lived mostly on farms, in villages and small towns scattered all over the land, with here and there an occasional large city. The bulk of the population were occupied in agriculture and its kindred industries. The home was the industrial unit, the center in which were practiced the arts and trades, every member of the household contributing his or her share, large or small, to the home industry. With the advent of the factory there has been a constant movement of population from the rural to the industrial and trade centers; cities have assumed huge proportions; areas that were before but scarcely inhabited have become the most densely populated sections of the country, witness the Charleroy and Liège districts in Belgium, the Ruhr Basin in Germany, Lancashire and London in England, New York and Pittsburgh in the United States. And this cityward movement still continues. It has been calculated that within a short period seventy-five per cent of the population will live in cities. This gathering of teeming populations, huddled over small areas away from the healthful country surroundings, naturally gave rise to problems of housing, sanitation, provisioning, policing and education, with which the national and local administrations have only recently begun to cope successfully. Not the least acute of those problems was that of education with which we are here especially concerned. Country life affords opportunities for growth, development and training, which the artificial city life does not offer. The country child lives and plays and works mostly out of doors; he early becomes familiar with the use of tools and all kinds of materials, is familiar too with plant life and animal life, and as he grows older and stronger he contributes his own share in the work of plowing, harrowing, planting, hoeing, harvesting, in the dairy or the barnyard. When he must look for employment at the end of the elementary school period he will find some form of occupation which offers variety, calls for some degree of intelligence, resourcefulness, freedom of action, and therefore is not likely to transform him into an automaton. Matters stand quite differently with the city child. If he has to leave studying at the end of the elementary school, he is commonly faced with the alternative of going either to an office or a factory. Unless he has shown exceptional capacities that have attracted the attention of his employers, the routine of office work will bring him some day into some form of specialized clerical labor which cannot pay him a living wage, and after a few years will unfit him for more intelligent and more remunerative occupations. Worse even is the lot awaiting the factory lad or girl. The factory system is based on minute division of labor. Ninety, or even one hundred and thirty processes are involved in the making of a modern shoe. Labor of this kind does not require intelligence or ingenuity or trained skill, but "hands" to feed the machine and remove the product. Day after day the worker has to perform this monotonous, lifeless, stupefying piece of work which gradually transforms him into a cog in the factory machinery.

The introduction of machinery made possible a huge increase in output which, combined with the new means of transportation and communication, led to a great commercial expansion. Trains and steamships now rapidly carry people and goods of every description along all the trade routes of the world; the telegraph and telephone at once report all important events in every part of the globe and they are narrated for us in the next morning's papers. Thus the barriers which custom, tradition, prejudice had raised between towns and states are gradually falling to the ground; local peculiarities in dress, festivals, home life, government, education tend to disappear; man becomes more and more a citizen of the world. To the influence of the Industrial Revolution can also be ascribed in a large measure the social and political changes of the last hundred years. It is directly responsible for the appearance of the "capitalist" and "working man." Before the advent of machinery, wealth and the power that goes with it were monopolized by the landed aristocracy and the wealthy merchants. The new inventions made it possible to exploit to the full the resources of the world. Investments in industrial enterprises yielded great profits and enormous fortunes were amassed by the investors, the "captains of industry" or capitalists. The great power wielded by these new "barons" lay not only in their wealth but even more in the ownership and control of the means of production. The peasant might be a serf and still retain some degree of economic independence from the fact that he had land out of which he could always eke out an existence; the artisan had his skill and tools with which he could always gain a livelihood, but the millions of landless and toolless factory workers were at the mercy of their employers, with whom they hardly had any personal relations; they were so many hands that could easily be replaced because the labor and skill involved in machine production is so small that women and even children can supply it. They were thus obliged to accept whatever terms were offered; their wages were low, the hours of labor long, the conditions under which they had to work were often unsanitary, even dangerous, their homes were dingy, crowded tenement houses, and they lived in constant fear of unemployment and starvation. Such conditions naturally bred discontent among the laborers and they soon realized that the only hope of improving their lot was through concerted action, the right to which they eventually won everywhere and have used to better their economic and political condition. Among other things they have secured better working conditions and wages, the limitation of child and woman labor, better provisions for the education of children at public expense, equality of all before the law and the extension of the right of suffrage. On the whole the material condition of the laboring man in the cities is far better today than it was one hundred years ago. Most of the evils following the sudden dislocation of the economic system produced by the introduction of machinery have been removed; the standard of food, comforts and sanitation, even in the humblest homes, has been greatly raised; labor of the roughest kind is being gradually eliminated; the workday has gradually shortened; holidays are more frequent, vacations more general; in short, people in general have much more leisure than they had formerly and the question that naturally arises is: how will they enjoy it?

REFERENCES

Cambridge Modern History.
Mantoux, P., La Revolution Industrielle au XVIII siècle.
Robinson, J., and Beard, C., The Development of Modern Europe.
Sedgwick, W., and Tyler, H., A Short History of Science.

PUBLIC LETTER WRITER

CHAPTER VIII

SCIENCE IN THE SCHOOLS

OUR SURVEY OF THE WESTERN SCHOOLS around 1750[1] has shown us that in spite of the "realistic"[2] movement the schools in which scientific subjects were taught were then still the exception. Some degree of success rewarded the efforts of the eighteenth-century reformers to reintroduce[3] science into the schools or even establish institutions in which the scientific element was predominant. The teaching of geography, physics, nature study, mathematics was a distinct feature of the instruction given in the Philanthropinums that sprang up in Germany in the latter part of the century. Most of those institutions were short-lived but they existed long enough to exert a profound influence on subject matter and method of teaching in Teutonic schools. Some elementary science with practical applications to the trades was also taught in the Sunday schools and industrial schools conducted by the Brothers of the Christian Schools in France, but these institutions disappeared in the political whirlwind at the close of the century. Hecker's "real" school at Berlin has already been mentioned. Under Hecker's successor it was organized into three courses, a pedagogium for higher learning, a school of art with courses in commerce, engineering, the fine arts, mili-

---

[1] See ch. II.
[2] See Vol. II, ch. IX.
[3] The medieval liberal arts course made ample provision for the scientific element; the disappearance of that element from the course of study was due to the influence of the sixteenth-century humanism.

tary science, etc., and a German or industrial school. The full development of the "real" school, however, did not take place until much later. To the latter part of the eighteenth century also belongs the foundation of the first higher schools for business or industrial purposes: commercial schools, schools of agriculture, forestry, engineering, architecture, technology.

The complete reintegration of the scientific element in the schools has been a slow process, the work mainly of the nineteenth century and a consequence of the scientific trend of the age and the Industrial Revolution. The pioneer work of the Philanthropinists which has just been referred to aroused a widespread interest in science in German lands and the Pestalozzian movement which spread to most German states during the first decades of the nineteenth century contributed much to make studies in elementary science general. Geography, now considered the connecting link between the sciences of nature and the sciences of man, was taught throughout the whole elementary period. Drawing, too, was incorporated into the course of study of every grade and in the upper grades introduced the student to the study of geometry. Arithmetic taught throughout the course was later connected with instruction in algebra and geometry in the upper grades. Elementary physics, physiology, botany, zoölogy were introduced into the middle and upper grades. The time allotted to these scientific subjects varied, according to the subject and the grade, from two hours to four hours a week. Before the middle of the century science had been recognized as one of the branches of the Volkschule curriculum in most German-speaking countries.

Science in the German elementary schools,

Of more recent date is the introduction of science into the elementary schools of other countries. Some elementary science, under the guise of object lessons, was introduced into the English infant schools, which after 1830 became quiet common in English- the English, speaking countries; the teaching of science and drawing was promoted in England by the Department of Science and Art, especially after 1860; but until 1900 the "3 R's" were the only required subjects in English elementary schools; government grants, determined by results, controlled the teaching of other subjects; of those, geography and science were the most popular and have now become part of the compulsory course. The general introduction of elementary science into the French schools dates from the Law of 1833, which followed Cousin's Report on Prussian Education and was the foundation upon which the whole system of elementary education has been developed. The Law provided for the establishment of two classes of elementary schools, the primary and higher primary. The primary schools the French, were to provide instruction in the "3 R's." In addition to more advanced work in those subjects the higher primary schools were to offer instruction in geometry and its applications, drawing, surveying, physical science, natural history, geography, history and music. The Law emphasized instruction "in the history and geography of France and in the elements of science," with their applications to everyday life. The introduction of elementary science into the schools of other European countries is of more recent date still, and it was due mainly either to German or French influence.

In the United States the elementary school curriculum continued to be the traditional one until about the middle of the nineteenth century; the average elementary school offered instruction in reading, spelling and English grammar, while those of a higher type added writing, arithmetic,

geography, and history. Geography was the first additional
subject to gain some sort of general recognition in the elementary schools, as is evidenced by the comparatively large
number of geographies and atlases published before 1850 for
elementary school purposes. Through the influence of
Horace Mann physiology had gained a footing in some of
the New England schools before 1840, but it
the American   was not generally made a compulsory sub-
elementary   ject until much later. Object lessons intro-
schools.   ducing to some elementary science were
gradually included after 1840, when the
influence of the Pestalozzian movement began to be felt in

the country. Nature study as such did not gain recognition
until much later. The modernizing of the elementary school
curriculum in the South American republics, in Japan, more
recently in China and other countries, has been going on
during the last fifty years under the influence of the United
States or the leading European nations.

It has been noted before that one of the legacies of the
Renaissance was a type of secondary education from which

all science had been virtually banished. The restoration of
science to its rightful position as one of the
essential elements in a liberal education   Science in the
began with the realistic movement, par-   secondary
ticularly its last phase, sense realism, which   schools in
through Francke's Institutions at Halle
gained a foothold in German schools. Those institutions in
which the realien, *i.e.,* scientific subjects, occupied such a
prominent place became the mother house of other schools;
they showed how the teaching of the traditional subjects
could be combined with technical and industrial training;
they supplied Protestant Germany with teachers and private
tutors trained in the atmosphere of realism, and they published text books for the teaching and study of the "real"
subjects. It has been noted, too, that one of Francke's followers, John J. Hecker, was the founder of the Berlin "real
school," an imitation of the one existing at Halle. Hecker
was entrusted by Frederick II with the organization of the
Prussian school system. He prepared the Ordinances of 1763,
whose purpose was "to banish from the
country the ignorance which is so harmful   Germany,
in its effects and so great an obstacle to the
spread of Christian ideals. . . ." It was hoped that "by improving the schools our subjects will be made morally better
and industrially more efficient." Those beginnings of the
realistic trend in the German secondary schools received
additional impetus from the Philanthropinist movement,
though, to the credit of the realists of the Francke type, it
must be said that they would not countenance the radical
principles of the Enlightenment. "True realism, says J. Fr.
Hahn, Hecker's collaborator, must be sought in the things
that promote a quiet and peaceful conscience."[1] The efforts
of the Philanthropinists supported by the encyclopedic tend-

[1] Quoted by Biedermann, Altes und Neues von Schulsacher, Vol. VIII (Programme of the Berlin Realschule).

encies of the age could not fail to have some influence on the curriculum of the German secondary schools; modern subjects were added to the course of study, but the spread of this scientific movement was checked for a time by a humanistic revival. The new German classicism, the heart of which was the appreciation of Hellenism, as we see it in the works of Winklemann, of Herder, Lessing, Schiller, and Goethe, the makers of classical German literature, won for Greek a position it never had occupied in humanistic studies. None the less, the ancient classics never regained in the German secondary schools the sway they had formerly held. In 1816 a uniform course of study was provided for the Prussian State secondary schools, the gymnasium and pro-gymnasium. The studies were Latin, Greek, German, mathematics, history, geography, religion and science. Though but two hours weekly were allotted to the last subject, it retained its hold on the classical secondary institutions until the school reorganization of the second half of the nineteenth century. Science also found a home in the few "real" schools existing at the beginning of the century, and the old humanistic institutions—gymnasiums, lyceums, pedagogiums, collegiums, Lateinische schools, academies—which could not meet the requirements of the 1816 reform; those institutions were permitted to continue as middle-class schools under the name Burgenschulen. The "real" schools which from their inception had been the fosterers of scientific studies in the schools were definitely organized in 1859. They were divided into two classes: "Real schulen Erster Ordnung," schools which offered six- and nine-year courses, including Latin, and had the privilege of one-year military service; "Real schulen Zweiter Ordnung," schools offering a six-year course without Latin and having their own leaving examinations without any privilege. In 1882 the nine-year "real" schools offering Latin were recognized as "real" gymnasiums, the other nine-year "real" schools being styled "Ober Realschulen."

In England the reintroduction of science into the secondary schools coincided with the foundation of the nonconformist academies in the seventeenth century. This early scientific movement practically came to an end with the decline of the academies in the next century, and a revival of popular interest in science had to await the controversy on the respective educational merits of linguistic and scientific subjects in the second quarter of the nineteenth century. This controversy, which at first was headed by the phrenologist, George Combe, and centered around the schools of Edinburgh and Glasgow, gradually assumed national proportions and enlisted on either side the leading scientists, writers, and politicians of the time. The immediate result of the controversy was the establishment of "secular schools" so-called, in opposition to the age-old, flourishing humanistic schools of the country. The controversy also did much to hasten an investigation into the England, work of the nine "Great Public Schools" of England (1861-1864) and a little later that of hundreds of other secondary schools. The investigation revealed an almost total absence of the sciences in the curriculum of the old English secondary schools, and its immediate outcome was the introduction into the course of study of a "modern side," including natural history, physics, modern languages and history. As noted before, the Department of Science and Art, combined with that of Education in 1898, did much to foster the study of the sciences and practical arts. Schools or classes providing instruction in those subjects were granted a subvention, and one of the noteworthy features of English education during the last fifty years is the steady increase in the number of "science schools" and "science classes."

In America as in England the academies were the first

modern secondary schools to offer instruction in science. Franklin's Foundation in Philadelphia, which opened its doors in 1751 and later evolved into the University of Pennsylvania, was probably the first of the American academies. In purpose and subjects taught, it resembled much more the German "real school" than its English namesake. The Phillips Academy at Andover, Massachusetts, founded in 1788, may be taken as typical of the more common American secondary schools in the next fifty years. America,   The foundation grant of the school states that its purpose is: "to lay the foundation of a public free school or academy for the purpose of instructing youth, not only in English and Latin grammar, writing, arithmetic, and those sciences wherein they are commonly taught; but more especially to teach them the Great End and Real business of Living . . ."; it is further declared that "the first and principal object of this Institution is the promotion of True Piety and Virtue; the second, instruction in the English, Latin and Greek languages, together with Writing, Arithmetic, Music and the Art of Speaking; the third, practical Geometry, Logic and Geography; and the fourth, such other liberal arts and sciences or languages as opportunities and abilities may hereafter admit and as the Trustees shall select." The academies rapidly multiplied during the first half of the nineteenth century. It has been estimated that by 1850 there were in the Eastern and Middle West States over six thousand academies with more than twelve thousand teachers employed and nearly three hundred thousand pupils of both sexes enrolled. Unlike the earlier Latin grammar school, the academy was not bound up with the college. Its chief purpose was the practical one of preparing for business or the rising new professions. Of the many new subjects offered by the academies the most commonly found are algebra, astronomy, botany, chemistry, general history, United States history, English literature, surveying, intellectual philosophy, declamation, and debating. An interesting feature of the history of the academies is that they were for a time the teachers training schools of the country. The first American high school (Boston, 1821) offered instruction in geography, navigation, surveying, astronomy and natural philosophy. Those that followed generally maintained the same attitude towards science, but for a long time the instruction on the whole remained confined to the use of the text books; it was only towards the close of the century that the laboratory method became common.

If we except the short-lived Port Royal schools, military academies and a few congregational colleges, French secondary schools remained overwhelmingly humanistic to the end of the eighteenth century when they were swept away by the Revolution. The Central Higher Schools established in 1795 to replace them offered many scientific subjects, but, lacking sadly in internal   France. organization, they were suppressed by the Law of 1802, which made provision for two types of secondary schools: the lycées, which were State institutions, and the communal colleges licensed by the Government but otherwise municipal or private schools; the colleges usually offered only a part of the lycée courses; in both institutions scientific subjects were taught from the first. The importance of the scientific element in the secondary school course of study has steadily increased since then. In what is called the section of modern, *i.e.*, non-classical humanities, the scientific course of study is a fair equivalent of the corresponding course in the German "real" schools. Other countries with a modern school system have followed the lead of one or the other of the above, and they all have now a more or less modern secondary school course of study.

It has been noted before that, except for the introduction of classical philology, classical literature, and some changes in theology and law following the Protestant Revolution, university courses of study were still, toward the close of the seventeenth century, substantially what they had been in the thirteenth, which means, among other things, that the teaching of the sciences never suffered in the universities the eclipse which befell it in secondary schools. The Faculty of Arts course included the three philosophies, meta-

Science in the Universities:

A LESSON IN PHYSICS GIVEN BY L'ABBÉ NOLLET

physical, moral, and natural, the last one corresponding more or less to what is now called natural science. On the other hand, it is true that the response of the universities to modern science was at first half-hearted, when it was not decidedly antagonistic. With very few exceptions the one ambition of the teaching staff in all universities seems to have been to transmit to the following generation the body of knowledge they had received from their predecessors and to admit no innovation which had not already been approved by experience. Down to the end of the eighteenth century the real centers of the scientific study of nature were the scientific societies commonly referred to as academies. In Germany the first university to embody the modern scientific spirit was that of Halle, founded in 1694, but the real departure from the traditional university work in science took place a century later with the founding of the University of Berlin in 1809. High attainment in some special branch of knowledge and the ability to advance that knowledge, much more than teaching skill, determined from the first the selection of its professors. Specialization in some field and productive scholarship were the ruling principles for the work of both students and teachers. For this purpose the seminar, in which small groups of advanced students investigate and discuss special problems under the direction of a professor, was given a prominent place in the work of the university. The fruitfulness of this new policy was soon made evident by the important contributions of the University of Berlin to the advancement of learning. The other German universities have gradually adopted the Berlin plan: the lecture, the seminar, laboratory investigation, research, the doctorate and academic freedom in study and teaching. Thousands of students from all lands, among them a large number of Americans, have flocked to German universities and brought back to their own country the German method of university work which is now well-nigh general.

The introduction of the modern sciences into the curriculum of American colleges and universities began around the middle of the eighteenth century with the foundation of Kings College, now Columbia University, and the Academy and

Charitable School, later the University of Pennsylvania, which has already been referred to. The other colleges soon followed the lead of those two. Around 1825 there began to be advocated complete freedom in the selection of subject by students and with it the importance of scientific training in this industrial age. The system was inaugurated at Harvard in 1769 by President Elliott. Two years previous to this Cornell University had been founded "upon a basis of complete freedom, with a strong bias in favor of the scientific and technical subjects." Since then the ascendency of science in the United States' colleges and universities has become general, and they occupy today a prominent position in the curriculum of higher education.

It is characteristic of English conservatism in education that as late as 1850 the pioneer industrial nation should still let scientific instruction develop independently of the universities, in a host of scientific societies founded in the eighteenth and nineteenth centuries, and in the
England, College of Chemistry and the School of Mines. The first degrees of doctor and bachelor of science were given by the University of London in 1860. At that time neither Oxford nor Cambridge had as yet made any progress worth mentioning in the teaching of the sciences.

The first step towards the promotion of higher scientific instruction in France was the foundation by the Convention of a number of special institutions of higher
France. learning which have already been referred to and were reorganized and added to by the Law of 1802, but the universities which had been suppressed by the Revolution were not re-established and organized along modern lines until the close of the century.

The reintegration of science into the curriculum did not proceed unchallenged. A lively controversy arose between the partisans of the old order of things and those of the new, as to the respective merits of humanistic and scientific studies. The controversy, which at times became somewhat heated, was carried on for decades, and it will occasionally flare up again even today. The question at issue, which really belongs to the province of the philosophy of education, can only be treated here in the briefest of outlines. The traditional course of studies, *Humanistic* with its stress upon language, is the best one *vs.* scientific yet devised to develop and discipline mental *studies.* powers: such was and still is, in the main, the humanists' contention, to which the scientists took exception. Some of them, *e.g.,* Huxley, claimed for science a "disciplinary" virtue not a whit inferior to that of the classics; others denied outright the possibility of a general discipline of intellectual powers and they supported their claims with a vast array of experimental data; all of them claimed for science a greater practical value, in an industrial age like our own, than is the case with the humanistics. At bottom, however, as it very soon developed, the whole incident was not so much a controversy over educational values, as a conflict between two radically opposed views of human nature, human life, and therefore of education. If man is a product of nature, if his destiny is to live in, and some day vanish into nature, then the sooner and the more thoroughly he becomes acquainted with nature and its forces, the better. If, on the other hand, we admit the presence in man of something which transcends physical nature, if we believe that man is man only because he can rise above his material surroundings, that his real destiny lies beyond this life and the world of sense, then evidently the sciences of nature can be nothing else than a minor element in the content of general education.

The influence of the scientific trend of modern thought

upon education has not been limited to the introduction of new subject matter into the school curricu-

The science of
education:
before the
19th century;

lum; it has been extended to the whole field of educational theory and practice and has been responsible for the appearance of a new science, the science of education, which today has its place in the college and university curriculum by the side of the old social sciences. This "scientific" treatment of education, let it be remarked in passing, was not an entirely new venture. The Republic and the Laws of Plato, the Politics and Ethics of Aristotle contain remarkable illustrations of a systematic treatment of education, and it is also worthy of note that those two pioneers of pedagogy as a science treated it from the social viewpoint. Quintilian's *De Institutione Oratoria* and Cicero's *De Oratore*, though somewhat perhaps lacking the breadth of view and loftiness of purpose of the Greek treatises, also emphasize the relation of education to society and the State as their very title would suggest. The literature of the early Church and that of the middle ages abound in writings dealing with education, but none of them taken singly gives us a comprehensive view of education. It is only when we consider the teachings of the Church as a whole and her centuries old educational policy that we come to realize that no important element of the educational process has escaped her notice, and that her deep, yet simple wisdom, is our safest guide in determining the relative importance of those elements.

Many educational treatises appeared during the Renaissance, but they are as a rule chiefly confined to a consideration of humanistic studies for purposes of personal culture, and not a few breathe a spirit that is alien to Christian education. A noteworthy exception to this treatment of education is Vives' *De Tradendis Disciplinis*, which is by far the most remarkable educational treatise of the Renaissance.

Vives' name was obscured in later generations, but nineteenth-century scholarship has traced the permeating influence of Vives on the pedagogy of later ages, and it may also be noted here that his treatise *De Anima* is considered by many as the starting point of modern psychology. Though he belonged to a previous generation, Vives may be classed with the Didacticians or Innovators of the late sixteenth and early seventeenth centuries, whom we may consider as the pioneers of modern pedagogy: Peter Ramus, Richard Mulcaster, Francis Bacon, Wolfgang Ratke, Amos Comenius, among others. We have seen (Vol. II, Chapter IX) that the fundamental principle of the new pedagogy advocated by the Innovators was, that education is a natural process whose laws or principles are discoverable in nature. This conviction was responsible on the one hand for the introduction into the school curriculum of new material selected from the natural sciences, and on the other for the formulation of a new pedagogy, the best illustration of which is Comenius' *Didactica Magna*. While this new pedagogy was remarkable for its breadth of view, it was sadly deficient on the psychological side; the Innovators insisted upon the study of the child and an adaptation of the educative process to the activities of the growing mind, but the knowledge of those activities was still rather scanty. The high-sounding principle of "education according to nature" amounted in practice to the teaching of the vernacular instead of Latin in the early school years, the use of illustrated text-books together with a method based on some real or fanciful analogy between the processes of nature and those of the human mind; with that there was a tendency to remedy the defects of purely formal training by the introduction into the school curriculum of a mass of bits of information concerning nature, man, his activities and their products, the home, the school and studies, the city, the state, war, religion, etc.

The pioneers of a modern science of education were mainly concerned with the question of knowledge and its assimilation by the learner. With Rousseau and his followers interest is shifted to the child; the study of education becomes a study of the educative process in the individual, a study of natural inclination, disposition, interest, of the growth and development of the child and the ways and means of adapting the educative process to the workings of the growing mind, to the interests and instincts of the child. Like its inspirer, Rousseau, and the age that produced him, the young science of education was for a time stubbornly individualistic, ignoring the bonds connecting the individual with the community, present and past, and thus isolating nineteenth-century education from its historical development. On the other hand, by insisting upon the study of the child's nature, the training of his senses, by demanding that the experience of the child be made the starting point of his own coöperation with the teacher, it has pointed out the way to a much needed improvement in classroom procedure. This "psychological tendency" in educational theory and practice coincided with a new trend in psychological studies which began with Locke's *Essay on the Human Understanding* (1690), its appeal to inner experience, its emphasis upon the use of the method of analytic introspection which rapidly grew in popularity and gave to English psychology the strong empirical bend it has ever since preserved. Psychologist after psychologist has described in detail the experiences through which he passed in the perception of objects and the formation of ideas. The more daring among them, Hartley, the two Mills, Bain, Spencer, following the lead of Hume, have denied the reality of any power different from the senses back of our higher intellectual life, and have attempted to explain even the highest and most spiritual conceptions of our mind as the outcome of sensation and association. The more conservative representatives of English psychology, while not denying outright the existence of a spiritual principle of human life, are satisfied with avoiding any treatment of, even reference to, rational or metaphysical psychology. This materialistic tendency of modern psychology has been strengthened and accelerated by some of the new elements in Western life which have already been alluded to: the secularization of education, the theory of evolution, the unprecedented interest in the sciences dealing with nature, in general, the whole trend of contemporary civilization. None of those new elements in Western life must of necessity lead to materialism, but the fact is that they have contributed much to the focussing of the attention of the age upon the physical approaches to reality. In non-English-speaking countries the surrender to empiricism and phenomenalism was not as unconditional as it was in England and America. In France there was in the nineteenth century a marked reaction against the crude materialism which followed the first inroad of English empiricism. Some French psychologists have even attempted to build up a genuine philosophy of the soul upon the inductions of empirical psychology. In Germany, the classic land of metaphysics, pure empiricism did not win the day either. While the old conception of psychology as a philosophical science has generally been abandoned, many German psychologists have insisted upon using introspective experience as a starting point for a doctrine of the immortality of the soul. Yet, the fact remains that in non-Catholic normal schools, colleges, universities, text-books in psychology are often little more than treatises on physiological phenomena and that the science of education is today permeated with the influence of this one-sided conception of psychology.

The first important contribution to the science of education in the nineteenth century came from Pestalozzi, but, as we have seen before, it is well to bear in in the 19th mind that much of what is usually con- and 20th nected with the name of the Swiss reformer centuries. was contributed to the theory and practice of education by his co-workers or followers. In fact, the clear statement and philosophical implications of the ideas advocated by Pestalozzi, and the actual transla- tion of those ideas into concrete schoolroom practice was to a large extent the work of generations of teachers and theorists who followed Pestalozzi's leadership. Pestalozzi's aim was to establish the closest possible correlation between elementary instruction and the activities of the child's mind, in order to further a "harmonious development" of mental powers through a mastery of the materials of instruction. This conception of education, not fully carried out until long after Pestalozzi's death, had several important results: the introduction of object lessons in the elementary stage of instruction and the use of objective teaching at all stages, an emphasis upon mental arithmetic and a more scientific study of geography; in general a reform in the teaching of the elementary school branches. On the other hand, Pes- talozzianism is responsible for the formalism which until recently prevailed in the teaching of elementary school branches to the neglect of the content and special technique of those subjects. Pestalozzi's experiments at Neuhof and Stanz, where he tried to improve the condition of the poor and the mentally or morally defective by a combination of manual labor and instruction, formed another important contribution to the science of education; they were partially responsible for the appearance of a voluminous literature dealing with industrial education and the care of abnormal children.

Pestalozzianism was but one phase of a school reform which had its origin in the eighteenth century and is not even now completed. Numberless teachers have contributed their share, large or small, to the practical side of the reform, while the dominant philosophy of the age has supplied the inspiration and some kind of metaphysical background. Kant's philosophy, closely related to the early phase of the reform, exerted a deep influence on the education of the period; it not only supplied some of the content of higher education and outlined its methods, but it offered in the "autonomous fulfillment of duty" a new path to happiness. Kant's (1724-1804) direct contribution to the science of education, notes of university lectures on pedagogy, contained nothing original, apart from what is carried over from his philosophy; it is a restatement of the doctrines, or rather a combination of the doctrines of Rousseau and Locke; more original are Fichte's (1762-1814) *Addresses to the German Nation*, in which he urged a thorough reorganization of the German school system along the lines of Pestalozzian pedagogy. Hegel (1770-1831) wrote no separate treatise on education, but his philosophical writings, chiefly his *Philosophy of Right* deal at some length with the sociological aspect of education, and his school addresses as Rector of the Nuremberg Gymnasium, give us his views on the theory and practice of teaching. Many of Hegel's students tried to work out the pedagogical implications of his philosophy. Rosenkranz' (1805-1879) *Philosophy of Education* is probably the best illustration of those attempts. It describes education as a process of "self-estrangement" and of identification with the self of those ideal elements which make up culture, but at first are foreign to the self. Rosenkranz worked out his Philosophy of Education, physical, intellectual, moral, religious, from the Hegelian principle. In still another way, though indirectly, the science of education was deeply influenced by the philosophy of Hegel through the latter's influence on some of the school subjects. His teachings, though here he shares the honors with Schelling (1775-1854), were to a great extent responsible for the reform of geography, the systematizing of philosophy, the recognition of aesthetics as a new and separate science, the application of the historical method to the various departments of learning, in general, for the establishment of the principles of scientific research work. Another early contributor to the science of education was Schleiermacher (1768-1834), theologian, philosopher, pastor and educator. Like Fichte's and Hegel's, his interest in education was that of the philosopher. Pedagogy, he teaches, is one of the "technical disciplines" which branch out from ethics. It is closely related to political science, the science of religious organization, and the "community of language and knowledge." The basic relation of education is that of learning and teaching and the medium of the activities it connotes is the school in the broadest sense of the term. Schleiermacher carried out only part of his plan for a philosophy of education, but some of his ideas have proved highly stimulative to subsequent educational theorists. To the same period belong several important contributions to the history of education, among them Schwarz's (1776-1857) *General History of Education* and Karl von Raumer's (1783-1865) *History of Pedagogy* from the revival of classical learning down to our own time, "the first to draw upon original sources and of permanent value in spite of partisan spirit in religion." Barnard's *American Journal of Education* has made the work familiar to American readers. The study of original sources has proceeded ever since and it has yielded a rich harvest of information which has helped correct a number of misconceptions of education in centuries gone by.

With the possible exception of Rosenkranz, the philosophers whose contributions to educational theory have just been outlined were interested in the science of education insofar as it is connected with some branch of philosophy. In Herbart, on the other hand, we meet a philosopher whose main interest in philosophy was in the problem of education, its aim, its methods and possibilities, and who treated the science of education as a science by itself with ethics and psychology as auxiliary sciences. Ethics tells us what the final end of education is, the formation of noble, cultivated moral characters; it is goodness of will. Psychology, Herbartian psychology, shows us how this goodness of will is attained, through the process of apperceiving knowledge and the development of many-sided interests. Herbart is thus led, on the one hand, to treat in detail all the steps connecting knowledge and volition, and on the other, to explain at great length the Herbartian maxim, "Make your instruction educative." The value of Herbart's contribution to the theory and practice of education, as pointed out before,[1] does not lie so much in the so-called Herbartian method of instruction, of which there was at one time much slavish imitation, but in his (Herbart's) insistence on the importance of the ethical aim, the value of interest and wide culture, the use of rational principles in teaching, the importance of the teacher's work. On the other hand, it will not be amiss to remark again that some features of his theory have been severely criticized. His conception of the soul, if carried to its logical consequences, will in educational practice lead to a rigid determinism, for, according to Herbart's account, every volition is the result of a "circle of thought" which functions automatically, independently of any power of free choice, which for that matter is denied by Herbart. What then, one may wonder, becomes of the pupil's individuality on which Herbart himself insists so much? It has also been pointed out that the Herbartian maxim, "make instruction educative," is nothing else at bottom than a revival of the old Socratic error that "knowledge is virtue"; that the ethical aim, as conceived by Herbart, is in the last analysis self-culture; that the stressing of

[1] See ch. VI.

interest in education will in practice, if not in theory, result in losing sight of the worth of effort. Furthermore, Herbart's system of education not only fails to take in the historical factors in education, but hardly goes beyond a consideration of the effects of education upon the individual.

In opposition to the Herbartians who emphasize instruction, methods of teaching and therefore the teacher's work, stands another school of educationalists, who insist upon the importance of self-activity in the pupil. In conformity with present usage it will be referred to as the Froebelian school, but that should not convey the impression that Froebel was the sole originator of that school nor even, in some respects at least, its most remarkable representative. In *The Ruling Principle of Method Applied to Education* Rosmini-Serbati[1] developed independently of Herbart and Froebel a theory of education which anticipated much that is now considered as fundamental. "The child," he says, "at every age must act." Education really consists in regulating this activity. Independently also of the influence of Froebel the Salesian Institute has established hundreds of schools whose work embodies the more important principles of the German reformer. The Montessori system and some of the reforms advocated by John Dewey, though bearing evidence of Froebelian inspiration, show a remarkable degree of originality and independence of treatment.[2]

In recent years, pedagogy, following the lead of psychology, has resolutely entered the field of experimentation. The pedagogy of Pestalozzi, Herbart, Froebel, had only been experimental in the sense that it was partly the result of their observation of mental processes in children. There is also a certain kind of experimentation which has been going on in the schools in the last two or three decades. Teachers, supervisors, principals, superintendents have suggested and

[1] See ch. VI.
[2] See ch. VI.

tried all kinds of plans and devices to improve the administration of the schools, their courses of study, the methods of teaching arithmetic, spelling, reading, writing, geography, history, the ways of dealing with defective or refractory children, the use of the text-book, of the free period, and many other matters of this kind. While conceding that experimentation of this type may lead to good results in some specific points, educational experts have pointed out that a large part of the data it supplies is scientifically valueless, because the conditions under which the experiment is made are not always carefully observed and the results obtained have not been well tabulated. There can be no true experimental pedagogy, they claim, without the methods used in all experimental sciences, particularly those applied in psychological experiments; besides, experimental pedagogy should be closely related with a number of other sciences whose results can throw light upon educational problems: psychology, of course, with its various branches, and logic, ethics, aesthetics, biology, physiology, anatomy, ethnology, anthropometry, pathology, the science of statistics; even the physical sciences can assist in the solution of the problems facing experimental pedagogy. Furthermore, education will not reap all the benefits which might accrue to it from experiments unless they are made in special institutions where the conditions of experimentation are under the control of the investigator. This last requirement has led to the establishment of so-called experimental schools, commonly affiliated with Teachers' Colleges; the Lincoln School of Columbia University, New York, is probably at present the best illustration of this kind of institution. Foremost among the questions investigated by experimental pedagogy in recent years have been the causes of retardation, acceleration, elimination involving the kindred question of test and measurements. Tests of some kind have ever been used by the schools as a means to classify pupils, to determine their promotion from one class to a higher one, the efficiency of teachers, the amount of financial support which a particular school or school system should receive, but now an attempt is made to give to school tests the precision and finality of the mathematical sciences. Countless experiments have been made to bring in some degree of refinement in methods of testing, to supply teachers and administrative officers with "measuring sticks" that will enable them to evaluate with some degree of accuracy, the efficiency of the teaching or administrative procedure in any given case. And pedagogy has appealed for aid in this matter to anthropology and psychology. The attempt "to read" the character of individuals in some external sign is, of course, as old as the human race. For a long time divination answered the purpose, then came palm reading not yet out of fashion; the first attempt at some sort of scientific method seems to have been made by the Italian physicist, Porta (1543-1615), who at one time was much interested in the study of physiognomy; Gall (1758-1828), Spurzheim (1778-1831) and others, were convinced they had found a reliable index of a man's character in the shape of his cranium; others preferred to rely upon handwriting. The English anthropologist, Francis Galton (1826-1911), was probably the first to attempt "to measure" what we call today "individual differences." Galton's purpose, however, was not to supply diagnostics to physicians, or psychologists, or pedagogues. His interest lay in the question of eugenics, i.e., the means of improving the race through a process of scientific selection. His inquiries belong in the main to the field of anthropology. Aside from the work done by experimental psychologists, alluded to before, the first attempts to "measure" mental aptitudes were made by a few pathologists, in an effort to draw up more accurate "psychical inventories" of patients than was usual in clinics. A number of articles appearing in journals of psychology both in Europe and the United States during the last decade of the nineteenth century is the first evidence we have that interest in "mental tests" was no longer confined to psychiatrists, but the novelty did not enter the stage of pedagogical usefulness until 1905. In that year appeared in the "Année Psychologique" Binet and Simon's *Méthodes nouvelles pour le diagnostic du niveau intellectuel des anormaux*. What distinguished the Binet-Simon tests from previous psychological experiments of the same class was that they were intended for the benefit of the school, that they were not confined to sensory reactions and, more especially, that they were more or less graded. Since then the method has been much perfected, its scope widened and its applications multiplied. A technique has been developed which meets the most exacting scientific requirements. Devised at first for the sake of abnormal or subnormal children, the method is now applied to all classes and grades, and it has even received interesting applications in the great economic world beyond the school.

The interest in the testing and measurement of mental capacities and achievements, especially in the United States, has been little short of marvelous, during the last two decades. And there is as yet no sign of abatement. Not a year passes without its crop of publications to be added to the already voluminous literature on the subject, and it is undeniable that this literature as a whole is a substantial contribution to the administrative branch of the science of education. Tests scientifically devised and conducted will lead to a clearer, more accurate notion of the pupils' capacities and achievements, will yield more reliable results from the comparison of pupil to pupil, class to class, school to school, will enable authorities to reach a better grading of pupils and therefore to obtain a better adaptation of subject matter and method to the mentality of a class or any group of pupils in a class. All of which should ultimately result in a substantial gain for education. But one may wonder if too much is not expected from what belongs after all to the mechanics of education. What test will reveal anything worth while of home influence upon the child, of his associations out of school, of the zeal or indifference of the teacher, of his magnetic or uninspiring personality, of the amount of personal effort put forth by the young scholar in the performance of daily tasks, of the growth or deterioration of character? Those are, it seems, the elements that really count in education, but they are too subtle, too elusive, to permit of any measurement in terms of q's or y's or x's. Important gains to the science of education have also come from the discussion of questions that were brought to the front by the political or industrial revolutions, the researches of anthropologists among the primitive races of Asia and Africa, of archaeologists among the ruins of ancient civilizations, of historians in the archives of chancelleries, municipalities or ancient seats of learning, in general by the progress of the biological and social sciences and particularly of the historical sciences.

REFERENCES

Armstrong, H., The Teaching of Scientific Method.
Coulter, J. M., The Mission of Science in Education (Science II, 12, pp. 281-293).
Dryer, C., Science in Secondary Schools.
Eliot, C., Educational Reform.
Galloway, R., Education, Scientific and Technical.
Greene, H., and Jorgensen, A., The Use and Interpretation of Educational Tests.
Huxley, T. H., Science and Education; Lay Sermons.
Monroe, W., De Voss, J. and Kelly, F., Educational Tests and Measurements.

CHAPTER IX

NATIONALISM AND SOCIALISM

NATIONAL SCHOOL SYSTEMS

PARADOXICAL THOUGH IT MAY SOUND, THE treatment of nationalism and socialism in the same chapter has been suggested by the similarities, nay the very close relationship of those two apparently opposed conceptions of life. Both conceptions spring from that deep-rooted tendency which draws man to his fellowmen; both emphasize community life over against individual life, the claims of the group over against those of its members; but whereas socialism usually views society as a whole, nationalism concerns itself with some particular society or "nation" as distinct from, even opposed to other "nations." It hardly needs to be remarked that, in one form or another, nationalism and socialism are, and must be, as old as the human race. Sparta is a classical example of the socialistic state in antiquity. The tribes of primitive and semi-civilized society, the city states of ancient Greece and Italy, the communes of medieval Flanders and Italy were so many small "nations" with a high degree of homogeneity and cohesive strength, which was not possessed at first by the modern nations. The latter, some of them for quite a long period of time, were mere agglommerations of peoples with different dialects, traditions, customs, held loosely together by some sort of political organization and allegiance to a common sovereign. The inhabitants of the country known today as France, for instance, are still sometimes referred to as Normans, Bretons, Flemings, Gascons, etc., and traces of those heterogeneous origins of the French nation can still be found in local dialects and customs.

Modern nationalism is, in the main, a product of nineteenth century politico-economic life, but its origins can be traced as far back as the close of the Middle Ages. Prior to that time the western peoples, whilst paying allegiance to a local prince or king, had considered themselves, above all, as members of the great Catholic family, with Rome as its centre and the Pope as its visible head. Medieval history abounds in illustrations of this "international" character of western society; one of especial interest to the student of education is the "international" character of the medieval universities; a young man could, in the course of his studies, pass from one seat of learning to another without in the least jeopardizing his academic status. He would find everywhere the same organization, general regulations, curriculum, methods of teaching. If he received his "degree" from a university empowered by a papal charter to grant the privilege of teaching everywhere, "jus ubique docendi," he could rest assured that his teacher's license was valid in every Christian community.

The first signs of a modern nationalism, that is to say, a sense of loyalty to a larger state than the primitive, or ancient, or medieval "nations," appeared in fifteenth century England, France, Spain, Portugal and Scotland. National consciousness of this type was in France and England one of the consequences of the Hundred Years' War; in Spain, of the centuries-old crusade against the Moors and the union of the country under the joint rule of Ferdinand and Isabella; in Portugal, of the rivalry with Spain in overseas conquests; in Scotland a consequence of the struggle for independence from English rule. This early modern nationalism was furthered by the religious wars of the sixteenth and early seventeenth centuries, when political rulers proceeded to determine what the religion of their subjects should be. The dynastic wars of the next hundred years gave it a further impetus and by the middle of the eighteenth century it was fairly well established in most western lands. It was not as yet, however, the kind of nationalism that we know today, being still a sort of popular loyalty to a sovereign or line of sovereigns. Paramount devotion to a political nation, founded on a community of language, culture, economic interests, is a thing of the last hundred years. Its first advocates were the eighteenth-century philosophers of the Bollingbroke type, and its prime movers were the forces let loose by the French and the Industrial Revolutions.

There was much that called for well-deserved criticism in the traditions, the social and political institutions of the eighteenth century and the Enlightenment did not fail to make good capital out of it. In the name of reason and humanity, its philosophers, particularly in France, inveighed against tyranny, privilege, social and political inequalities; they clamored for reform and they expounded nationalistic doctrines which found an echo in the declamations, laws, reforms and wars of the French Revolution. France was to be one, indivisible, democratic, republican, egalitarian and secular. Every tendency toward provincial autonomy must be fought; the will of a highly centralized state must be enforced in every phase of the nation's life, in every part of its territory. Class distinctions, guilds, religious and other traditional associations were suppressed because they were incompatible with the new order of things. The freedom of association was declared to be a "natural right" of man, but any faction which appeared to be lacking in loyalty to the revolutionary conception of French nationality was to be rooted out; in fact, for a time every kind of association was forbidden with the one exception of the "clubs of patriots,"

The origins of modern nationalism;

a sort of semi-private, semi-public societies for the propagation of the revolutionary principles at home and abroad. Every citizen, it was asserted, had the "natural right" to publish and read whatever he would, but it was not long before the ruling faction of revolutionaries had monopolized this freedom of the press by cutting off the heads of those who "misled" the people.

Fully aware of the value and need of a new education for nationalist propaganda, the revolutionaries suppressed the old schools and devised a system of new ones, state supported and state controlled schools, where all children, now declared to be state property, would be thoroughly grounded in the national language and the gospel of liberty, equality, and fraternity. Catholic Christianity, for centuries the religion of France, was at first accepted by the Revolution as the necessary, though not the ideal, religion of the country, but it was made to serve national ends through a "civil constitution of the clergy." A little later on, however, it was proscribed as dangerous to liberty and republicanism, and in its place there was installed the new religion of the twin goddesses, Reason and "La Patrie," with its own patriotic symbolism and ritual; this new religion in turn was replaced first by the religion of the Supreme Being, then by a number of quaint little sects claiming, each one of them, to be the best expression of the religious creed of the Revolution. Eventually the Church regained some of its former influence in the country, but the state retained its leadership in education, charity and social welfare work which it has since thoroughly "secularized."

It could hardly have been expected that the rulers of Europe would remain idle, in the face of this bold challenge of the French Revolution to the established forms of government and the traditions of centuries. Burke's "Reflections on the Revolution in France," published in 1790, fairly well expressed the sentiment of the ruling classes everywhere on the political and social changes which were then taking place in France. If the French revolutionaries still entertained any doubts as to that sentiment, those doubts were dispelled by the joint declaration of Pillnitz (1791), to the effect that the rulers of Austria and Prussia considered the restoration of order in France an object of "common interest to all sovereigns of Europe." We are not interested here in the details of the twenty-three years' war which followed, but we must take note of two features of that war which are closely related to the subject of this chapter: the use of a new system of warfare and the awakening of the dormant national consciousness outside of France. At first, in self-defense, as their only means of salvation against an encircling coalition, the revolutionaries appealed to the "nation in arms." Every able-bodied young Frenchman became liable to conscript military service; the government claimed the right to requisition any material, or supplies, or assistance for national defense. The armies thus created not only removed the menace of invasion, but also became schools of nationalism at home and powerful agencies for revolutionary propaganda abroad. The mingling in the same army units and for a common service, of recruits coming from all social ranks, often from widely separated regions, their induction into military service with solemn rights and patriotic orations, the incessant appeal to their sense of duty and devotion to France could not fail, as is shown by the history of the wars of the French Revolution, to develop patriotic fervor.

The purpose of French revolutionary propaganda abroad is clearly stated in a decree issued by the National Convention in December, 1792, after its armies had begun to overrun the neighboring states. "The French nation," so runs the decree, "declares that it will treat as enemies every people who, refusing liberty and equality or renouncing them, would maintain, recall or treat with a prince and the privileged classes; on the other hand, it engages not to subscribe to any treaty nor to lay down its arms until the sovereignty and independence of the people, whose territory the troops of the Republic have entered, shall be established, and until the people shall have adopted the principles of equality and founded a free and democratic government." That aim, the French military machine failed to achieve for the time being; the fruits of its revolutionary propaganda were to appear only years after the close of the Napoleonic wars, in the chronic state of revolution in Europe between 1820 and 1848. What the presence of the French armies succeeded in achieving at once was the arousing of a national spirit which in the end proved to be more than a match for French nationalism. We need only refer to the rise of the Spanish nation against Napoleon's armies and the German War of Liberation in 1813. Apart from the fervor of its devotion to the Fatherland, this nationalism, aroused everywhere by the presence of a hateful invader and oppressor, had, of course, nothing in common with the nationalism of the Revolution. The French Jacobins had received their inspiration and principles from the Enlightenment, particularly Rousseau's doctrine on the state of nature and his Social Contract; they had done their best to build up a French nationality on the ruins of the past. Outside of France, on the other hand, nationalism, at that time at least, professed everywhere reverence for the past, for the country's traditional institutions, for local customs and a degree of local autonomy, for the national language, the national literature and culture. In justice to France, however, it must be said that she too possessed a few nationalists of this type, like de Bonald (1754-1840), who were no less patriotic than the most fervid Jacobins, but whose national enthusiasm, instead of being aroused by the Revolution, found its inspiration in historic France.

A priori, one would be tempted to assume that the In-

dustrial Revolution was fundamentally opposed to nationalism, that the economic forces it has generated must, in the
long run, bring peoples into a condition of vital inter-
dependence. Railways, automobiles, steamships, the telephone, the telegraph, the radio, the aeroplane link one
country more and more closely with every other country. News agencies keep us informed day by day of the
trend of events the world over. People undertake today a
voyage from New York to London, or Paris, or Rome, with
no more concern than they would formerly take a trip from
New York to Boston, or London to York. The exchange of
raw materials and manufactured commodities is becoming
more and more international, and so are credit and banking,
the demand and supply in labor. Newspapers, reviews, national and international societies or congresses keep every
country in contact with scientific researches and discoveries,
literary, or artistic, or political, or religious movements taking place at home or in other countries. All of which, it
seems, should accelerate the progress of cosmopolitanism.
And yet the fact is, that nationalism is still very much
with us, and it even looks as though it had succeeded in
enlisting the Industrial Revolution in its service. If the new
means of transportation and communication tend to break
the barriers between states, they also have been used to link
more closely regions and provinces within national bound-
aries; they have made possible intensive nationalist propaganda, a highly centralized supervision and control of
schools, of the political, social, economic activities of the
nation. The economic life of industrialized nations depends
on international markets, but still more on national
consumption. Labor and capital may have, and do have
international affiliations, but they are organized in accord-
ance with national laws, to serve first of all national purposes. Socialism, a child of the Industrial Revolution, which
at first seemed to be intent upon the international organiza-

tion of the proletariat class, gradually gave up the idea as
utopian; it has been satisfied with national organizations,
and time and again it has proved no less "patriotic" than
the "bourgeois" parties in helping to carry out policies for
the national interest.

Like every important movement in the last three or four
hundred years, nationalism has been the subject of much
philosophizing. All sorts of theories have been propounded
to account for its origins and evolution, its variations from
one country or one generation to another, to explain the
very nature of the concept "nation." What constitutes a nation? What mysterious bond holds together in one great
family, Englishmen, or Frenchmen, or Germans, or Ital-
ians? Certain theories emphasize the objec-
its   tive elements of the national makeup:
philosophy   race, physical surroundings, culture, language, tradition, government; other theories,
on the other hand, stress the subjective, personal
elements; they hold that what makes a nation out of any
community is the idea or feeling or conviction on the part
of its members that they belong, of their own free will,
to a certain community, which has a personality of its
own, made up of a number of elements which are held
together by the national consciousness. A detailed critical
exposition of those theories belongs to the provinces of
sociology and philosophy, but it may not be amiss to remark here that in the discussions on this subject there
sometimes creeps in a certain confusion between nationalism and something very akin to it, though not identical
with it, and which for lack of a better term we shall
call "statism" or "politism." It is the doctrine of the
supremacy, even deification of the state, as we see it per-
sonified in the rulers of imperial Rome. Driven out of
Western political life by Christianity, it reappeared first in
a mitigated form with the teaching of Roman law at Bo-

logna. The emperor-king Frederick II and Philip the Fair of France, with the aid of their subservient jurists, were among the first rulers in Western Europe to apply the doctrine in the government of their dominions and their relations to the Church. The "Defensor Pacis" of Marsilius of Padua and Machiavelli's "Prince" are probably the best expositions of the doctrine in medieval and early modern times; it was known in the seventeenth and eighteenth centuries under the name of the "divine right of kings." In modern times the French Jacobins were the first to apply it to a republican form of government and the German philosophers Fichte and Hegel were its first well known exponents.

FICHTE

When Germany lay prostrate at the feet of Napoleon after the battles of Jena and Auerstadt, Fichte was one of the first to point out to his countrymen that the only hope of national regeneration and reconstruction lay in a complete reform of education, along the lines and in the spirit of national culture. Fichte's plan of educational reform and conception of nationality are outlined in his *Addresses to the German Nation*, which became the gospel of German nationalism and remain to this day the best known of his works. According to Fichte the essential, fundamental element of nationality is "culture." A group of men do not constitute a nation because they happen to dwell in the same country, or possess certain common racial characteristics; they form a nation when, and only if, they enjoy a common intellectual patrimony, when there is among them community of language and literature, artistic sentiment and scientific conceptions, community of beliefs, traditions, economic life. Most characteristic of national life, says Fichte, is language, because, better than any other element of culture, it expresses the psychology and genius of the people, their reactions to their environment and their views on life; and because of this community of language all Germans belong to one and the same family, the German nation, and that too, in spite of the artificial, arbitrary political divisions.

With Hegel the foundation of culture is not only national, but political, nation and state become synonymous. The state is not merely a political institution, concerned with the maintenance of order, the protection and defense of individual and national interests; it is the supreme, ideal social institution, antecedent and superior to the family, the local community, the nation and the Church. It is the foundation, the fountain-head and preserver of rights, material goods and culture. It is the law, it is the absolute. Its preservation and welfare should be the set purpose of all its citizens, because their welfare, nay their very existence as civilized people, is conditioned by the existence and welfare of the state. National culture, education, progress are products of political life; suppress the state and they must perish.

The relation of this Fichte-Hegelian conception of nationality to the function of education, and its bearing upon it, are obvious. If culture is at once the spiritual capital of the nation and the very condition of national life, it follows that the prime function of education, its chief purpose, is to preserve national culture, *i.e.*, national life, to enrich and transmit it. Education is to be national in aim, content, spirit, organization and methods. Education could have no better, no higher aim than the welfare and progress of the nation. Its finished product is not the man of culture, but the highly educated German, who is thoroughly im- bued with the spirit of national culture, effi-   and relation cient, self-supporting, contributing his own   to education. share to national welfare and progress, an intelligent, zealous protagonist of national culture and na- tional interests.   The school curriculum must, of course, remain what it has ever been: the instrument for mental development and discipline; but it has another, no less important function to perform; it must be an agency for national education, it must be the vehicle of the national spirit and national creed. Heretofore religion has been the central, essential element in the educational content. It must now yield this position to the national subjects: the national language, national literature, national art, national geography, history and civics, national legends, traditions and folklore, which must be the core to which all other sub- jects should be related. The family and the Church can no longer be the chief educational agencies, because the youth of the land belong to the state, because education is a state affair; its temple, its home, is the state owned, state con- trolled school; its priest and missionary is the teacher. Such in substance is the nationalist philosophy of education. It has been put into practice in most countries with varying degrees of thoroughness during the last one hundred years. Bol- shevism, Fascism and Action Française are its more recent labels.

Leaving aside references by writers on the socialist move- ment to utopian theories of classical antiquity and the Ren- aissance, like Plato's *Republic*, Plutarch's *Life of Lycurgus,* More's *Utopia* and Campanella's *City of the Sun*, the origins of socialism, such as we know it today, can be traced to the writings of eighteenth century social theorists like Meslier, Mably, and Rousseau. William Godwin's *Inquiry Concern-*

ing Political Justice, published in 1793, is one of the earliest expositions of the more radical conceptions The origins of socialism, and Babeuf's *Conspiracy* the of modern first attempt to translate those doctrines into socialism; practice through violent means. The French Revolution, in Babeuf's opinion, had in the main only profited the middle class. The economic condition of the French proletarians was still just as bad as before, if not worse; they should organize a revolution of their own for the purpose of "equalizing worth and abolishing poverty." Babeuf's *Conspiracy*, however, was nipped in the bud, his party was suppressed, and he was sent to the guillotine.

In the early years of the nineteenth century an Englishman, Robert Owen (1771-1858) and two Frenchmen, Comte Henri de Saint Simon (1760-1825) and François-Marie Fourier (1772-1837) attempted by peaceful means to carry out Babeuf's doctrines of social reform. The essential and common feature of their plans was the establishment of model communities in which the people would share the profits of their work. Louis Blanc (1811-1882), the leading French "socialist" of the next generation, advocated the establishment by the state of "workshops" in which the working men would choose the managers and divide the profits. Meanwhile the social and economic problems growing out of the development of the Industrial Revolution attracted everywhere the attention of economists, politicians, philanthropists, social workers and theorists of all creeds. The theories and principles which form today the body of socialism as a system of philosophy, the economic, that is, materialistic conception of history and society, the theories of "class war," "surplus value," etc., were being gradually formulated by radical thinkers in England, France, Germany, even Russia. Those principles and theories were organized into a system by Karl Marx (1818-1883) with the aid of his friend and brother-Hebrew, Friedrich Engels, first in the *Communist Manifesto* of 1848 and a few years later in the much more elaborate form of *Das Kapital*, which even to this day is the economic creed of the immense majority of socialists. "Proletarians of all lands, unite!", the closing sentence of the *Communist Manifesto*, became a reality with the organization of the "International Workingmen's Association" which originated in an informal gathering of English, French and Belgian laborers at the London Exposition in 1862 and became a permanent society two years later. Due chiefly to the opposition of Bakunin and the anarchist school this "First International" came formally to an end in 1876, but it had achieved its main purpose in making workingmen realize the international character of capitalism and their own grievances. The successful organization of the socialist movement is to be ascribed to another German Jew, Ferdinand Lassalle (1825-1864), the real originator of the German Social Democratic Party which became the model according to which were organized socialist parties in other countries. This brief historical survey of the socialist movement will help us, it is hoped, in gaining a clearer view of its philosophy to which we must now turn.

Leaving aside a consideration of the various shades of socialism, *i.e.,* Marxist socialism, reformed socialism, syndicalism, communism, collectivism, anarchism, bolshevism, etc., which has no place in a book of this kind, we shall confine ourselves to a brief study of the main tenets of the system insofar as they bear upon education. The essence of socialist philosophy is probably best expressed in the old aristotelian dictum that "man is by nature a political (social) animal," if we read it to mean that what is essentially human in man is a product of community life. Man is not a human being, says socialism, because of certain attributes, among them a tendency to seek the companionship of

fellowmen, which are supposed to be inherent in his nature;
he is not born a man in the truly human
its sense of the term; he becomes a man
philosophy through society, because society alone can
provide the conditions under which spir-
itual life, *i.e.*, the truly human life is possible. Are not
religion, traditions, morality, language, literature, science,
art, economic and political activities essentially social
phenomena? What would become of the individual without
his social environment? The individual's personality, his
moral character, his whole life are fashioned by the conditions of his surroundings. His thoughts, feelings and volitions are in the main prompted, directed by his social environment. The language he speaks is part of the social
inheritance and it came to him through intercourse with his
fellowmen; so it is of his beliefs, his views on life, on nature
and society, of traditions and customs; it all came to him
from the community, through social agencies, the family,
the Church, the school, the library, the newspaper, the thea-
ter, etc. Individual life as such is a nonentity, for it is nothing else at best than a mirror of social life which alone has
any reality, and that means, among other things, that the
only sound view of culture and its branches is the social
view. Language, literature, art, science, philosophy, religion
are various expressions of community life in any given age
or country and they should therefore be treated as such.
Ethics and morality, for instance, have in themselves nothing absolute, final or transcendental; they are a social creation. That which benefits the community is good; that
which may prove harmful to the community is evil. Good
and evil are relative; their character varies with time and
country. What is good at a given time, in a given community may become an evil at another time, in another
community. So it is with religion; society creates it, fash-
ions it to its own image, and for its own particular pur-

poses; remove religion from its social background and it ceases to possess any meaning or reality.

Like naturalism with which it has much affinity, socialism views life as an essentially physical process. Social life is synonymous with economic life. Social questions are invariably treated by socialism as questions of the body: sanitation, factory conditions, employment of women and children, wages, hours of work, housing conditions, unemployment, pauperism and the like. These, to be sure, are excellent ends in themselves, but lacking the spiritual leaven of Christianity they cannot solve the "social question," for the very simple reason that being purely economic they can only minister to bodily wants; they cannot satisfy human aspirations; likewise, and for the very same reason, this is true of the socialist dream of an equal distribution of earthly goods under state supervision. Socialism has nothing to offer that would bridge the chasm between boundless human desires and the possession of material goods, which it teaches men to regard as a "summum bonum" and which from their very nature are so limited in quantity, quality and duration.

From those conceptions of society, human nature and human life there flows an educational programme which in many respects is the very antithesis of the traditional curriculum; its protagonists like to refer to it as the "education of the future." It is expounded and discussed at great length in a host of articles, pamphlets, books, which have appeared within the last forty years in Europe and America; *The School of the Future, Integral Education, The School of Activity, The Free School, The Common School, The Workingman's School, The New School*, are the more common labels attached by its advocates to this new type of education. The American, John Dewey, the Frenchman, E. Durkheim, the Germans, P. Natorp and G. Kerschensteiner, the Russians, A. Lunatcharsky and Mme. Lenine, the Spaniard,

F. Ferrer,[1] are the best known exponents of the innovation. Many isolated attempts have been made, particularly since the close of the World War to carry out parts of the programme assigned to the "New School." Russia is the only country, so far, that has tried to carry out the programme in its entirety. A brief description of the and relation more salient features of the Russian experito education ment, together with citations from the pronouncements of those in charge of it will give us an idea of the animus and general trend of "integral" socialist pedagogy. Let it be remarked to begin with that consistency is one of the things one should not look for in the system. Time and again we are brought face to face with glaring contradictions between theory and practice, between promises made by socialism and their actual realization. Freedom, we are told, is the principle upon which the bolshevist school, like the bolshevist political economic system, is founded. "But," remarks Mme. Lenine, "autonomy is out of the question for the school, because it would be a dangerous weapon in the hands of 'bourgeois,' reactionary propagandists."[2] As a safeguard against that danger the school is placed under the joint control of the people's commissars, a committee of parents and a council of public instruction made up of delegates from the local civil administration, teachers and students; the people's commissars, of course, always reserve the right to modify, or even set aside the decisions of the other two branches of the board of education. "The aim of the socialist school," writes P. Birukoff, "is to form 'integral' men, fit for any kind of work, whether physical or intellectual."[3] In other words, the aim of the socialist school is to turn out men who, as the occasion may

---

[1] All of them belong to the second half of the nineteenth and the twentieth century.
[2] Madame Lenine, Une école Socialiste.
[3] Birukoff, P., Rapport sur le premier congrès international des étudiants socialistes, p. 237.

require, can be shoemakers, carpenters, locksmiths, street-cleaners, chemists, engineers, and what not! Such at least was the interpretation of the pronouncement by the Russian proletariat in the early days of the Revolution. E. Vander-velde, one of the leaders of the Belgian Socialist Party, re-lates that in the Donetz mining district, managers, engineers, accountants, were compelled to exchange their positions for those of the men in the pits who, most of them illiterate, thus had their opportunity to run the mining busi-ness. Needless to say, the experiment was shortlived.[1] Socialist assertions to the contrary notwithstanding, the truth of the matter is, in this question of educational aims, that socialism is not interested in "forming men," not interested in the "integral" development of man's physical and intel-lectual capacities; its one set purpose is to turn out cogs for the huge economic machine it seeks to control. Useful, "free," yet compulsory manual work occupies the central position in school activities. In the early stage of school life, with children of three to seven years of age, there can be no question, of course, of this "free" manual work being "use-ful"; its chief purpose is to familiarize the child with the atmosphere of socialist life, but during the following periods, in late elementary and in secondary education, manual work is expected to be productive economically; a close relation is then established between the school and the surrounding industrial life.

Education is free, public, co-educational, of the same gen-eral polytechnic character for both sexes, received in the same type of schools all through Russia up to the age of sixteen; boys and girls can then attend whatever higher school they like. A thoroughly levelling system, indeed; what results it will achieve the future will tell. In order to foster the spirit of "free association," thus preparing the rising generation for an efficient participation in the socialist

[1] Vandervelde, E., Trois aspects de la révolution russe, pp. 28-29.

state, the administration of the schools is, in a generous measure, under the control of its students; they have a right to send delegates to the teachers' meetings, they have a say in the preparation of schedules, courses of study, questions of attendance, discipline, appointment, retention or dismissal of teachers. Freedom, independence for the young is the motto of bolshevist education and the young, of course, take advantage of it to the full.

It is hardly necessary to point out:

1. That a system of education which does away with effort, self-control, takes it for granted that the problem of educating the young has been solved when school life begins;

2. That the conditions of school life are not and cannot be a replica of the conditions of social, industrial life;

3. That a systematic unification of schools and school programs, by ignoring the fact of diversity of talents and aptitudes, runs counter to nature and shuts the door to progress;

4. That a school system which extols manual activities at the expense of intellectual work condemns the community to hiring its leaders from other countries.

No mention has been made of the family in this very brief expose of "integral" socialist education. Like the Church and other traditional institutions of "capitalistic" society the family thus far has been looked upon as an enemy. The educative influence of home life has been practically nil since 1918.

The first signs of a tendency to build up state school systems have been recorded in connection with the influence of the Protestant Revolution on the schools,[1] the beginnings of Christian education in America and the eighteenth century school reforms.[2] The complete realization of that tendency's aim has been achieved in the last one hundred and fifty years with Germany in the lead, and in Germany with Prussia in the vanguard of the movement. In 1808 there was

[1] See Vol. II, ch. V.
[2] *Ibid.*, ch. VII.

created in Prussia a Department of Public Instruction organized as a branch of the Department of the Interior. One of the first steps of the acting head of the new Department was to send seventeen Prussian teachers to Yverdun, in order to study Pestalozzian aims and methods. Upon their return to Prussia those seventeen teachers were appointed directors of training institutions or superintendents of schools. Wherever men could be found either in Prussia or in other states who were imbued with the Pestalozzian spirit and were able to apply the Pestalozzian methods of instruction they were induced to enter the Prussian school system. In this way were Pestalozzian ideas soon at work in the elementary school and there was achieved in a few years an educational reform which proved to be a telling factor in national regeneration. In order to give stability to the reform many teachers' seminaries were established and those who desired to enter these institutions were carefully selected. By 1840 Prussia had thirty-eight teachers' seminaries and approximately thirty thousand elementary schools; a new spirit had been infused into elementary education and the position of the elementary school teacher had been raised to the rank of a profession. The schools referred to here were known as people's schools (Volkschulen); they were gratuitous and attended mostly by the children of the lower classes; their course of study extended over a period of eight years, but did not directly prepare for the secondary schools; the only further training a pupil could obtain after completing the people's school was through a commercial or industrial or continuation school. Parallel to the elementary schools were the intermediate schools, Mittelschulen, with one more class than the people's school and offering a modern language during the last three years; they were attended by the middle class children whose parents could not

State School Systems in Germany,

afford to send them to a secondary institution and yet could pay the lower fees of the middle schools.[1]

Alongside the reforms of elementary schools there went a complete reorganization of secondary and higher institutions. In 1807 the Department of Public Instruction was changed from a bureau of the Department of the Interior into a separate Ministry of spiritual and Instructional affairs. In 1825 governing school boards were established in all the provinces of the kingdom and made responsible to the Ministry for Education in Berlin. By this time a well organized state school system had become an accomplished fact. A few years previous to the establishment of the provincial boards a unified plan for the preparation and examination of prospective secondary school teachers had been put into effect. The examinations were to be conducted by University professors for the State; those examinations, of course, presupposed attendance at a university for some time, and they were to bear upon all gymnasial subjects, allowing the selection of a specialty. Pedagogical seminars were established at the universities in which candidates for secondary school positions could receive some pedagogical training. Later on, more stringent regulations still were issued for the appointment of secondary school teachers, as for instance a year of trial teaching before appointment. A similar reform was made in other departments of the national civil service, the main feature of which was the leaving examination (Maturitätsprüfing). In 1834 the passing of such an examination became a prerequisite for entering nearly all branches of the State civil service. One of the consequences of this regulation was the unification of the curriculum in the then existing secondary institutions. All nine year schools now assumed the name of Gymnasien and adapted their course of study to the State requirements; Latin, Greek, German,

---

[1] Conditions in elementary education have been slightly altered by the establishment of the Republic.

mathematics, history, geography, science and religion were to be taught in all those schools for so many hours a week with the classics in the lead. Secondary schools which could not meet the standards of the nine year classical course were classed as Pro-gymnasien or else as Burgenschulen, *i.e.*, middle class or intermediate schools. The few real schools (Realschulen) then existing were permitted to continue as middle class institutions. As a consequence of further legislation there were at the close of the nineteenth century six classes of secondary schools; the traditional Gymnasium with the classical languages as its main feature; the Realgymnasium with Latin but no Greek and a nine-year course: the Oberrealschule with a nine-year course but without either Latin or Greek; below those institutions were the Pro-gymnasium, the Realpro-gymnasium and the Realschule which did not carry the student more than six years and had a curriculum corresponding to one or the other of the nine-year course institutions. The graduates of schools with a nine-year course of study were granted the privilege of studying at the universities in all or some of the university subjects according to the type of school from which they came. The preliminary training needed to enter a secondary school could be obtained at the people's schools, or middle schools, or in a Vorschule, a sort of preparatory school attached to the secondary school. During the last decade of the century there appeared a new type of secondary school known as reform school, whose curriculum was so organized as to make possible without any appreciable loss of time to the boy, his transfer from the classical or semi-classical course to the scientific and vice versa.

Though the universities are legally State institutions, being established only by the State or with the State's approval, they are not generally governed by legislation but by their charters and decrees from the ministers of public education. They are mainly supported by the State and managed internally by a senate and rector, the latter elected annually by the full professors from their own number. The work of the Prussian universities is now carried along the lines of the reform introduced at the foundation of the University of Berlin which is recorded in another chapter of this volume.[1] Closely related with the elementary, middle, and secondary schools and the universities there has been evolved in Germany a system of continuation, commercial, agricultural and industrial schools of all grades and description which gave the country her industrial and commercial leadership before the World War. During the last ten years there has been a tendency to unify still more the German school system by bringing the kindergarten everywhere under State control and by establishing a close relation between the curriculum of the common school and that of the secondary school and thus make the work of the first a preparation for entrance into the second.

Subordination to a central government which has been for centuries the tendency of French administrative policy is probably the most characteristic feature of the French school system. Its founder was Napoleon, but the form it has received in the main embodies the ideas expressed in the legislation of the Revolution and the suggestions made in the plans submitted to the Government by Talleyrand, Condorcet, Lakanal and others.[2] What Napoleon did was to shape ideas and suggestions into some sort of working order. All secondary and higher institutions were organized by him into a single corporation controlled by the central government and known as the "University of France, of France." The plan of this University provided for a two-fold system of secondary schools: the lycées, institutions of a national character, and the collèges or local institutions. The scope of the work

[1] See ch. VIII.
[2] See ch. IV.

of the collège was not usually so wide as that of the lycée, but in both, as everywhere then in Europe, it showed a strong classical bend. Reorganization did not result as it did in Germany in the creation of new types of schools but in the establishment of a sort of elective system in the old ones. The course of study is very much the same for all students during the first two or three years of school life; after that, there take place bifurcations leading to different types of courses devised to meet the demands of general preparation for the various careers. Preparation for entrance at the lycée or collège may be received in the primary school or in the preparatory department of the secondary institution. No provision was made in the original plan of the "University" for the secondary education of girls. Until late in the nineteenth century those who could afford it would attend some private institution where they would receive a preparation as prospective wives and mothers in the middle or upper classes, but in the last fifty years there have been founded many public and private secondary schools for girls which favorably compare with the same type of institutions for boys.

No state provision worth mentioning was made for elementary education until the reign of Louis Philippe (1830-1848). In the early days of that reign Victor Cousin (1792-1867) was sent on a mission to Germany and particularly Prussia to study the systems of elementary education, teacher training, organization and administration of the schools. His "Report on the Condition of Public Instruction in Germany and particularly in Prussia" made a deep impression in France. On the basis of that Report a bill was prepared which eventually became the law of 1833, the foundation upon which the French national system of elementary education stands. A primary school was to be established and maintained in every commune, or at least for a group of two or three communes, the State reserving the right to fix the minimum salary for the teacher and even to approve his appointment. The subjects taught were to be reading, writing, arithmetic, the metric system, the French language, morals and religion. In the department capitals and large towns there were to be established higher primary schools, corresponding more or less in nature and scope of work to the German Burgenschulen. Inspectors of primary education were to be appointed and normal schools under State control were to be established in every department. Subsequent legislation has developed the provisions of the law of 1833. Elementary education has been made compulsory between the ages of six and thirteen, normal schools in all departments have become an actuality, and there have also been established two higher normal schools, one for men and one for women, to train teachers for the departmental normal schools, those higher normal schools being independent of the original normal school founded during the Revolution to train teachers for the secondary schools. The higher primary schools which were suppressed under the Second Empire (1852-1870) have been re-established. "Ecoles maternelles" for children between two and six years of age and "infant classes" for pupils from five to seven years have also become a part of the primary school system. Supplementary courses of a technical character have been added to the primary curriculum and there also have been founded many continuation "schools of manual apprenticeship" together with five large schools for training in special crafts in Paris. The whole system has been secularized by the substitution of civic and moral instruc-

VICTOR COUSIN

tion for religion, by excluding members of the clergy from the public teaching staff and closing "free" schools conducted by the religious congregations.

The old French universities which had been swept away by the Revolution were replaced in Napoleon's plan by single faculties scattered throughout the country, in the various "académies" or administrative divisions of the "University of France." Of late years there has been a complete reorganization of higher education, the country going back to the old type of university. The degrees conferred are the "licence"

CHARTER HOUSE

or master's degree and the doctorate; licenciates intending to teach in the lycées may also win the "aggregation" through a competitive examination. The degree of bachelor which follows the completion of the lycée course is conferred after the passing of an examination conducted in each "académie" by a committee of university professors.

The building up of an English state school system did not begin until 1833. All English schools were of the "voluntary" or private initiative type. "The Society for the Promotion of Christian Knowledge" and "The Society for the Propagation of the Gospel in Foreign Parts," both founded around 1700 provided some facilities for elementary education in England and her colonies in the form of "charity" schools.

Other types of "voluntary" schools followed in the course of the eighteenth and nineteenth centuries, under various names: day schools, evening schools, children's churches, shoeblack brigades, bands of hope, clothing clubs, messengers brigades, ragged schools, orphans schools, reformatory schools, Sunday schools. Those types of "voluntary" schools, in the main, belonged to the eighteenth century though some continued in the nineteenth. Joseph Lancaster (1778-1838) and Andrew Bell (1753-1832) launched, independently of each other, it seems, another variation of voluntary education known as the "monitorial" or mutual system which was very flourishing in England and England, to some extent in the United States during the first half of the nineteenth century. The first school of this kind in England was probably that founded by Joseph Lancaster at Southwark, London, in 1798. It proved to be a remarkable success from the very beginning. Monitorial schools were soon established everywhere and there was founded a society first known as the "Lancastrian Institution," later on as the "British and Foreign Society," to foster the propagation of the monitorial system. The curriculum of the Society's schools included religion but permitted no denominational instruction of any kind. To the Church of England this non-conformist type of religious education appeared as a menace to its hold on the people and to forestall the danger there was organized a "National Society" for the establishment of schools in which would be taught the Anglican Catechism and Prayer Book. Doctor Andrew Bell, who had achieved some success in the use of the monitorial system at the Male Asylum of Madras, was put in charge of the schools. Though the monitorial or mutual system of teaching was not new at the beginning of the nineteenth century, it was the work of Bell and Lancaster which gave it prominence in modern times. In both the Lancastrian and Bell plans the system essentially consisted in this, that the teacher would teach the lesson to monitors or more advanced students, who would in turn impart it to groups of ten or twelve pupils for each monitor. Classroom work under those conditions could hardly be anything else than drill, memoriter work in the elements of reading, writing, arithmetic and religion. Discipline of a rather rigid character had to be enforced by all kinds of devices. The great service of the monitorial system to the cause of education in England was to awaken the nation to the need of a system of national schools and for some time to afford a substitute, though a poor one, for those schools.

The first step in the establishment of the English national school system was a parliamentary grant of £20,000 in 1833 for schools, following a reform bill which increased the suffrage, thus making it incumbent upon the government to educate the prospective voters to their new duties. The grant was increased to £30,000 in 1839 and government inspection of the schools was inaugurated. With the further extension of the franchise in 1868 the necessity of preparing great masses of the population for new responsibilities led to the passage, in 1870, of the Foster Bill, creating local boards for the establishment of public schools wherever needed. The voluntary schools shared in the government grants with the board schools, but the latter also received local rates. Religious instruction of a denominational character was forbidden in the board schools though never interfered with in the voluntary schools. The sharing in the government's grants was determined in all schools by the inspector's report. Further steps towards state control, were the passing of compulsory attendance laws, an extra grant to take the place of tuition fee, and the creation of a Board of Education. In 1902 the voluntary schools were admitted to a share in the local rates and the immediate supervision of

instruction was placed in the hands of a school board of
managers appointed jointly by the county councils and the
trustees of the schools. The bill of 1902 also extended the
powers of the Board of Education over the secondary schools
in an attempt to bring them into the national system of
schools.

Technically the English universities do not belong to the
national system of schools. They have preserved their autonomy and they are governed by their respective charters,
but they all breathe the same spirit of national educational
expansion and have enlarged the scope of their work to
meet the demands of the political, social and economic
movements of the last one hundred years. They are as a
rule admirably equipped for technical specialty and make
ample provision for the training of teachers in both the
theory and practice of their profession. While science and
technology are in many of them the subjects of chief interest, their curricula include a fair amount of classical studies,
thus uniting old traditions and the requirements of a scientific age. In most of them too women are admitted to share
equally with men in the benefits of higher education. This
scientific trend and liberal policy in higher education is one
of the characteristics of the new universities established in
the great industrial and commercial centers like London,
Manchester, Glasgow, Birmingham, but even Oxford and
Cambridge, the strongholds of conservatism in English education have yielded to the spirit of the age.

Universal education under state control has its most con-
sistent form in the United States but it was not reached at
a bound. We witnessed its beginnings in the middle of the
seventeenth century in the New England colonies which
may be said to have inaugurated the first real system of
public education. By the beginning of the eighteenth century, however, the once flourishing New England school
system was in a state of decline which endured for about a

century and a half. At the outbreak of the Revolution the
New England elementary schools, like those
in other colonies, were either private or   the United
maintained by some church or philanthropic   States.
society, and this state of affairs continued
well into the nineteenth century. Thus in the City of New
York a "Free School Society" known later as the "Public
School Society" was founded in 1805 to provide for boys who
were not eligible for the private or church or charity schools
existing at that time. The Society received many private gifts
from the legislature, the city and private individuals, and in
1828 it was even allowed the benefit of a small local tax.
For a number of years it supported many elementary schools
on a monitorial basis, but its most important achievement
was to awaken the people to the need of public schools. The
case is typical not only of New York but of other cities in
New York State and other States of the Union as well.

The young American Republic was theoretically committed to the doctrine of free public schools, but the people
were for some time unwilling to be taxed for their support.
The awakening and growth of a "public school consciousness," *i.e.*, a willingness on the part of the American public
to support out of the public funds a system of common
schools was the great educational event in American history
during the first half of the nineteenth century. The chief
centers of the movement were Massachusetts and Connecticut, and its leading protagonists were Horace Mann (1796-
1859) and Henry Barnard (1811-1900). During the twelve
years of his tenure as Secretary to the newly created Board of
Education of Massachusetts, Horace Mann carried on a vigorous campaign for school reforms. Most effective among the
means he employed were his annual reports on the condition
of the schools and the progress made during the year, and
the Massachusetts Common School Journal devoted to
spreading information concerning school improvement,

school law, the proceedings of the State Board, duties toward the school of school officials, parents and children. Due in the main to his efforts the appropriations made for public education were more than doubled, many new high schools were established, school attendance increased enormously and a full month was added to the average school year; two State normal schools were founded and the average salary of teachers was increased by more than fifty per cent. Many

new buildings replaced the old, inadequate and squalid school houses, and the methods of instruction were much improved.

Horace M a n n w a s mainly a practical reformer; his interest lay mostly in the material, administrative side of education. Henry Barnard, on the other hand, by temperament and training was mostly interested in the literary, intellectual side of school life, though he too occupied important

HENRY BARNARD

places in educational administration. He was for some time secretary to the Connecticut State Board, was then called to Rhode Island to become its Commissioner of Common Schools, and after a few years in that position returned to Connecticut to become Superintendent of Schools. For brief periods he was President of the University of Wisconsin and St. John's College in Maryland. He also had the distinction of being the first United States Commissioner of Education. Even in those positions, however, his main concern was in the common schools and educational literature. While still

Superintendent of Schools in Connecticut he had suggested the establishment of a national journal of education that would supply "a series of publications, which should, on the one hand, embody the mature views and varied experience of wise statesmen, educators and teachers . . . and on the other . . . serve as a medium of free and frequent communications between the friends of education in every portion of these great fields." He had hoped that the "American Association for the Advancement of Education" would help him to carry out the enterprise; when it failed him he undertook it upon his own responsibility. Time and again the work was interrupted by other duties, but it continued for more than a generation until at length over thirty large volumes had been issued, a splendid educational encyclopedia.

HORACE MANN

The United States public school system such as it exists today, was already, in essentials at least, an accomplished fact in the Northern States before the Civil War. It still had to be introduced into the South and there still remained much to be done in the North towards perfecting the system, but the principle had been firmly established, that the American system of education was to be democratic throughout—a public school supported by general taxation, free and equally open to all, non-sectarian in spirit and curriculum, controlled by the civil authorities and offering instruction from the very beginning of school life through the high school, and in some States even the university. At the beginning of the present century the principle had been translated into actual practice everywhere in the Union. That, however, let it be remarked, should not convey the impression that there is now in the United States a national, highly centralized system of schools such as obtains in some European countries. Education is regarded as a function of the separate States and local communities, and the extent of the control over education exercised by the civil authorities varies from State to State. The educational activities of the Federal Government are limited to information, advice and financial aid, carried on through the United States Bureau of Education, the Federal Board of Vocational Education and other agencies connected with the Departments of Agriculture, of Labor and of the Treasury. The Board of Education, created as a separate Department in 1867, was made a little later on a Bureau of the Department of the Interior where it has remained ever since. Its two administrative duties have been the direction of schools for the natives of Alaska and the supervision of the accounts of the so-called "land grant" colleges of agriculture and mechanical arts, made possible by the Morrill Act of 1862. In the last fifteen years the Bureau of Education has also been much interested in the promotion of research work in the various fields of education and in making educational surveys of states, local committees, and types of institutions. Its publications, partly free and partly sold at cost price, have done much to spread in the country an adequate knowledge of its educational conditions and needs. Of late there have been several unsuccessful attempts in Congress to transform the Bureau of Education into a Federal Department in which would be vested the whole control of education in the Union. Not until state consciousness has died out, however—and it is very much alive today—will any such attempt have chances of success.

The Federal Board of Vocational Education was established in 1917. Its function is to co-operate with the States in the maintenance of programs of vocational education of less than college grade in agriculture, trade and industry, and to prepare vocational teachers. The activities of that Board also include the administration of the Civilian Vocational Rehabilitation Act, whereby the Federal Government co-operates with the States in the vocational rehabilitation of persons disabled in industry. Federal educational activities also include agricultural education, health education, maternity education, education of the immigrant, support of the Indian schools and administration of schools in the Philippines and Porto Rico; these activities belong to various departments and are carried on through co-operation with allied agencies of the States. The only branch of the United States Educational System that comes directly under Federal control is the training of the land and sea forces; though even in this case there is again some co-operation with the States for the training of reserve forces.

To complete this brief survey of federal educational activity, mention should be made of Child Labor Legislation, initiated in Congress and submitted for ratification to the various States. Its only purpose is to stimulate educational progress in some States, especially for the period between fourteen and eighteen, which is not generally considered as a period of education but rather as one of supervised industrial employment. Apart from the federal activities referred to above, education in the United States is today, as it has ever been in the past, a state and local affair. In every State there is a school official, more commonly designated as State Superintendent of Public Instruction or State Commissioner of Education, who is in charge of the school administration in the state. The powers and salary attached to the office naturally vary from one state to another.

Introduced in the country as a private undertaking, kindergarten education for children between four and six years is now incorporated in the system of most cities to the extent of at least one year of training. Recent investigations, however, have shown that less than ⅛ of the children between the ages of four and six attend kindergartens. More recently there has developed a movement to promote the establishment of nursery schools for children below four. There are as yet few schools of that type, but researches and discussions dealing with child welfare show that there is in the country a general interest in this aspect of education.

The age of compulsory attendance at school varies from State to State as also the effectiveness of the enforcement of the law. Most States now make school attendance compulsory from the age of seven to that of sixteen, but in some States the limit is placed beyond that age. Differences in the ratio of attendance to the number of children are also very marked. In California and a few other States the ratio is as high as 80%, indicating a practically perfect elementary school attendance and a heavy enrollment of the kindergarten and high school, whereas in some other States the ratio of children at school between the specified ages is as low as 50%. Inadequacy of school provision and laxity in the enforcement of school laws in some States is also shown by the extent of illiteracy. In 1920 there were nearly five million illiterates in the United States, of whom more than three million were native born. The shortness of the yearly school period in some districts and the poor quality of teaching may account for such a large number of illiterates.

As late as 1910 the accepted school organization, irrespective of kindergarten and college, meant an elementary school of eight years or grades, followed by a secondary school of four years—the high school—the so-called 8-4 plan.

Within the last fifteen years this type of organization has gradually given way to a new policy of six years of elementary education followed by six years of secondary education, *i.e.*, three years of Junior High School and three years of Senior High School, or the 6-3-3 plan, which is now being rapidly put into effect everywhere. Occasionally the reform has gone beyond the high school by organizing the first two years of the traditional college course into the "Junior College."

Recent studies of curriculum arrangements have shown that the above-mentioned reorganization has meant much more than mere external change. The first year of the "junior high school" (seventh year of school life) is commonly used for the study of subjects common to all; electives are gradually introduced during the next two years, and the tendency seems to be to use the senior high school as the place for specialized work. The same policy obtains in the relation of junior college to the two years following it. Another consequence of the school reorganization has been the lengthening of the period of secondary education which used to be limited to the four years of high school, but has now extended downwards and upwards so as to include four additional years, and is brought appreciably nearer the European continental type.

One of the most discussed questions in American education today is that of curriculum revision. In 1925, three hundred public school systems were at work on the problem. The purpose of this movement is to make suggestions for what is styled "a growing curriculum" rather than to attempt the drafting of anything like a uniform course of study, and the movement has already produced some tangible results. A consideration of the time allotment in the new courses of studies shows a decided departure from the elementary curriculum policy of twenty years ago. The three R's have retained their position, but health and physical education now follow close upon the traditional subjects, and there is a tendency to stress art, music and other creative activities, which is a marked departure from the predominantly intellectual education of a generation ago. As to secondary education, limiting the period to the high school or its equivalent, statistics published by the United States Bureau of Education show that language and mathematics still occupy the leading position in spite of the elective system of studies and all that has been said and is still said about vocationalizing secondary education. Judging from the number of students who take it English is by far the leading subject; then follow in order of importance: algebra, Latin, music, geometry, civics, general science, ancient history, home economics, typewriting, bookkeeping, Spanish, manual training, physics, shorthand, biology, chemistry, hygiene and sanitation, agriculture and economics. German, taken by one-fourth of the high school students in 1916, was taken by less than 1% in 1921. Its place seems to have been taken by Spanish, but it has of late shown a rapid growth.

There are now in the United States some eight hundred universities, colleges and professional schools in which are enlisted some 700,000 students, the ratio of men to women being approximately two to one. Unlike elementary and secondary education, which is overwhelmingly public, higher education in the United States is still predominantly under private auspices, both as to the number of students and of schools. Most of those institutions are endowed, some indeed royally, and the gifts continue to pour in year after year. In the face of huge enrollments tending to lower the standard of university and college work, an attempt has been made of late to introduce "honors' courses" which stress the quality of intellectual attainment in higher education, and would, it is argued, set a higher academic standard for the average student than the system actually in use. The lack of uniform work and standards is far more conspicuous in American higher education than it is in elementary and secondary, and that too in spite of strenuous attempts at standardization made in the last twenty-five years. As to organization an American university is, generally speaking, composed of an undergraduate department, a college of liberal arts, requiring for admission a four-year high school diploma or its equivalent, a graduate department consisting of professional schools or colleges for the study of medicine, law, engineering, etc., requiring for entrance one or two years in the college of liberal arts; there are still many students, however, who prefer to complete the liberal arts college course and receive their bachelor degree before taking up studies in the professional schools.

The wide variety of educational conditions prevailing in the United States, which has been referred to several times, is perhaps best illustrated in the situation concerning the preparation, certification and compensation of teachers. For many years it was the general practice to require from prospective teachers in city elementary schools, two years of normal school training beyond the secondary school, and to require college education for high school teaching; of late there has been a tendency to strengthen the requirements. Professional training beyond the college is now required in many places for high school teaching, and elementary school teachers are recruited so far as possible among college, even university graduates. On the other hand the preparation of teachers is still far from what it should be in rural districts, where thousands of elementary school teachers can be found who have never completed their high school education. Compensation for teaching service varies no less widely, from four thousand dollars and above in some cities to less than five hundred in rural districts. As remarked before, while higher education is still mostly conducted under private auspices, elementary schools are now for the most part public institutions; of the more than twenty-two million children in elementary schools, only approximately two million are in private institutions, mostly Catholic parochial schools.

The four types of school systems outlined in the foregoing paragraphs have been imitated in more or less detail by other nations. The Prussian school plan has been most influential in Germany, the former Austro-Hungarian Empire, in Russia and Scandinavia; in lesser degree the plan has been imitated in smaller neighboring states like Holland, in Japan, China and America. The influence of the French plan has been paramount in Latin Europe and America, though one may find there elements borrowed from the school systems of the United States or England or Germany.

Differing in details of organization and administration, scope of government control, extent of state support, percentage of the population they actually reach, all national systems have this in common, that they are used for the promotion of the national culture, national ideals and national interest at home and abroad.

"Practically all modern nations are now awake to the fact that education is the most potent means in the development of the essentials of nationality. Education is the means by which peoples of retarded culture may be brought rapidly to the common level. Education is the means by which small and weak nations may become so strong through their cultural strength and achievements that their place in the political world may be made secure. Education is the means by which nations, strong in the strength of the past, may go through the perilous transition to the modern world, as has Japan and as will Russia. Education is the only means by which the world can be 'made safe' for the national type of organization."[1]

National unity in ideals, language and culture, national solidarity in interests, subservience to the State in all its

[1] Monroe, P., Introduction to "Teachers College Syllabi, No. 9. on Democracy and Nationalism in Education."

policies is today as we saw in the opening pages of this chapter the set policy of every nation, small or great, and because this national unity is "an artificial product which can be manufactured by education" the promotion of nationalism is everywhere made the paramount aim of the school. With those nationalistic aims there is everywhere, in degrees that vary with time and country, an admixture of socialistic philosophy, coming not so much from above as from the ranks of the teachers and student body, large numbers of whom, particularly in the great commercial and industrial centres have been bred in the atmosphere of the Marxian philosophy of life.

REFERENCES

Balfour, G., The Educational Systems of Great Britain and Ireland.
Barnard, H., American Journal of Education.
Boone, R. G., Education in the United States.
Browne, E. E., The Making of Our Middle Schools.
Cathrein, A., Der Socialismus.
Defourny, M., La Sociologie positiviste.
Dexter, E. G., History of Education in the United States.
Foerster, Fr. W., Christentum und Klassenkampf.
Gréard, O., Législation de l'instruction primaire en France.
Montmorency, J. E. G., De, State Intervention in English Education.
Paulsen, F., German Education.

CHAPTER X

CATHOLIC EDUCATION

IN THE COURSE OF OUR SURVEY OF EDUCA-
tion in the last four hundred years we witnessed the
gradual destruction of the vast and varied system of legislation and institutions which for centuries had served the
cause of Christian education. With the suppression of monasteries, of chantries, cathedral and collegiate chapters,
benefices attached to guilds, grammar schools, colleges and
other foundations, came the cessation of educational activity
connected with those institutions. In Protestant countries the
work of confiscation was accomplished at the time of the
Reformation, in the sixteenth century;[1] in France, Belgium
and Italy it began with the French Revolution;[2] in other
lands it took place in the nineteenth century and it is still
going on. Spoliation, however, never has changed nor will
it ever change the attitude of the Church towards education.
She may be robbed of what material goods she may possess
but she cannot give up her right to teach. Being a perfect
society she has the right to maintain schools of her own
which from their very nature are public,
though the State may consider them as private institutions. She has the exclusive right
to teach religion to Catholic children; when
parents or lay teachers teach it, they do it
with her express permission and under her supervision. She
does not, of course, deny the right of the State to levy taxes

The right of
the Church to
teach.

[1] See Vol. II, ch. IV.
[2] See ch. IX.

for education, to maintain a public school system, to compel attendance, to see that the laws of public health, public order and public morality are observed, but she considers a State monopoly of education as nothing short of tyranny, and she cannot approve schools in which the teaching of religion is omitted. Not only is religion the most important subject in education but its relation to the whole field of knowledge is such that the teaching of secular subjects will not bear its best fruit unless it be related to and vivified by religion.

A detailed history of Catholic educational activities the world over during the last one hundred and fifty years is of course out of the question here. All that can reasonably be aimed at in the following pages is a short description of the more salient features of that history with a brief explanation of the nature and purpose of Catholic education. With the firm establishment throughout the world, during the nineteenth century, of state jurisdiction in matters of education, ways and means had to be devised to safeguard the Catholic faith. A uniform plan of action was of course out of the question. The problem facing the Church was one that called for national, even local solutions, the consideration of particular circumstances of time and place, the greater or lesser degree of freedom allowed to Catholic action.

In Germany and Austria Hungary, before the World War, while the supreme control of the schools was vested in the government the ecclesiastical authorities were granted a degree of control and supervision which would vary according to circumstances and localities. In some districts, as for instance in the Rhineland provinces, the "confessional," *i.e.*, denominational schools, were the rule, whereas in others the problem of religious education was solved through simul-

Catholic education in Germany and Austria Hungary,

taneous, *i.e.*, mixed schools, the children of any given denomination receiving religious instruction from an official representative of their denomination who was a salaried teacher like the instructor in any other subject. The school systems of those countries were reorganized after the War but the status of Catholic education is still in the main what it was before.

At the dawn of the nineteenth century France was practically without schools. The old educational foundations had been swept away by the Revolution and in France, the congregations which for centuries had provided the nation with teachers had been driven out of the country. Reconstruction in this as in other

FATHER GIRARD

branches of national administration was the work of Napoleon and it was carried on in the spirit of state centralization. The decree creating the "University of France" declared that "public instruction, in the whole Empire, is confined exclusively to the University" and that "no school, no establishment for instruction, can be formed independent of the Imperial University, and without the authority of its chief." Except in the field of higher education the state monopoly was for a long time more theoretical than actual; alongside of state or city secondary schools there were many "licensed" religious colleges, and many primary schools were conducted by the Brothers of the Christian schools. There were over six thousand religious schools in 1850 and by 1870 the number had increased to nearly twelve thousand. In 1904 the Government ruled that "teaching of every grade and every kind is forbidden in France to the members of the congregations." The decree resulted in the closing of 14,404 out of 16,904 "congregational" schools. Since that time Catholic education in France has been re-organized by establishing private schools in which are employed laymen and laywomen or secularized members of the congregations.

In Belgium, state monopoly in education was one of the causes leading to the secession of the country from Holland in 1830. Catholics and Liberals, the two national parties, were then and remained for   in Belgium, some time in full agreement on the government's educational policy. Every one then was still convinced of the paramount importance of religion in the education of the young. The law of 1842, which received a unanimous vote in both Chambers made religious instruction compulsory in the schools, but dispensed dissenters from attendance. With the dissolution in the forties, of the Union which had won the country's independence, the Liberals, under the influence of the Masonic lodges, adopted a policy of systematic warfare on the Church and Catholic education. Brought to power in 1879, this for the last time, they drafted a school law which Belgian Catholics still refer to as the "Law of Misfortune." It was in every respect the reverse of the law of 1842; religious instruction was excluded from the schools and all graduates of free, *i.e.*, religious normal schools, were as such refused the state teaching certificate. The Catholic members of the legislature refused to take part in the discussion of the law thus compelling the Liberals to shoulder the full responsibility before the country. The Catholic masses were at last roused from their apathy. A vigorous campaign was organized

against the godless schools; free schools were opened everywhere, more than two thousand state teachers resigned,
most of them to teach in the "free schools" which soon had
to accommodate more than sixty per cent of the entire body
of school children. The elections of 1884 brought the Catholics back into power and there they remained uninter-
ruptedly until the beginning of the World War. The law
of 1879 was repealed; control of elementary schools passed
from the State to the communes which were to decide
whether or not there should be religious instruction in the
communal schools. All elementary schools whether communal or "free" schools were entitled to State subsidies,
whenever meeting the State requirements as to qualifications
of teachers, curriculum, examinations, etc. Such is still, in
the main, the status of elementary schools in the country.

The beginnings of Catholic education in Canada have already been briefly recounted. With the passing of this
French colony to English rule by the Treaty
in Canada,   of Paris in 1763, there began a policy of persecution aiming at the extinction of the
Catholic faith. Fortunately for Catholics the revolt of the
American colonies made the English government realize
the necessity of conciliating the Canadian Catholics who
were then granted many liberties heretofore withheld or
suppressed. The War of 1812 had a like sobering effect on
British officialdom when at the beginning of the nineteenth
century it tried to revive its policy of persecution of the
previous generation. Education in Canada as well as in the
United States is not a Federal matter. Each province has its
own system. In some districts, public schools are divided
into Catholic and Protestant; parents are free to send their
children to either type. In other districts the law does not
recognize any such distinction; denominational schools receive no State support. The administration and supervision
of State "denominational" school systems is also denomina-

tional. In the Province of Quebec, for instance, public schools are under the control of a Superintendent of Education, assisted by a council of public instruction which frames the school laws to be submitted to the government. The council is divided into two sections, Catholic and Protestant, sitting independently to discuss matters concerning either Catholics or Protestants and uniting to consider questions that interest both denominations. Besides the public schools there are in the Province many free, *i.e.*, independent Catholic schools which receive no State support and do not therefore come directly under State supervision. The latter type of Catholic school is, of course, the rule wherever the State does not recognize the public school upon a religious basis.

The English State school system is of recent origin. Beginning in 1833 with a modest yearly appropriation of twenty thousand pounds for school houses, the building of the system proceeded in true in England, English fashion during the next three generations, through the appointment of parliamentary school commissions, the granting of state subsidies to existing institutions meeting state requirements, and the foundation of new schools wherever conditions called for it. The building up of the system was still going on at the outbreak of the World War. Prior to 1833 English schools, all the United Kingdom schools as well, were either old institutions which had weathered the sixteenth century storm or new foundations due to Church or private initiative. The nearest approach to anything like state interference in matters of education was the enactment of Parliamentary Acts barring Dissenters from the Established schools, or, as in the case of Catholics, forbidding them to have schools of their own; besides, there was some sort of indirect supervision of teaching and teachers which the government exercised through the Established Church. Freedom of education in England began with the Relief Act of 1791 and Catholics immediately took advantage of it; when in 1847 they were admitted to a share in the government money grants there were already many Catholic schools to profit by the boon.

At the present time Catholic schools sharing in the local rates or imperial grants are considered public institutions and belong to what is termed the non-provided type of school. The building and its upkeep is at the expense of the trust body which sets it up. The school is under the management of six persons, two of whom are appointed by the local civil authorities and the others by the trust body that owns the school. The local authority of the school district controls and maintains secular instruction. The teaching of religion is, of course, under the control and at the expense of the trustees.

Several attempts were made by Catholics in the United States to obtain a share of the public funds for their own schools: by Father Richards of Detroit in 1808, in the Lowell (Mass.) plan in 1830, for St. Peter's and St. Patrick's schools in New York, in the Faribault and Stillwater plans in Minnesota, in Poughkeepsie, New York, in Savannah, Georgia, St. Augustine in Florida. Most of those attempts were unsuccessful. A petition of the Catholics in New York City in 1840 precipitated a school controversy in which Bishop, later Archbishop Hughes championed with great zeal and talent the cause of religious education. He claimed no special privilege for Catholics but rightly contended that as citizens and taxpayers the Catholics have a right to "a fair and just proportion of the funds appropriated for the common schools, provided the Catholics will do with it the same thing that is done in the common schools." Bigotry, however, was still running high in the state and when the petition came before the Legislature it was defeated. The Faribault plan, referred to above, was the occasion of another controversy which assumed nationwide proportions. The plan consisted in setting aside a certain time for religious instruction to be given gratis by Catholic teachers, and a time for secular instruction to be given also by Catholic teachers but to be paid by the state. The school was to be under state supervision for the secular part of its work. The plan was submitted to the Congregation of the Propaganda which decreed that ". . . it may be tolerated," but owing to local difficulties the agreement was discontinued. The general trend of Catholic opinion in the United States at present is against state aid which, it is believed, could be accepted only at the cost of independence leading perhaps, in the course of time, to partial decatholization of the schools. As early as 1829, at the First Provincial Council of Baltimore, the assembled bishops strongly urged upon the clergy and laity the necessity of establishing Catholic schools. The Council's pronouncement was reiterated and amplified in the decrees of subsequent Provincial or Plenary Councils, but it was only in 1884 at the Third Plenary Council of Baltimore that specific and precise legislation on the question of Catholic schools was enacted in the following decree:

1. Near each church a parochial school, if it does not yet exist, is to be erected within two years from the promulgation of this Council and is to be maintained in perpetuum unless the bishop, on account of grave difficulties, judge that a postponement be allowed.

2. A priest who, by his grave negligence prevents the erection of a school within this time or its maintenance, or who, after repeated admonitions of the bishop does not attend to the matter, deserves removal from that church.

3. A mission or a parish which so neglects to assist a priest in erecting or maintaining a school, that by reason of this supine negligence the school is rendered impossible, should be reprehended by the bishop and, by the most efficacious and prudent means possible, induced to contribute the necessary support.

4. All Catholic parents are bound to send their children to the parochial schools, unless either at home or in other Catholic schools they may sufficiently and evidently provide for the Christian educa-

tion of their children, or unless it be lawful to send them to other schools on account of a sufficient cause, approved by the bishop, and with opportune cautions and remedies. As to what is a Catholic school, it is left to the judgment of the Ordinary to define."

There are today in the United States over ten thousand Catholic schools of all kinds with a population of more than two million five hundred thousand. Of those schools a little over seven thousand are elementary, attended by more than two million children. When we reflect that this vast system is maintained by Catholics without any public aid, we have indeed some reason to feel confident about the future of Catholicism in the country.

The foregoing brief account of the Catholic elementary school systems in Germany, France, Belgium, Canada, England and the United States will enable us to form an opinion of what the system is like throughout the world if we bear in mind that wherever the Church is allowed some freedom of action the organization of her elementary schools is of one or the other of the foregoing types.

As a whole the Catholic school system includes the following classes of institutions: elementary (whenever possible parochial), secondary, normal, seminary Catholic elementary schools and university. Of the five divisions the elementary or parochial is undoubtedly the most important. It is the foundation of the whole system; on its proper organization and growth depends in a large measure the religious education of Catholics, as also to a great extent the success of the higher institutions of learning. When Catholic schools are free from state interference, as in the United States, they are organized into practically autonomous, diocesan systems, coming directly and exclusively under the jurisdiction of a school board approved by the bishop; otherwise the extent of ecclesiastical control is determined by the terms of the agreement between Church and State in matters educational. The main difference between the curriculum of the Catholic elementary school and that of the public school lies in this, that besides devoting at least half an hour daily to religious instruction, the Catholic school course of study correlates every subject with religion which is made to vitalize the whole educational content. For the rest, the curriculum is similar to that of the public school, and comparative studies of achievements by both types of school have shown time and again that the Catholic elementary school is at least as efficient as the public school in the teaching of the secular branches.

The vast majority of Catholic elementary school teachers are of course members of religious communities. The rules of the teaching congregations and the regulations of ecclesiastical authorities require that those teachers must receive an adequate training before entering the classroom. In order to meet these requirements most religious congregations have their own normal schools, whose work, when necessary, is supplemented by attendance at various Summer or Extension sessions in colleges or universities. On the whole the academic and professional preparation provided for in Catholic normal schools practically parallels that of the public teacher training institution with this very important exception: that all other things being equal, leaving aside all religious considerations, the spiritual training which religious teachers receive develops a keener, more practical, more sympathetic psychological insight than could be acquired by years of book study in lay institutions.

To the teaching congregations mentioned previously in the survey of Catholic education in the seventeenth century, many others have been   teaching congregations, added since. The Society of Jesus which, as   gregations, we saw in Chapter IV had been suppressed in 1773, was restored in 1814 by Pope Pius VII[1] and within

¹ See Vol. II, chs. VI and X.

a few years of the restoration was conducting flourishing institutions in many lands. The educational principles of the "new" Society are those of the "old"; they are the principles of sound pedagogy in all times and places, but a few innovations in subject matter and method have been introduced into the Ratio to meet the changed conditions in intellectual life. The revised Ratio of 1832, again modified by subsequent legislation, states, *e.g.*, that more time should be given to the teaching of the modern tongue, history, geography, and particularly of the natural sciences which have become of late such an important item in the school curriculum.

ROSMINI

Some of the teaching congregations are chiefly, if not exclusively, devoted to secondary and higher education, but most of them have been founded for the express purpose of teaching in the elementary schools though it sometimes happens that even those congregations eventually engage in secondary school work. One of the more remarkable of the lately founded congregations is the Salesian Society or Society of St. Francis de Sales, its patron saint, founded in 1859 by Blessed Don Bosco and definitely approved by Pope Pius IX in 1874. Few religious congregations have spread with such rapidity. In less than fifty years after its foundation the Society had three hundred houses distributed over Europe, Asia and the two Americas. The real object of the Institute is the training of boys, especially for the trades, but it also conducts secondary schools and seminaries, is occupied with the diffusion of good Catholic literature and is engaged in mission work. The pedagogy of the Institute which has much in common with that of Rosmini and Froebel is summed up in which the Salesians call the preventive system of education: win the heart of the child, do all that can reasonably be done to avoid punishment.

There are today, the world over, thousands of Catholic secondary institutions of varied description: colleges, collèges, institutes, high schools, academies, professional schools, industrial schools, etc. Most of those institutions provide a general academic education of from three to six years beyond the elementary school; some, like the American College, offer a general education with an admixture of semi-professional preparation leading to the university or higher professional institutions. Again some of those schools have a decidedly technical character; a few, like St. Louis in Brussels, and Notre Dame de la Paix in Namur, offer a course of study filling the gap between the elementary school and higher studies proper. The organization, curriculum, purpose of those institutions, like their name, are more or less dictated by local conditions, but they all have this in common: that their work and achievements whether in linguistic or scientific studies compares most favorably with the work and achievements of similar public institutions and what is far more vital, that they surround the boy or girl with a healthy Christian atmosphere and prepare them for a Christian life.

secondary
schools,

Seminaries, or institutions for the preparation of young men to the priesthood, are either preparatory or major, the difference between the two types lying in the fact that the major or "grand séminaire" offers courses in philosophy and theology

seminaries,

whereas the work of the preparatory or "petit séminaire" is usually limited to the teaching of language, literature, history and the sciences; preparatory seminaries are primarily intended to be feeders for the major seminaries. The Decree of the Council of Trent (July 15, 1563) has remained to this day the fundamental law of the Church in this matter.[1] In substance it states that every diocese is bound to maintain an institution in which a certain number of youths will be prepared for the priesthood. Poor dioceses may combine for that purpose, large ones may have more than one seminary. Religious congregations of men, in whose membership there are priests, usually have their own houses of studies independently of diocesan seminaries. There are also in Rome a number of colleges of a national character, or maintained by religious congregations, where young men receive the usual preparation for the priesthood or pursue higher studies with all the advantages that Rome offers for research work or ecclesiastical training. As an illustration of those advantages might be cited here the Roman Institutes established by civic and ecclesiastical authorities for the purpose of historical and biblical research, particularly in connection with the Vatican Archives. The standards now accepted in the preparation for the priesthood are certainly high ones, but the recent Apostolic Constitution "Deus Scientiarum Dominus" will raise them higher still. Taking into consideration the scientific exigencies of the time the Holy See sets forth in that Constitution very strict regulations for the granting of degrees to theological students, who will now be required to possess not only a profound knowledge of the sacred sciences but "also of the other sciences closely allied to them."

The capstone of the Catholic school system, as it is of other systems, is the university. Most Catholic universities,

[1] See Vol. II, ch. VI.

like non-catholic ones, have one or more coördinate colleges or schools: colleges or schools of theol-
ogy, law, medicine, dentistry, engineering,   universities.
social science, education, journalism, etc. In
several instances some of those colleges or schools have a
nationwide or even a worldwide renown. The pride of the
Catholic university, however, and its chief concern as well,
is its system of philosophy, the philosophia perennis, which
was elaborated in Greece, was organized into a splendid system by the great thirteenth century Doctors, Albertus Mag-
nus, Saint Bonaventure, Saint Thomas Aquinas and Duns
Scotus, and has been lately adapted to modern ways in
philosophical discussions through the movement known in
Catholic circles as neo-scholasticism. Inaugurated around the
middle of the last century by writers like Sanseverino
(1811-1865), Gonzalez (1831-1892), Stockl (1823-1895),
the movement received in 1879 the solemn approval of the
Holy See in the Encyclical *Aeterni Patris.*
Neo-scholasticism retains the essence of the   Neo-
teachings of medieval scholasticism on God,   Scholasticism.
reality, the nature and destiny of man, the
origin, elaboration and nature of knowledge, the freedom
of the will. It rejects, as untenable in the light of modern
scientific discoveries, theories of physics which medieval
philosophy had grafted upon its principles. Saint Thomas
himself had warned his contemporaries that they were as-
sumptions and therefore subject to change.[1] The general
lines along which neo-scholasticism should proceed are thus
set forth by Leo XIII in the Encyclical *Aeterni Patris,* referred to above. "If there is anything that the Scholastic
Doctors treated with excessive subtlety or with insufficient
consideration or that is at variance with well-founded teachings of later date, or is otherwise improbable, we by no

[1] See Vol. II, p. 192.

means intend that it shall be proposed to our age for imitation. . . . We certainly do not blame those learned and energetic men who turn to the profit of philosophy their assiduous labors and erudition as well as the results of modern investigation; for we are fully aware that all this goes to the advancement of knowledge." The neo-scholastic movement which was for a time more or less confined to Italy gradually spread to other countries, where it rejuvenated and modernized the teaching of philosophy in Catholic in-

A PUBLIC DEFENSE AT LOUVAIN

stitutions and led many scholars to make important contributions to the subject and its history. The "Institut de Philosophie" founded at Louvain in 1891 by Pope Leo XIII, for the special purpose of teaching Thomistic philosophy in connection with history and science was from its inception and is still now one of the chief centers of the neo-scholastic movement. Keeping in touch with the progress of physics, chemistry, geology, biology, and a host of allied sciences neo-scholasticism has shown victoriously that Catholic philosophy has nothing to fear from the findings of science or the theories born of those findings.

In order to do full justice to our subject we should now consider the educative influence of the Catholic home, the doctrines and rites of the Church, her missionary work, her retreats, her sodalities, and all the activities of Catholic Action. All these are edu- *Other educa-* cative agencies in the best and highest sense *tional* of the term, but the limits within which *agencies.* we must keep the treatment of the subject forbid anything beyond the mere mention of other educative agencies than the school. By way of conclusion to this survey, of necessity very brief, of Catholic education in modern times, we shall now inquire a little more closely into the nature and purpose of Catholic education and bring out in all its significance, if possible, the one element in that system of education which differentiates it from other systems.

Religious education, we know it, is the characteristic feature of the Catholic school, but not equally clear to all of us perhaps is the nature of this religious educa- tion. To many, if not most people, religious *The essence of* education means that so many hours are de- *Catholic* voted every week to some sort of dogmatic *education.* instruction, explaining to a class, according to their intellectual capacity, the teachings of the Church on the Creator and his creatures, man's nature, his position in the universe, his origin and destiny, his duties to his Lord and Maker, to his fellowmen and to himself, in brief, on the teachings of the Catholic Church and on her rites. Instruction of this kind is and should be, of course, a part of Catholic education, because Christianity is a doctrine, or rather a system of doctrines, that needs exposition and explanation. But Christianity is something else than an appeal to the intellect, something more vital than doctrinal subject matter calling for explanation. Christianity is first of all and most essentially a Person and a history; it is the history of a Man, of the only Man whose history was recorded before He was born, the history of Him who is the Truth, and the Way and the Life, it is the history of the Son of Man and

Son of God. Christianity, the word itself tells us that much at least—is Christ, in His Person, in His Life and teachings. The Christian is the disciple whose intelligence and will gladly surrender to Christ through faith and love, who shares abundantly in the life of his Master. And so it is that the one purpose of religious education in Catholic schools is to teach Christ, to reveal Him to the mind and the heart of the child, of the boy and girl, to win them over to Him, to make of them followers of Christ. And so it is too that religious education in the Catholic school is not, cannot be limited to a course on religious doctrines; the influence of the Christian religion should extend to every situation in life, it should be felt in the teaching of every subject, because that religion should be the very life of the Christian.

SOURCES

The archives of the Vatican, diocesan chancelleries and religious congregations.

REFERENCES

Brück-Kippling, Geschichte der kath. Kirche im Deutschland im Jahrh., IV.
Burns, J. A., The Catholic School System in the United States.
Chauveau, P., Instruction Publique au Canada.
De Wulf, M., Scholasticism, Old and New.
Goyau, G., L'Ecole d'aujourd'hui.
Graham, Balfour, Education Systems of Great Britain and Ireland.
Maritain, J., Art et Scolastique; The Things that Are Not Caesar's.
The Official Catholic Yearbook (Kennedy and Sons, New York).
Verhaegen, H., La Lutte scolaire en Belgique.

CHAPTER XI

THE MODERN EDUCATIONAL SYSTEM

A GENERAL SURVEY

THE TITLE OF THIS, OUR LAST CHAPTER, IS apt to convey some misconception which it will be well to dispel at once. Quite frequently the term educational system is used for school system and from a certain viewpoint the confusion is justifiable. School education has nowadays assumed proportions it never had in the past; schools have multiplied far beyond the dreams of even their most ardent advocates; they are doing their best to satisfy needs which formerly were met by other institutions, they have been articulated into a well-knit system. But even so, if words are to be accurately used, the two terms, educational system and school system, should not be identified.

Besides the school, the modern educational system includes many agencies, some of which may have an even greater educative influence than the school: the home, the church, and the apprenticeship system, museums and libraries, literary, artistic, scientific, sportive societies, newspapers and periodicals, traveling, the theatre, the radio, whose importance as an educative agency is likely to grow every year. For reasons at once obvious the following survey will be chiefly concerned with the modern school system, leaving the treatment of the other educational agencies to works of a wider scope or of a more special character.

Generally speaking, the modern school system comprises three main divisions, elementary, secondary and higher, but there is great diversity, sometimes even in the same country, in the organization of these divisions. Until quite recently the accepted school organization in the United States was an elementary school of eight years or grades followed by a secondary school period of eight years evenly divided between high school and college. In some districts the elementary school covered only seven years, while in others it would cover nine. In addition to this, at least one year of kindergarten education was and is still provided for in most cities as part of the school system. The upper branch of the organization included universities, professional and technical schools. There was no counterpart in the system for what is known in Europe as the intermediate or middle school which provides a semi-general, semi-vocational instruction for boys and girls who have completed the elementary school course and do not intend to enter the secondary school. Many children left school as soon as the law on compulsory attendance would permit, most of them by that time having reached only the sixth grade. A comparatively small percentage of all children entering the first grade reached the ninth year, and many of them, otherwise talented youngsters, did not continue in the high school because its traditional course of study was ill suited to their natural talents. Of late years there has been a strong tendency in all the States to require children to stay in school till at least the age of sixteen, in some States that of eighteen, and as a consequence of the extension of the period of compulsory attendance, provision had to be made for the instruction of boys and girls who were compelled to stay in school and had no talent or felt no disposition for the work of the traditional four-year high school. The junior high or intermediate school has been established to meet this situa-

Main divisions of the system in the United States,

tion. Its main purpose, in keeping with the spirit of the compulsory attendance laws, is to keep boys and girls under school training, irrespective of their ability to pursue the traditional academic studies, in order to make them better members of society than they would otherwise be. It usually combines the old seventh and eighth grades and the first year of the senior high school. It first offers to its students a common group of required subjects intended to supply a certain amount of common culture for adolescents, and later differentiates its course of studies in order to give individual students that education which best corresponds to their particular abilities and probable vocations.

Though this junior high school idea has made great headway, it is still in the experimental stage, and the intermediate school, which has been for generations a feature of European school systems, is still an exception, though an important one in the United States.

This junior high school movement has been paralleled in recent years by a similar movement in college education. The junior college is an institution doing two years of college work beyond the high school. It has developed partly as an upward growth of the high school and partly as the result of a new policy of smaller institutions to do thoroughly the work of the first two years of college life, rather than to spread superficially over all the courses of a modern college or university. Another striking feature of the United States school system is the large number of private colleges and universities; of the 800 odd institutions listed under higher education more than three-fifths are conducted under private auspices, and the royal gifts pouring in year after year to those schools enable them to hold more than their own against State or city institutions.

In a sense there is no German school system, no more than there is a United States school system. The various

States forming the German federation have remained independent in their domestic affairs, and the Germany, existence of certain institutions in any part of the country is no guarantee that they exist in other parts. Elementary schools, gymnasiums, universities, are the main institutional features of the system as a whole, but side by side with those there have developed many other types of schools. Again institutions bearing the same name and subject to similar regulations may differ greatly from one another because of differences in local traditions or spirit of the people. On the whole, the German policy in educational administration has been a combination of the French and English attitudes in such matters; sudden transformations and extreme centralization have been avoided; the school system has been organized to some extent through the definite plans of the governing body; a degree of uniformity in types of schools, curriculum, methods of teaching has been secured, but not at the expense of local needs for individuality.

England never had anything approaching a national school system until the close of the nineteenth century and the building up of that system is typical of the history of English institutions. It is not the result of theorizing or long-considered plans, but of a series of experiments, of compromises directed by conflicting forces, the Church, the State, private enterprise, philanthropic endeavor, new theories of education. It has the England, noteworthy distinction of combining respect for tradition with due regard for the requirements of new social and economic conditions, of satisfying the legitimate claims of the State without destroying local liberty and initiative. The old Latin schools dating back from the fourteenth and the fifteenth centuries have been allowed to preserve their old tradition by the side of others established in more recent times and modern in scope and tendencies. Oxford and Cambridge have retained their peculiar organization, but beside them there are other universities of recent foundation with entirely different tendencies and characteristics. Elementary instruction continues to be given in private schools or schools founded by various denominations and religious societies. The State has been satisfied with aiding and supplementing private initiative by money grants, the foundation of new schools wherever the old foundations were unequal to the situation, by setting up certain minimum standards in teacher training, curriculum, attendance, school accommodations and by co-ordinating local educational efforts.

Of quite a different type is the French school system, which originated at the close of the eighteenth century with the violent measures of the Revolution, but did not take some sort of permanent shape until Napoleon turned his attention to a general reorganization of education. The law of 1802 supplemented by the Imperial Decree of 1808 provided for three grades of schools, primary, secondary and higher or special, all of them under State supervision. The central and local administrations were to share in the burden of France. maintaining the schools, but a large part of the expenses was to be covered by tuition fees. Private and Church institutions were allowed to operate under certain conditions, the main one being a State license for the employment of teachers. Those are the main lines along which the organization of the French school system has proceeded from the time of its foundation. Its general tendency has been towards a State educational monopoly, which it had virtually become at the outbreak of the World War. Most schools by that time were public schools; religious instruction had been replaced by ethico-civic instruction, and teachers were required to be "neutral" in religious matters. Since the close of the War a more liberal policy seems to prevail;

many private schools, mainly denominational, have been allowed to operate again with some degree of freedom; State control is now exercized in an indirect way through the examinations which give access to most careers; since such examinations are State controlled, all schools are compelled to conform to State programs of instructions.

Those four school systems, American, German, English, and French, may be taken as typical of all the others; there is in all systems at least a tendency towards uniformity and centralization, but the strength of the tendency and the extent to which uniformity and centralization have been achieved vary from one country to another; in some countries, as for instance in Italy, French influence seems to be paramount, whereas in others the tendency seems to be to follow the lead of the United States, or Germany, or England, or again to combine elements borrowed from various sources.

The three main divisions of the school system, elementary, secondary and higher, should normally correspond, for every individual, to childhood, early and middle adolescence, late adolescence and young manhood, in terms of years, to the periods of five to twelve years of age, twelve to nineteen and nineteen to twenty-four or twenty-five. But experience shows that millions never reach the secondary school, notwithstanding inducements of all kinds and the most generous provisions made by State and city for the education of the masses. This fact had been overlooked by the framers of early compulsory attendance legislation. They shared the illusion of the Enlightenment concerning man's intellectual capacities and its prejudices against the past. All children were to be trained for so many years in the same institution; it might be a rural or city school, public or private, but in purpose and type of work it was everywhere fundamentally the same. It soon became evident, however, that if the school was thus to assume the sole burden of training the young, individual differences and local needs must be taken into consideration: subject matter and method of instruction must be adapted to the mental capacity even of the dullest child; special classes or special schools must be established to meet a variety of needs. The full realization of this program has been the work of the last two generations. The elementary school system, such as we have it today, includes, in addition to the common, traditional elementary school, many other institutions having in common this one characteristic: that the elementary studies form the chief, or at least a large, part of their curriculum. There are, first, those schools which may be considered as variants or extensions of the common elementary school: kindergartens, day nurseries, crèches, middle schools, industrial schools, continuation schools, Sunday, evening or summer schools, city and rural schools; then there are those institutions caring for destitute or wayward or otherwise abnormal children, such as orphan asylums, protectories, reformatories, schools for the blind, the deaf mute, the feeble minded; there are finally the institutions for training elementary school teachers: normal schools, teachers seminaries, teachers colleges.

Though the preparation of the elementary school teacher has received much attention in the last hundred years, there is still much divergence in both theory and practice on the subject. In Germany, some States like Saxony and Thuringia require of prospective elementary school teachers a three-year preparation in the university; in Prussia the State requires the nine-year secondary school course as a general preparation, to be followed by a two-year professional preparation in a pedagogical seminary, while other States still retain the special normal schools based on a five-year elementary education followed by two years of practical training in a pedagogical institute. In England a change of policy is now being gradually introduced in the methods of training and certifying teachers. Formerly prospective elementary school teachers would serve for some time as apprentices or pupil teachers in elementary schools, receiving instruction from the head master or, when Teacher circumstances permitted, in institutions training. known as pupil teacher centers. A preliminary examination known as Queen's and then as King's scholarship was the standard test for admission to a training college, and the normal qualification for employment as uncertificated teacher. At present the first qualifying examination is usually the school certificate examination following on a four or five years' secondary school course. The prospective teacher may then serve as a student teacher for one year before he begins work as an uncertificated teacher or enters the training college, or else he may proceed directly from the secondary school to the training college. The tendency seems to be in favor of the latter course. There has been of late a like tendency to raise the standards of eligibility requirements for elementary school teachers in other countries. Thus in France the academic professional preparation will be entrusted to the lycées in which a normal section will be established for that purpose. Formerly the requirements were graduation from a normal school beyond a higher elementary school course. In the United States the standard preparation for city schools was for a long time two years of training in the normal school beyond the high school. Recently there has been a tendency to transform the normal school into a four-year normal college. In rural communities, however, the standard is still much lower; a large percentage of elementary school teachers have only received a high-school preparation and in some districts many elementary school teachers have not even completed the high school.

Success in teaching, it seems to be fully realized at last, like success in any profession is contingent upon a combination of at least three factors: natural talent, knowledge and practice. The talent to teach is commonly presupposed in its students by the normal school, but because of the long course in theoretical preparation unfitness is not detected until the teacher is actually at work in the classroom. It has been suggested that a practical test of a candidate's professional fitness be included among the requirements for admission into the normal school. Such a test would certainly reduce the number of misfits, but it would also bar from the profession candidates who might through training develop remarkable teaching ability. Besides, the natural talent for teaching is usually more or less one-sided; a teacher will show remarkable skill in the handling of a certain subject or the use of a certain method and will be merely normal or even fall under the average in the teaching of other subjects and the use of other methods. Would a practical entrance test detect every candidate's forte, which might more than outweigh possible deficiency along some lines?

Efficient instruction and classroom management call for skill in the art of teaching, the result of natural talent and experience; the prospective teacher should first get the benefit of the experience of others by observing the work of trained teachers and then practice the art of teaching under the guidance of tried masters. But much more is required from the teacher than the skillful application of the rules of his art; intelligent teaching presupposes a knowledge of the laws and principles upon which the art of teaching ultimately rest, and in the process of teacher training theory and practice should be closely related and supplement one another. Besides this knowledge, theoretical and practical, of methodology which is the technical part of his professional training the teacher should be acquainted with the system of education in general, as well as with the special kind of school in which he intends to teach; he should know something of the system of education in the past and of its relation with other social forces; he should have a clear conception of the end of education, its agencies, its forms, its content; he should study their relation to ethics, psychology, logic, sociology. Back of this all there should be a solid academic preparation. No less than the lawyer, the physician, the engineer, in short, all those who occupy positions of trust and responsibility in the community, the teacher needs breadth of culture to enrich his own life and that of those that will be committed to his charge, to be a credit to the profession, to feel at ease and exert his own due share of influence in society. But academic preparation means much more for the teacher than breadth of culture. All teachers, including even those in the kindergarten, are concerned with instruction of some kind; they have to impart at least part of the knowledge they have acquired, and they should know much more than they have to teach. Thus, for example, a mastery of elementary school arithmetic implies some knowledge of the theory of numbers and the elements of algebra and geometry. It is not requiring too much of the elementary school teacher that he should hold the four-year high-school diploma, and that high-school teachers should have graduated from a college of good standing. Even then it will require on the part of teachers much diligent study in the preparation of daily lessons before they can feel perfectly at home in the subject they have to teach.

To all this an important element is added in the preparation of the religious teachers. As novices, the members of religious congregations have to go through a period of at least one, often two years of spiritual preparation, through prayer, self-renunciation, meditation, the constant practice of self-control and self-denial, and after the completion of the noviceship not a day passes in the life of the religious without a few hours given to spiritual exercises. Aside from the deep influence those exercises must have upon the character of the teacher, they cannot fail to vitalize what knowledge he may have acquired of psychology through experience and book learning, and they constantly keep before his mind the real purpose of education, to uplift the individual, to raise him above the world of sense, bring him nearer and nearer to his Lord and Maker.

From time immemorial the teaching of reading, writing, arithmetic, has been the primary object of the elementary school, and the common test of its efficiency today is still proficiency in those branches. To those fundamentals of elementary education Christianity added religion, which for centuries remained in the center of the curriculum. Religion was everywhere, as it is still in Catholic schools today, not only a matter of instruction but one also of practice. It was at all points correlated with the life of the Church, its general or local forms of worship, its traditions, its aims and ideals. The new pedagogy Curriculum born of the Enlightenment has banished reli- revision. gion from the public classroom and in its place has enthroned "lay ethics," with a multitude of subjects which have made of the elementary school course of study some sort of a popular encyclopedia. Formerly teacher and pupil could devote all their time to a few essential subjects; they have now to divide it among a multitude of studies and school activities which vary with any new theory which happens to catch the fancy of pedagogues. In point of fact "curriculum revision" has become quite a fad of late years, and, in keeping with the spirit of the age, this curriculum revision is carried on in true "scientific style": gathering text books, teacher's helps, courses of study for every possible type of school and from as many countries and localities as possible, establishing committees, conducting experiments, marshalling statistics, drawing up and discussing reports. The scope, methods, purposes of those investigations vary somewhat from country to country, but there seems to be everywhere a tendency to incor-

porate into school work more of the life actually surrounding the child and to make the school serve national
aims. It is most unlikely, however, that curriculum revision
will result in any radical departure from the present system
of studies, for no new element has as yet appeared, nor is
likely to appear in twentieth-century culture, which could
take the place of the age-tried branches of the elementary
school curriculum. There will be a re-arrangement of time
allotment for the various subjects, new devices will be suggested in methodology, but the course of study will emerge
from the hands of the commissions substantially as it has
been in the past fifty years. The one change which would be
of any real consequence to the child and society is the restoration of religion to its former position in the school curriculum, but present indications do not point in that
direction.

A glance at the classification of schools in the different
national systems soon reveals the fact that there is as yet
no general agreement as to the meaning of the phrase "secondary schools." Institutions listed in one country as secondary are classed as elementary, or partly elementary and
secondary in another, and the line between higher and secondary schools is not always clearly drawn
The Secondary either. To define the secondary school as an
education institution whose instruction follows that
period. given in the elementary school, or as one
which prepares for the university, or again
to try to define it in terms of the age of the pupils received
or through a differentiation of subjects taught would hardly
help clarify the situation. The statement that a secondary
education is a continuation of elementary school work is
meaningless, unless we know exactly where school instruction ceases to be elementary. To speak of the secondary
school as preparatory to the university is to lose sight of the
fact that many boys and girls never proceed nor intend to

proceed to the university, yet expect to receive at school an adequate preparation for their calling. To define the secondary school as one that makes provision for boys and girls between the ages of, let's say, twelve and seventeen is not very accurate either. As a matter of fact, many secondary schools receive students under the age of twelve and keep them to the age of eighteen or nineteen. The simplest and easiest way out of this difficulty it seems leads us back to the traditional conception of the elementary school and university. So long as the student has not mastered the elements of knowledge and skill which he needs to be capable of study he belongs to the elementary school. And when he has become capable of self-dependent study, using the instructor in the same sense in which he utilizes the library, or laboratory, or office consultors, then he has reached the region of the university. Between those two regions lies that of the secondary school. Under normal conditions it should be reached at the age of ten and have been explored before twenty. It is the period in formal education in which the school utilizes the best in the cultural capital of the race to develop fully and train all the latent capacities of the student, to develop intelligent attitudes towards his environment, high and just standards of moral and aesthetic values, to develop the student's ability to study and think for himself, to help him discover his own special ability and to form a strong, sterling character. The German gymnasium or the French lycée are probably the nearest approach to the institutional equivalent of the period.

The preparation of secondary school teachers is still in some countries the work of special institutions, higher normal schools, but the general tendency is now to entrust it to the university. The usual minimum requirement for admission to the examination leading to a license is the bachelor's degree or its equivalent. The following additional requirements are also quite common: the candidate must have studied at a university for a period of from two to four even five years and must have practiced teaching for at least two years. The study of methodology which occupies such a prominent position in the preparation of the elementary school teacher has always been relegated, and rightly so, into the background of the preparation of secondary school teachers.

The vocational aspect of education has become in the last hundred years a topic of general importance. In a certain sense all education is vocational in that its purpose is to prepare one in a general or particular way for some occupation or vocation. Liberal education in ancient Greece and Rome was vocational in that it prepared for the life of the statesman, philosopher, orator. The education of the knight in medieval times, of the gentlemen in the post-Renaissance period was vocational insofar as it prepared for special activities. Training for the practice of medicine, law, engineering, commerce, teaching, the ministry, are other illustrations of vocational education, though here the term professional would be more in keeping with English usage. Nowadays, however, the term vocational is commonly restricted to what might be termed the lower range of industrial education. It is the modern counterpart of the old apprenticeship system which has been described in a previous volume[1] and was practically driven out of industrial life by the Industrial Revolution. Under that system young helpers learned not merely the technique of some single process, but the "arts and mysteries" of a craft as well, and they remained throughout the formative period of adolescence under the direct influence of a master responsible to the corporation for the technical training of the young artisan and his moral character. With the introduction of machinery and its consequent division of labor, the

Vocational education.

[1] See Vol. I, ch. VII.

artisan of former days has given way to an army of machine workers, performing one small mechanical process over and over again and knowing nothing of the work done beyond their own limited sphere. One of the purposes of vocational education is to counteract the deadening effects of this mechanical type of occupation upon the individual, by keeping him for as long a period as possible under the liberalizing influence of the school, and to that purpose the period of compulsory school attendance has been extended in many countries to the age of sixteen or even seventeen.

The vocational movement is chiefly economic. It began in the second half of the nineteenth century with the recognition of the need for a readjustment of the old apprenticeship system to the modern conditions of commerce, industry and farming, in order to increase national production, prestige and power. Germany has been most prominent in this movement for industrial efficiency. In no country have the central and local authorities or private organizations made such efforts to provide vocational training for every one, from the lowly laborer to the director of the great manufacturing establishment. In 1925 there were in the country over 12,000 full-time continuation and vocational schools of the greatest variety of types, irrespective of secondary and higher institutions of this class. Attendance at a vocational school of some kind is compulsory in most States. Germany has also taken pains to articulate the work of the school for general culture with that of the vocational or professional institutions. France also has given much attention in the last fifty years to vocational preparation, though her efforts seem to have been confined chiefly to secondary and higher institutions. Agriculture and the dairy industry in Denmark, Holland, Belgium owe much of their flourishing condition today to agricultural education. The latter country also possesses what is probably the most highly developed system of vocational education for the preparation of artisans and small traders. Switzerland's economic progress in the last twenty years is due to the development of skillful artisanship through appropriate vocational training. England awoke to the importance of this type of education only in recent years, when she realized that her position as a great commercial and industrial country was threatened by other countries better equipped for economic competition. The Fisher Act of 1918 which reorganized the English system of education contains important provisions concerning vocational preparation. There is still much progress to be made, but the foundations of a national system of vocational preparation have been laid. In most countries the control of vocational schools is divided among the various departments of Government Administration, commerce, industry, labor, according to the type of school, or else they are placed under the joint control of anyone of those departments and that of education.

Vocational education is of comparatively recent growth in the United States. Not being pressed by the necessity of feeding a surplus population, and being endowed with enormous natural resources, the people of the United States were satisfied with selling their raw products, letting other nations do their shipping, and importing their cheap labor and trained workers. Aside from college preparation for agriculture and engineering, some manual training and commercial education of a purely clerical character, very little advance had been made in vocational education in the United States by the close of the nineteenth century. The country's awakening to the importance of this kind of education came in the first decade of the following century, when it began to feel the keenness of European competition in world trade and the necessity of being thoroughly prepared for the economic battles of the future. The Presidential Commission appointed in 1913 to inquire into the matter reported that there were in the country over 26,000,000 persons engaged in agriculture, manufacturing and mechanical pursuits, not 1% of whom had received an adequate preparation for their occupation. Attention was called to the startlingly backward position of the country in the matter, the consequent loss to wage earners and the nation, and the danger threatening the country's position in the international markets. The Smith-Hughes Act of 1917, based upon the best of European experience in the matter, made the beginning of what will, in the course of time, develop into a splendid national system of vocational education. The plan is based on co-operation between State and Federal Government, the States providing at least as much money as the Federal Government appropriates for vocational education; provision is made for vocational training in agriculture, home economics, commerce, the trades and industries. The courses of less than college grade are intended for persons over fourteen years of age and they are arranged to meet the needs of full-time and part-time students: those who intend to enter and those who are actually engaged in some industrial occupation.

An interesting phase of the movement for vocational training is the recent development of vocational guidance which aims to give to parents and children information with regard to trades and other occupations, and the best method of entering or preparing to enter them. While the methods and agencies vary, the purpose is everywhere the same; it is not to secure employment for young people, but to help them select and prepare for that "vocation" best adapted to their own talents and disposition, to save them from entering the first occupation that offers, regardless of the future.

Higher education.

We have seen in a previous chapter that the condition of higher education around 1750 was still substantially what it had been a hundred years before. The universities were still the only institutions of higher learning and their organization, studies, methods, had undergone little change since the Renaissance and Reformation. They were local, at best national institutions, with the four traditional faculties of theology, law, medicine and arts, all of them, with very few exceptions, offering the traditional subjects taught in the traditional ways. The scientific movement of the seventeenth and eighteenth centuries had left them unaffected. The first important change took place in the Faculty of Arts; its name was gradually changed everywhere into that of Faculty of Philosophy and the three philosophies, moral, natural and metaphysical, formed the substance of its course. As a result of the expansion of science certain parts of these philosophies developed into independent sciences: physics, mental science or psychology, jurisprudence, natural law, politics, economics, which became objects of study on the part of specialists who did not concern themselves with the rest of philosophy. The new philosophies which developed outside of the universities around the scientific discoveries of the sixteenth and seventeenth centuries gradually found their way into the Faculty of Arts. Scholasticism was displaced by Cartesianism in some universities, by the Baconian and Newtonian philosophy in others, and these new philosophies in turn have been displaced by others, Kantian, Hegelian, positivist, etc. In fact, outside of Catholic institutions, the teaching of philosophy within the last two hundred years has been kaleidoscopic, and there is probably no subject today whose academic status is more unsettled, in its scope, organization, methods, trend of instruction. Philosophy used to be considered a fitting capstone to a liberal education and the necessary background of expert knowledge, but today in many institutions it has been practically crowded out of the undergraduate department by premature specialization and confined to the graduate department with the result that men otherwise remarkable specialists in their own chosen field complete their higher studies without that broad, intelligent outlook upon life which alone a serious study of philosophy can give.

The progress and subdivision of pure and applied science, and the expansion of trade and commerce in the last hundred years have led to the establishment of new departments in the universities and the foundation of new schools preparing for the major positions of industrial life. A few schools of this kind already existed in the eighteenth century, but they were in the main merely trade schools giving a more or less formal instruction in connection with training in the trade. The first higher technical school was established in France in 1747, a special engineering school for bridges and highways (Ecole des Ponts et Chaussées) and a little later was founded the Ecole des Mines for the training of mining engineers. Mention has been made of several institutions of higher learning founded during the Revolution and Napoleon's reign; others have been founded since. In addition to her universities, revived by the law of 1896, France possesses today a number of higher schools some of which have been incorporated into some university, like the Higher Normal School now attached to the University of Paris, while others have remained independent institutions. Among these are the following: the Collège de France, which offers courses of lectures in various subjects by the most distinguished specialists of the country; the School of Living Oriental Languages; the Ecole des Chartes for the training of archivists and professors of history; the Museum of Natural History providing instruction in all the branches of natural science and particularly their applications to industry and commerce; the Ecole Polytechnique for the training of artillery officers and engineers; the Ecole Centrale des Arts et Métiers, which, though slightly lower in rank than the others, is still one of the best technical schools of the country.

In German lands there were founded in the eighteenth

or early nineteenth century a number of trade schools most of which have since developed into technical schools of the highest rank. The oldest one was the mining school established at Schemnitz in 1760; then followed those at Charlottenberg in 1799, and in the first decades of the nineteenth century at Prague, Darmstadt, Carlsruhe, Munich, Nuremberg. Others have been founded since. Germany's position well in the front rank of technical education is due to the early and active realization by her manufacturers and the Government of the economic importance of thoroughly trained technicians. No student is admitted into a higher technical school until he has received the equivalent of a twelve years' course in the preparatory schools. To secure the degree of "Diplome Ingenieur" he has to take courses requiring practically four years of study and in addition he must spend at least a year as a special apprentice in some establishment co-operating with the schools in the training of industrial officers. In the courses provided in such establishments the student is shifted through the whole plant and is given opportunity to study all the processes and methods which are appropriate for his instruction. In order to receive credit for the courses he must hold a certificate of proficiency from his employer. This method of technical preparation which has proved highly efficient has been adopted more or less by all industrial nations.

In England the great center for higher technical education is the City and Guilds of London Institute which exists "for the establishment of or for assistance to trade schools, for the conduct of examination in technology, and for subsidizing other institutions in London, or in the Provinces, having cognate subjects." The City and Guilds of London Institute maintains a number of technical institutions in the metropolis and provinces. While the older universities of the United Kingdom have been rather slow in their response to the industrial movement, the new ones, as remarked before, like London, Birmingham, Bristol, Leeds, Manchester, Liverpool, were from their inception centers of scientific studies which contributed much towards English industrial supremacy in the nineteenth century. Of late the fear that this supremacy was seriously imperiled by Germany and the United States has focused public attention upon the methods of training the industrial leaders of Great Britain. Many suggestions have been made for the improvement of the work in the technical schools, but the consensus of expert opinion is that no serious improvement can be accomplished until there is adequate training in the elementary and secondary schools.

The first school of technology in the United States was the Rensselaer Polytechnic Institute founded at Troy by Stephen Van Rensselaer in 1824, but it did not develop into a full fledged college of engineering until about 1850. It was only after 1860, however, when the demand by the growing manufacturing interests for technically trained men became acute that foundations of that kind became common. A marked stimulus to the growth of technical education came from the Land Grant Act of 1862 for the "endowment, support and maintenance of at least one college (in each State), where the leading object should be, without excluding other scientific and classical studies, and including military tactics, to teach such branches of learning as are related to agriculture and the mechanical arts." Technical education has grown apace in other industrial nations. Zurich in Switzerland, Delft in Holland, Louvain, Liége, Brussels and Ghent in Belgium, Rome, Milan, Turin and other cities in Italy, Madrid in Spain, to cite but a few, possess technical schools of the highest order which are modeled chiefly after those of France or Germany. The early type of engineering was rather comprehensive, but the rapid expansion of science and the field of its applications to industry, commerce, agriculture and life in general has made specialization imperative. Today there is at least a dozen of special types of technical education in such related fields as architectural, civil, metallurgical, mining, electrical, chemical, etc., engineering.

The first school of agriculture appeared in 1806; it was a branch of the Institute conducted at Hofwyl by Fellenberg for nearly forty years. Many imitations soon appeared in Switzerland, southern Germany, France, England and the United States. France, until a recent time an essentially agricultural country, soon took the lead in the development of agricultural education. Before the middle of the century it had more than twenty agricultural schools in operation in various parts of the country. Today France possesses one of the best organized systems of agricultural education. All rural schools provide instruction in agricultural subjects according to the needs of the district. There is a farm school in each department, and there are several higher agricultural schools located at central places, with a national agronomic institute at the top of the whole system. In the United States there was some agitation for agricultural education in the early decades of the nineteenth century, but with the opening of the new West to farming and the change of the East to manufacturing this agitation died out. It reappeared in the middle West around 1850, and its first tangible result was the foundation of the Michigan Agricultural College in 1857 and two years later of a "Farmers High School," which a little later became the Pennsylvania State College. It was not, however, before the close of the century that a real interest in agricultural education was awakened in the United States. The first typically agricultural high school was opened in Minnesota in 1888; ten years later a dozen more had been established and today agricultural instruction is given in thousands of schools, elementary, secondary or higher, in addition to experimental stations established by the national, State or local authorities. Strenuous efforts have also been made during the same period to regenerate rural life in other countries, in Germany, Holland, Belgium, Denmark, England, Italy, Australia, Japan, China, the Philippines.

One of the most remarkable and certainly the most praiseworthy achievement of science has been in medicine, surgery and public hygiene. Within the last sixty years instruction in those subjects has been entirely transformed. The traditional, uniform course of studies has branched off into many lines of specialization and what used to be the exception, viz., the use of the laboratory and practice under expert guidance at some hospital, has now become the rule everywhere. A similar transformation has taken place in veterinary medicine, and a broad, entirely new province, that of plant pathology, has been added to the field of medical science. Formerly confined mostly to the task of curing, medicine is no less concerned today with detecting and preventing the spread of the germs of disease in persons, animals, plants and goods. Sanitation in building, public health, medical inspection of school children, quarantine service with ample medical staff to cope with disease have become a part of the public administration in all civilized countries.

Another important phase of educational activity in the last hundred years has been the greater attention given to the education of orphans, neglected or defective children. From her very inception the Church made it incumbent upon the Christian community to take care of the orphans as well as of the sick and poor. The placing out of orphans was a common practice in early Christian days. The Apostolic Constitutions commend them to the special solicitude of the bishop. He is to have them "brought up at the expense of the Church and to take care that the girls be given, when of marriageable age, to Christian husbands, and that the boys should learn some art or handicraft and

Education of defectives.

then provided with tools and placed in a condition to earn their own living." During the middle ages the monasteries, convents, guilds and other foundations were the shelters where the orphans learned a trade or received the liberal education that would prepare them for some profession. In modern times the care of orphans, abandoned children, children of the poor, is inseparably connected with the name of St. Vincent de Paul and the Sisters of Charity who gradually spread all over the world and since their foundation have been looked to for the protection of the orphan and have been the inspiration of other organizations seeking to perform the same work. On the American Continent, however, the first orphan asylum was due not to French but to Spanish inspiration. This was La Caridad founded by a Spanish order in Mexico in 1548. The first orphanage founded on what is now United States territory was that established by the Ursulines at New Orleans in 1727. Today there are probably more than three hundred Catholic institutions of that kind in the country with a population of at least 60,000 orphan inmates. In those countries which adopted the sixteenth century Protestant Reformation the care of orphans came to be considered a public duty, though here and there orphans would be cared for in private institutions, e.g., in Francke's Institution at Halle. In England, they were cared for under the provisions of the Poor Law, being apprenticed and indentured, or if too young committed to "such of the wards appropriated to female paupers as may be deemed expedient." In the treatment of the indigent no distinction was made between child and adult. The same conditions prevailed in Colonial America and continued after the War of Independence. Everywhere during the last three-quarters of a century orphan asylums have rapidly increased in number and an earnest endeavor is made to give destitute children their full share of the blessings of a good education.

No attempt was made in ancient times to instruct the blind and deaf mute. They were generally looked upon as mental defectives, and the deaf mute were even considered by many as being under the curse of Heaven. Sympathy for and care of those unfortunates begins with Christianity. From the earliest times the Church made provision for their material and spiritual needs in hospices, and here and there attempts were made to teach them some handicraft. One of the most famous institutions of that kind was that established at Paris towards 1260 by St. Louis, King of France, the Hospice des Quinze Vingt, where 300 blind persons were housed and instructed. Undoubtedly the blind, deaf and mute received a modicum of education in institutions of this kind, but the means were so inadequate that the problem of this special education remained unsolved until the second half of the eighteenth century. Attempts had been made to devise special processes for the instruction of these abnormals in

DE L'EPÉE

the sixteenth and seventeenth centuries, but the first school for the deaf mute was opened in Paris in 1760 by Abbé Charles Michel de L'Epée (1712-1789), and the first school for the blind was opened at about the same time by Valentine Haüy (1746-1822), who was trying to do for the blind what de L'Epée was doing for the deaf mute. Today all civilized countries possess institutions of learning and industrial training schools for the blind and deaf mute.

Surveying modern education from the vantage point that we have now reached we can see that present-day educational tendencies are still inspired in a large measure by the philosophy of the Enlightenment. Immediate usefulness still remains the more common standard in appraising the respective values of studies. The diffusion of knowledge, useful and diversified knowledge, among the masses is the chief purpose of most schools today as it was designed by the eighteenth century theorists, and in this spreading of varied, useful information, the school has received the powerful aid of the book, the press in its various forms, the moving picture, the radio and all sorts of industrial and commercial exhibitions. To be educated nowadays means to be well-informed, not to be well schooled as in former times. Man's gaze is fixed even more firmly today than it was in the eighteenth century upon his immediate material surroundings; his goal is the conquest of nature. The road of progress and to happiness, we are told, lies but in one direction: a better knowledge of nature, a better use of all its forces for greater material ease and comfort, a complete liberation from the trammels of tradition, a well-developed, keen, alert intellect, ever ready to grasp at every opportunity of bettering one's condition materially. Schools of all kinds have multiplied even beyond the dreams of the Encyclopedists, their doors have been opened wide to all comers and the school system has become in the hands of the State a huge machinery for social control and national expansion. The pedagogy of the twentieth century is still ruled by the worship of intellectualism and method so characteristic of the Enlightenment and its early nineteenth century disciples, but in some respects it shows a radical departure from the trend of eighteenth-century thought. The French Revolution and the phenomenal growth of Napoleon's power had opened men's eyes to the consequences of the Enlightenment's contempt for the past, its cosmopolitanism and individualizing tendencies. The fear had become general at the beginning of the nineteenth century lest all nationalities would be swallowed in the French Empire, and all national

Summing up.

institutions would be destroyed. The violent reaction which set in carried Europe to the other extremes. The national spirit was now everywhere encouraged; the intensive cultivation of national characteristics became the avowed purpose of education, to be followed later by an intensive preparation for national survival and national supremacy. Social efficiency, the present-day slogan in education, everywhere is the twentieth century counterpart of Rousseau's fierce individualism, but the fear has already been expressed in many quarters lest the true interests of individuals be submerged under this undue stressing of the welfare of the group.

One commendable result of the nineteenth century reaction against some of the ideals of the Enlightenment has been the revival of interest in the past and historical studies. The strong national animus with which certain studies were at first carried on was gradually toned down by the scientific tendency of the age, and the result has been a saner, fairer view of the past, of its contributions to the present and the value of tradition. If it could not be said that the study of history has brought in a genuine revival of Christian ideals in education, it could not be denied either that there is today a better knowledge of the great contributions of Christianity to civilization, culture and education, and a readiness to admire the ideals which saved Europe from a return to savagery, reared the great Gothic cathedrals, gave wings to Dante's genius and fired the zeal of countless pioneers of civilization among the natives of America and Africa. The most evident result of the historical revival, insofar as the school is concerned, is the importance now attached to the study of history, the new method of teaching the subject and the use of the historical viewpoint in the treatment of the whole content of education.

History now occupies in the curriculum a position second only to that of language, and the teaching of the subject is no longer limited as before to a mere record of wars, battles, treaties, great deeds of generals, statesmen and kings. The teacher of history is now asked to help his pupils understand and explain modern life in the light of its historical background. The course in language is not considered complete without a study of the early forms of the mother tongue and their transformations all through the ages down to present usage. Greek and Roman antiquities are studied not in Renaissance fashion to develop the aesthetic sense, but to show us the origins and development of some of our intellectual possessions. The teacher of religion uses the narrative, *i.e.,* the historical method of presentation, and tries to bring home to his pupils the importance of Christianity in the development of Western civilization. The history of inventions and discoveries has its place in the scientific course of study. The study of the history of education is now an integral part of the professional preparation of the teacher who is thus made to realize that if our education owes much to intellectual movements of the present it is in the main a fruit of the past. Not all the applications of the historical principle however have been equally happy; witness those inspired by the theory of evolution, witness the extravagance of the so-called, now happily dead, Culture Epoch Theory. Then, too, it has happened that too much importance was attached to the process of development of a subject and correspondingly too little to the intrinsic worth of that subject. A mere historical survey of philosophy, or language, or literature, or science, or Christianity will most certainly not extract from those subjects all that the student should get from them. After history has said its last word, the facts of religion, philosophy, language, literature and science still face us to be taught and learned through the method best adapted to each.

Never before has the content of general school education been so wide in its scope or so diversified in its materials. Subjects that once belonged to the university or technical or professional school have been brought within the reach of the secondary or even elementary school pupil, without, however, losing their function in higher education, while sometime elementary or secondary school subjects have been likewise expanded upwards or have branched off into new school subjects. New sciences and new branches of scholarship which for a time belonged to the province of pure scientific research have been introduced into the curriculum of the higher or even the lower schools. If the classics have lost somewhat of their hold on the school, the loss has been compensated, in some degree at least, by the introduction of modern languages into the curriculum of the secondary school, and the technique of language teaching has been substantially improved by the results of linguistic researches and the alliance of language with history resulting in the new science of philology, the study of which has become a part of the professional preparation of the prospective teacher of language. Linguistic studies have lost none of their value for mental discipline, but they have become in addition a gateway to various types of culture. School mathematics has remained in form essentially the same as before, though its scope has been enlarged. Wider still has become the scope of the natural sciences; the importance of the natural sciences in everyday life, in the trades and industries, demands that the students in all schools for general education be familiarized with at least the elements of natural science. Music and drawing, which formerly were taught only exceptionally in the elementary and secondary schools, have become an integral part of their curriculum. The elementary school takes up the study of civics, of local and national history, to which are added in the secondary school economics, ancient, medieval and modern history. Illustrations of all kinds, pictures, maps, charts, diagrams help the student in the mastering of the written record. Closely allied to the instruction in history and the natural sciences is the teaching of geography, which seeks to give man a knowledge of his whole habitat and the material conditions under which civilization and culture have originated and developed, while astronomy introduces the student to the wonders of the heavens. It is to be regretted that in many school systems philosophy has been confined to so narrow a field that its educative value is practically nil or else it is broken up into new sciences which are treated as separate university subjects. Philosophy thus loses the universal, unifying quality it had formerly when it was the capstone of general education. Greater still by far is the loss from the absence of the Christian element which the irreligiousness or indifference of the age has driven out of the school curriculum. Such as it is, it cannot be denied that the modern school curriculum contains a wealth of splendid materials. Whether or not it proves to be a more powerful, more efficient instrument than the slender curriculum of former days will depend on the way and the spirit in which it is used, and that in turn depends on the teacher, on whether or not his purpose is to use the course of study as a means to humanize the young minds entrusted to his care.

INDEX